Dangerous Positions

Dangerous Positions

Mixed Government,
the Estates of the Realm, and the
Making of the
Answer to the xix propositions

MICHAEL MENDLE

THE UNIVERSITY OF ALABAMA PRESS

*Publication of this book was made possible, in part,
by financial assistance from the Andrew W. Mellon Foundation
and the American Council of Learned Societies.*

Library of Congress Cataloging in Publication Data

Mendle, Michael, 1945–
   Dangerous positions.

   Bibliography: p.
   Includes index.
   1. Great Britain—Politics and government—1485– 1603.
2. Great Britain—Politics and government—1603–1649.
3. Church and state—England—History—16th century.
4. Church and state—England—History—17th century.
5. Estates (Social orders)—England—History—16th
century. 6. Estates (Social orders)—England—History—
17th century. 7. Presbyterianism—History—16th century.
8. Presbyterianism—History—17th century. I. Title.

DA315M45   1985   942.06   83-4798
ISBN 0-8173-0178-X

For Gillian

Contents

Preface / ix

Introduction / 1

1. The *Answer to the xix propositions* / 5

2. The Idea of the Estates of the Realm / 21

3. The Sixteenth Century: Mixed Government and the Estates to the Rise of the Presbyterian Movement / 38

4. Presbyterianism and the Estates, ca. 1580–1603 / 63

5. Dangerous Positions, 1603–1637 / 97

6. The Revival, 1638–1641 / 114

7. The Reversal, 1641–1642 / 138

8. The Answer / 171

Appendixes

1. Hyde's Religious Position in 1641 / 184

2. Henry Parker and *A question answered* / 187

Notes / 189

Bibliography / 227

Index / 247

Preface

Historians' debts must be acknowledged, for seldom can they fully be repaid to those to whom they are owed. Perhaps the most to be hoped for is that restitution will be made to others in the name of the profession; in the chain of prefaces one may glimpse a greater chain of personal and professional generosity, the *traditio* of scholarship itself. For the individual, however, the debts remain what they are—unpaid because they are unpayable bills.

In this spirit I thank first Richard Vann of Wesleyan University and the Department of History of Washington University for many kindnesses and helpful guidance. My dissertation supervisor at Washington University, John Pocock (now of Johns Hopkins University), is owed this acknowledgment and more. I began my professional training as his student and so I remain. I also have been especially encouraged and assisted by Conrad Russell and Valerie Pearl. Derek Hirst has been most generous. Others whose help I acknowledge include Esther Cope and Maija Coles. Development of parts of Chapters 4–6 was assisted by a grant of the Research Grants Committee of The University of Alabama. The index owes much to Lynn Johnson's assistance.

Forrest and Ellen MacDonald have been devoted friends of this book. Forrest's inexhaustible stock of literary expertise saved me from countless infelicities and worse. He saw paths where I saw none. Ellen typed the manuscript once and some of it again and brought consistency to notes, text, and bibliography. Like the others whom I name, they cannot be held responsible for the errors of the book, but to them is due much of the credit.

I dedicate this book to my wife, Gillian. This is not the place to thank her. It is a place to give thanks for her.

All textual quotations from English or Scots have been modernized in spelling and capitalization. Abbreviations and contractions have been expanded; italics and other manipulations of fonts have been suppressed. Word forms almost always have been left untouched. In a few cases punctuation has been silently emended. A few major divergences from these rules are indicated in the notes.

The need for bibliographical reference dictated a different course for titles of works published, or first published, before 1800. Here original spelling has been preserved. However, shifts of fonts have been suppressed and only initial capitals and those required in normal prose have been retained. Foreign titles follow the appropriate current national and linguistic conventions. Modern English-language titles follow standard modern publication practice in matters of capitalization.

Dates in the body of the text and notes take the year to begin on 1 January. Dates of books in citations are supplied as they are given on the title page. However, inferred publication dates assume the year to begin on 1 January.

Dangerous Positions

Introduction

In eighteenth-century England it was a commonplace that government was by crown-in-Parliament. Everybody knew that this arrangement represented a fusion of the three "estates" of the realm—king, Lords, and Commons—and also that it was a "mixed" polity, combining the three classical forms of government by the One, the Few, and the Many. Such happy symmetry was not, however, the way things always had been. Traditionally there had been another reckoning of the estates: bishops (or clergy), lords temporal (or nobility), and the commons. That reckoning and the one suggested by the language of mixed government were different and had, at times, been antithetical. How, in the sixteenth and seventeenth centuries, the two conflicted, and how ultimately a redefinition of the estates compatible with mixed government came to prevail, are the subject of this book.

For a variety of reasons, the story hitherto has not been told satisfactorily. Perhaps the most important reason has been that the complexities of the two sets of ideas, as they combined and recombined over time, match up poorly with customary divisions of scholarly labor. Accordingly, though most of the relevant printed and manuscript sources have been mined, the story itself usually has been marginal to the topics of the scholars who have used them. For example, at crucial points Scottish religious ideas and issues become involved in the story, and students of English constitutional history have been disinclined to explore those seemingly tangential subjects. On the other hand, the theologically oriented students of religious history, to whom those subjects are central, scarcely have known what to do with the scattered and seemingly irrelevant traces of secular language in their sources. To complicate matters further, each of the anatomies of the

English body politic had medieval and ancient roots, investigation of which takes the student still further from familiar paths. As a consequence, such studies of mixed government by the estates as have been made suffer from unfamiliarity with and indifference to many strands in the story.

Such difficulties beset the work of Corinne Comstock Weston, whose considerable scholarly enterprise has been devoted to the mixed constitution in Tudor and Stuart England. Not least among her signal services to historical scholarship has been the interest she has revived in a royal statement of 1642—a document central to the present study—called the *Answer to the xix propositions*. But, assuming that the *Answer* was the foundation for much later seventeenth- and eighteenth-century political and constitutional thought, Weston unfortunately allowed that thought to guide her search for antecedents of the *Answer*.

The result was a great deal of confusion. Weston did ask some of the pertinent questions (the narrowly political and constitutional ones) of some of the relevant materials (constitutional statements or decontextualized constitutional snippets in other sources) and received some confused answers. Yet she failed to investigate, or to investigate thoroughly, such other important matters as the significance of estates, the arenas of conflict, and the puzzling absence of use of the language of mixed government for several decades in the early seventeenth century. Nor did she exploit certain internal contradictions of the *Answer* as a lead into a complex problem; rather, she ignored them in a determinedly unidimensional reading of the document, just as she brushed aside the force of the objections to the *Answer* by Edward Hyde, the king's principal adviser on policy statements at the time. Similarly, she ignored or failed to give due consideration to the wealth of information pertaining to the period 1640–1642, when the idea of mixed government by the estates of king, Lords, and Commons was a staple of the opposition, not of the crown. And above all, Weston encountered difficulty stemming from failure to perceive the full dimensions of the subject—Scottish as much as English, ecclesiological as well as political, all of it changing through time. Hence it is not surprising that in her first book on the subject she attempted, unsuccessfully, to prove that there was a body of antecedents of the *Answer* and that in her second book she reversed herself and attempted, again unsuccessfully, to prove that there had been no true antecedents.

Enough has been said to suggest that the story that follows is rather complex. Because it is complex, it may be useful to sketch it here in general and simple outlines. The traditional enumeration of estates, medieval in origin, was functional: those who pray, those who fight, those who work. This enumeration was a fixture in English thought as well as in Continental, though its relationship to English institutions in general and to Parliament in particular cannot be expressed in a simple formula. Whatever the relationship, the concept of these three estates, under the king, routinely was accepted in the later fourteenth century and throughout the fifteenth.

The idea of the tripartite anatomy of government—the One, the Few, the Many—was borrowed from classical antiquity and introduced decisively into England by mid-sixteenth-century humanists. Some of those who used the concept did so in a way that had leveling implications, but this approach was neither universal nor inherent in the idea. In principle, at least, it could have coexisted peacefully with the traditional idea of the estates.

Things did not work out that way because, beginning in the 1580s, a religious dimension was infused into both formulations. The pivotal event was the characterization of the One, the Few, and the Many as "estates." To reckon the king as one of the estates obviously was to reduce him to the level of the other estates and thus to aggrandize the power of Parliament and to minimize the prerogative. Moreover, the inclusion of the king necessarily excluded the bishops or the clergy from separate standing or status.

The aggressors, so to speak, in this reformulation were James VI and his Scottish bishops, who in combatting their presbyterian opponents insisted that the bishops were an estate. The Scottish presbyterians in fact had not resorted to the alternative enumeration of estates made possible by the language of mixed government, but their English counterparts soon did so. Thus by the 1590s king yokers and monarchists alike came to regard mixed government by the revised estates as a code language for presbyterianism and to regard the traditional estates as a code language for the royal supremacy and episcopacy, at least in certain contexts. Perceiving the former position as dangerous to the crown—no bishop, no king—James declared it treason in Scotland to hold that the bishops were not an estate of the realm. In England it was not made treasonable to hold that position, but it was made dangerous to the holder when Elizabeth's privy council declared it to be seditious. Hence the virtual disappearance, during the early decades of the seventeenth century, of nearly all talk of mixed government by the revised estates.

The dangerous language of episcopal exclusion from the estates was revived with a vengeance by the rebellious Scottish Covenanters of the late 1630s. As the troubles of Charles I spread to England, the language in its

English form was rapidly taken up by the parliamentary opposition, and for two years it served the opposition well. Then came 1642 and Charles's abrupt—albeit incomplete—reversal of positions in the *Answer to the xix propositions,* matched by an equally partial but equally surprising abandonment of mixed government by some of the leading parliamentarian tacticians and writers. The *Answer,* thus, was no less troubled than the moment of its appearance, the eve of a civil war. One hardly should have expected anything else. But just what did the *Answer* have to tell a perplexed nation?

1
The *Answer to* *the xix propositions*

"The experience and wisdom of your ancestors," said the *Answer to the xix propositions,* molded "the constitution of the government of this kingdom" out of the "three estates" of monarchy, aristocracy, and democracy—king, Lords, Commons.[1]

With these words, Charles I inadvertently opened one of the great political and constitutional debates of the English Civil War; with them he launched what became, as the debates died off, one of the great constitutional orthodoxies of English history. With them, too, he closed out a large chapter in the history of English political thought, a chapter that as recently as two years previously had him avowing a contrary constitutional doctrine, a chapter that was the offspring of the struggles of presbyterians and episcopal partisans in England and Scotland in the days of Elizabeth and James.

Opening and shutting are, in this instance, metaphors and exaggerations, though pardonable ones. The words of a king do have a way of dramatizing historical and intellectual processes that were more diffuse and less striking. It is not a small irony, then, that Charles in all likelihood did not even read these words of his and that the document in which they appeared was the result of a logistical bottleneck in the war of words that preceded the outbreak of armed fighting in 1642.

In December 1641, Edward Hyde had begun to write the king's public papers. It was good for Hyde's soul to write for the king; Hyde always needed the last word, but seldom did it come in debate to the young lawyer whose talents and ambitions were not yet matched by the power he craved. Writing for the king, however, posed serious threats to Hyde's safety: matters would have been extremely sticky for Hyde if he, who still sat in the

Commons, were proven to have been the source not only of royal replies to parliamentary messages but also of the earliest information on the parliamentary documents themselves. Accordingly, in March 1642, when Hyde was drafting virtually all the king's responses, Charles himself devised an elaborate and personally exhausting security system to protect his still-secret councilor from discovery. Apart from Hyde's close associates Lucius Cary, Viscount Falkland, and Sir John Culpeper, no one but the king was to know of Hyde's work. His drafts were to be sent directly to the king. In spite of Hyde's bad hand, Charles alone would transcribe every word of Hyde's drafts before giving them over even to the incorruptible Edward Nicholas, Clerk of the Council and Secretary of State. The declarations grew longer, but Charles never wavered in his resolve to protect Hyde. His transcriptions "sometimes took him up two or three days, and a good part of the night." After each, Charles burned Hyde's draft.[2]

The system remained intact for a while after Hyde came to join the king at York late in May 1642. The answer to the parliamentary declaration of 26 May, a document of some eight thousand words, was the last that Charles brought to the council board "in his own hand writing." Only then did Hyde, who had been lying low outside York, begin to resort to the court without ruse or pretense. It was no doubt as great a relief for Charles as for Hyde that the secret no longer needed to be kept.[3]

But when Hyde came to York he had lost time; also he had lost contact with the inside intelligence that had been his in London. The answer to propositions framed after Hyde had left London—the Nineteen Propositions of 2 June—was undertaken by his friends Falkland and Culpeper because Hyde "had so much work on his hands, as they believed he would not be able to despatch soon enough." Completing their reply, they routed it to the king, then to Hyde, to "peruse it, and then cause it to be published." At this point in his account, which is quite his usual mixture of deviousness and truth, Hyde skirted a sensitive question: whether Charles actually had bothered to read the *Answer to the xix propositions,* as it came to be called. This occasion would have been Charles's first respite from *ad litteram* knowledge of all that issued in his name, a course that had caused him to spend "more than half the day shut up by himself in his chamber, writing." Doubtless Charles glanced at what Falkland and Culpeper laid before him. How likely, however, was it that he would alight upon the words cited at the beginning of this chapter, words buried midway in a manuscript of nine thousand or so words? Because, as Hyde himself remarked, "the answer was full to all particulars, and writ with very much wit and sharpness," a busy king could excuse himself from doing much more than satisfy himself on that point.[4]

Hyde did fall upon the words in question. They and a few amplificatory phrases that followed were his sole objections to the document: Culpeper and Falkland had their three estates wrong. The king was not an estate "but the head and sovereign. . . . in truth the bishops make the third estate." On those grounds Hyde "did not advance the printing of it." Hyde was in a delicate position. He felt forced to choose between his friends and his duty to the king. With perhaps more tact than judgment, he attempted to forestall the unfortunate decision. He simply told the king that the declaration said nothing that had not been said in the earlier squibs ("which was true," he added). To protect Falkland and Culpeper, "of whose affection to the church . . . his majesty was always jealous," Hyde said nothing about the offending words. The king was satisfied. Falkland and Culpeper were not. Arriving in York after Hyde, they were surprised to find their reply unprinted. Falkland bitterly charged Hyde with his undeniable vice: Hyde disliked it, the viscount said to Hyde's face, "because he had not writ it himself." Hyde gave him the text, and Falkland had it printed without further delay, "of which the king was afterwards very sensible." Charles was not allowed to forget the words in his own declaration that he had failed to read and that Hyde failed to call directly to his attention out of fear that his friends would lose royal favor because of them.[5]

In his thirty-fourth year, Hyde already was touched by an old man's prissiness. His objection to a very few words in the *Answer* reasonably could be taken as a mark of a quirky scrupulosity. In truth, however, Hyde did not consider his objection at all trivial. A point of fact was involved—who or what was or was not an estate. But it was not a fact upheld for the sake of a schoolboy's truth, like the correction of a small-change error made in one's own favor, a duty undertaken in the sacred name of arithmetic. Rather, Hyde, without being fully aware of it, felt that a whole way of life, a civilization was threatened in these few words. To think in this fashion, of course, is to join prudery to passion, learned accuracy to the irrational; it is too much to ask of men in such situations that they be entirely capable of analyzing their own minds.

But Hyde's own words tell the tale. The *Answer*'s denomination of the "estates" —king, Lords, and Commons—did one thing by assertion and another by negation. By including the king, it left out the bishops, the representatives of the clergy. Hyde could not countenance leaving out the clergy, an act that already had been accomplished by the bill to exclude the bishops from their votes in the Lords, a bill Charles had accepted in a moment of near-panic late in February 1642. It was "a great alteration in the frame and constitutions of Parliaments"; it was "a violence, and removing landmarks, and not a shaking . . . but dissolving foundations, which must leave the building unsafe for habitation." It would be "pernicious" not to resist "so antimonarchical an act."[6]

Hyde's words, so far as we have seen them, were those of the politician, but they were also those of the believer.[7] Hyde would not separate the two roles or their responsibilities. Drawing upon a commonplace in which he desperately believed, he thought church and state were like "Hippocrates' twins." And the "church of England," he concluded upon his examination of religion with "more pains" than politicians "use to do," was "the most exactly formed and framed for the encouragement and advancement of learning and piety, and for the preservation of peace, of any church in the world." To divert its revenues was "notorious sacrilege." The "impulsion of conscience" drew him to oppose "all mutations" in the church.

The error about the estates was one such mutation, and although Hyde actively opposed it he later thought it a particular manifestation of Providence, a judgment for sin. Hyde saw the error of the estates as a result of the mutual jealousy of common lawyers and churchmen. Their self-destructive hatred was "an instance of the Divine anger against the pride of them both," of the churchmen who thought they were peers (and not an estate on their own) and the lawyers too driven by short-sighted resentment to see that the "great and unwieldy body of the clergy" could be governed only by bishops and that their own mystery would not have "the same respect and veneration from the people, when the well disposed fabric of the church should be rent asunder."[8]

The king, the law, the church: all three were menaced by the error about the estates in the *Answer,* menaced not separately but conjointly. The same three categories of king, law, and church were also the organizing principle of Hyde's own self-description in the *Life.* His own integrity of personality consequently was threatened by his two friends' persistence in their mistaking of the facts.[9] To make matters worse, the occasion of the *Answer* was not the first but the second time Hyde had been humilitated by it.[10] Yet he knew his friends meant no harm to him, nor to the king, the law, the church. Hyde loved his friends still, and, grievous and personally upsetting as their error was, he could not bring himself to tell Charles about it. At the time of his final opportunity to control the publishing of the *Answer,* he gave the copy to Falkland, knowing it would be printed.

The sky was falling, but Hyde could not bring himself to give the alarm. Why? There is a simple answer: the sky was also not falling, and Hyde knew that as well as he knew that it was. The error that menaced a civilization was part of a tract designed to preserve it, at least to identify the threat of its collapse with the cause of Charles I against his Parliament. The pursuit of that cause had drawn Falkland and Hyde to Culpeper, had bound them together through the exquisite friendship of completely trusted fellow conspirators, had brought them to such a close agreement about king, law, and even the church that Hyde could not allow himself to act on his instincts. The obverse of Hyde's paralysis was Falkland's and Culpeper's stubbornness; as determined as Hyde was to correct them, so were they insistent of their own rectitude. And Hyde believed them; he believed, that is, in their devotion to the same cause. And if Hyde's stuffiness could not allow him to recognize it, Falkland and Culpeper (especially the latter, it would seem) had in their very "error" found an argument that was so terrifying to parliamentarian apologists that the most important of them, Henry Parker, could not bring himself to answer it.[11] What was worse still, was that it was Parker's own argument. We could continue: in the long run, Parker was wrong to be so frightened.

Wheels within wheels; Byzantium, not England; opera plots, not political thought: the reader has a right to protest. But the *Answer* was an equivocal document of a paradoxical period; the *Answer*'s origins and effects were not different. It will not do to dismiss any of it, even if we must keep an uncomfortably large number of items in our minds or if we have to approach our text as if it were a bomb with two fuses, one set to go off as a result of disengaging the other.

But much of the difficulty of situating the *Answer* in its several contexts can be gleaned by analysis of the text itself. On any strict reading, the *Answer* said too much, contradicted itself, pulled in different directions. Depending upon what one chose to notice, the *Answer* meant one thing or another. That fact alone goes far to establish why Hyde could turn himself in circles over its implications. Although it is not part of this essay to consider the future of the *Answer* after its immediate publication, the same analysis will show why both parliamentarians and royalists had cause alternately to fear and to cheer the *Answer.* Undeniably, the *Answer*'s influence did not come from its originality, for there was little in it that had not been said before by either parliamentarians or royalists. Nor did the influence derive solely from the fact that the *Answer* was issued in the king's name; there were several more incisive and certainly better written royalist declarations than the *Answer,* but no one except a few specialists pays mind to them now. Its influence, rather, came from its equivocation and confusion: it forced men to think, to play with their minds rather than their fingers, as musicians say.[12]

The same analysis of the *Answer*'s inconsistencies serves another, nearer purpose: it raises the issues and themes pursued in this book. The *Answer*'s double-talk revealed an inability of its authors to speak clearly about the most elementary facts of English politics and English history. Falkland and Culpeper were intelligent men, and if they spoke with forked tongues it may be that they had given themselves no choice.

The Nineteen Propositions of Parliament of 2 June 1642 were presented to Charles as "the most necessary effectual means" of settling the distractions of the kingdom.[13] The leading demands amounted to nothing less than a request for surrender of virtually all Charles's executive power to the control of the remnant of men who claimed to be the two Houses of Parliament. Much of their content was to be found in other documents going back as far as John Pym's Ten Propositions of June 1641, but the naked listing of so many of them together was as arrogant, to the royalist mind, as the prefatory and concluding professions of humbleness and duty were a "mockery and scorn."[14]

The *Answer,* then, was a reply to a demand for a joint tenancy of executive power. Almost every line of the *Answer* was strained to a rebuttal and denial of this general position. The celebrated part of the *Answer* about the estates came in the midst of an assault upon the fourth proposition, the most outrageous of the lot, that Charles be denied the rights of any other father to raise his children and arrange their marriages. (An earlier, brief drift into the language of estates was prompted by the second proposition, a scheme to give Parliament control over the privy council.) In the main, the *Answer* did its work well. Its "wit and sharpness" could equal Hyde at his best. The two houses, it railed, would leave Charles with the "twigs" of kingship:

We may be waited on bare-headed; we may have our hand kissed; the styles of majesty continued to us; and the king's authority declared by both Houses of Parliament, may still be the style of your commands; we may have swords and maces carried before us, and please our self with the sight of a crown and scepter.[15]

Such "asperities and corrasives" did not go unnoticed in the Commons.[16]

But the *Answer*'s weaknesses arose from the same overflow of outrage that gave it power, for that outrage contributed to an entanglement of wildly different, ultimately opposed structures of thought. One pattern was quantitative, emotional, and linked to the *Answer*'s view of the estates. This structure tended to regard the whole of the Nineteen Propositions and the underlying parliamentary politics in terms of the most extreme construction that could be put on the two houses' actions. It judged all in terms of the worst, an approach that presumed a hierarchy of indignities. The other pattern was qualitative and functional. More coolly, it discriminated by kinds of proposals rather than by degrees of abuse; and it was at odds with the logic of the language of the estates of king, Lords, and Commons. Its whole point was to insist on such a difference between the king and the two houses that a common covering term, such as estate, was inappropriate for all that it was used. Passion thus was bound up with one of these structures—the famous one having to do with the estates—but it affected both, simply because rage obscured the reasoning when qualitative rather than quantitative matters were at issue.

The analysis in terms of the worst case took its cue from a common perception among royalists: the houses had gone beyond making Charles their equal and had made him their inferior. Rights that he had shared equally with them had been menaced, particularly his right to join with the other two "estates" in assent to laws made in Parliament. Irresistibly—for there was history behind it—the denomination of the king as an estate suggested the equality, commonality, and functional identity of each estate's share in legislation. But the correspondence of estates and Parliament also created a back pressure on the meaning of kingship. The parliamentary structure that made it possible to see the king as an estate also made it necessary, precisely to the extent that the parliamentary constitution was taken to be either the whole constitution or the controlling part of it. The revised anatomy of estates characteristically had functioned as a code, as at least a latent symbol of parliamentary sovereignty or, not quite the same thing, parliamentary omnicompetence.[17]

Of course, parliamentary action required the assent of the three "estates." Nothing could be worse than to deny the king his equality; the language of estates began therefore with built-in resentment that this most equal, most parliamentary construction of the role of the king had been violated. In a brief excursus into this idiom, somewhat before the celebrated passage on the constitution, the *Answer* had responded to the second of the Nineteen Propositions, which demanded parliamentary control of the privy council. The *Answer* did not reject this demand on the ground that the privy council was not intrinsically subject to parliamentary control but rather on the ground that the king was as entitled to take advice as freely as were any of his subjects. It was an inequality—an inferiority— that the Lords and Commons should have the freedom of their consciences, but not the king. "Our vote is trusted by the law, to our own judgment and conscience." Therefore "most unreasonable it were that two estates, proposing something to the third, that third should be bound to take no advice, whether it were fit to pass, but from those two that did propose it."[18]

That point was made well enough. It is also excellent testimony to the parliamentary matrix of the three estates of king, Lords, and Commons that a point about the privy council was referred to the parliamentary context and that the goal of the second demand was interpreted as a bringing of the king not to the rank of the houses but to a level beneath them. If the *Answer* had pursued this line of argument consistently, it would have employed an emotive and quantitative model throughout. The consistency would have been accompanied, presumably, by obligatory and strained references of all points in dispute to the parliamentary component of the constitution. All would have brought into consideration as an instance of this extreme case of the king leveled beneath the houses, beneath his equality with them as an estate.

However, there was another way to view matters in dispute, one that bore an organic relation to the facts with which it was concerned, just as the parliamentary partnership did to the idiom of three estates. It was a logic of quality and function and was no more amenable to strategies of measurement than is any other distinction of kinds. No point of equality and commonality possibly could be involved; rather, the discussion was carried along in terms of separation and, indeed, noncommensurability. And, most critically, this logic was used—in this part of the *Answer* and later—to explain why the king rejected the demands he did, why he refused assent to the militia bill, why his conscience would lead him to reject the parliamentary way, why he would not allow himself to be brought to the equality suggested by his rank as an estate.

Later ages have had an easy familiarity with notions such as the separation of powers; earlier eras were equally at ease with the traditional functionally distinguished estates. The classical-humanist terminology of constitutions also was prone to accord specific qualities, including functions or virtues that might be functions, to its categories of the One, the Few, the Many. Hindsight, foresight, and peripheral vision seem to agree that a functional description could accord with notions that evolved out of the *Answer* and that fairly could be seen as underlying the *Answer*. For all this, the notion of functional discrimination was alien to the *Answer*'s concept of estates, which had been a leveller from the beginning. Thus when the same passage that has been examined introduced a scarcely disguised notion of function and separation through repeated use of the word "proper," it cut directly across the grain of the three estates of king, Lords, Commons. It stressed their inequality—really their lack of a common measure; it stressed not their joint sphere of activity but their unique roles, removing Parliament from the center of vision; it established a nonquantitative standard of judgment, eliminating the logic of the extreme case. Rather, the standard was now whether king, Lords, and Commons each stayed within the bounds of what was "proper"—a word that by continued usage as well as origin commingled senses of ownership and suitability.

In this way, the facts of the king's right could be rescued, but only by divesting the word "estate" of all the emotive, egalitarian, quantifiable sense that it bore and for which reason it was used. Thus when the *Answer* viewed the two houses (alias estates)—particularly one of them, the Commons—as overstepping the boundary of the "proper," the implication was that the two houses had meddled in areas simply beyond the rights of Parliament. But it was only an implication, because the *Answer* was caught between its two thought-structures and oscillated confusedly between them.

The passage in which the crux occurs can be summarized as follows: when the Commons had functioned by itself as a court, when also (though this is less clear) it had undertaken to countermand interim injunctions of the Lords concerning religious obedience, "one estate" had done what was "proper for two." When the houses had seized control of the might and money of the kingdom and had declared null the commissions of array ("our legal directions"), two estates had undertaken what was "proper for three" (because these actions involved the omnicompetence of Parliament). Yet, oddly, it was not proper for three either; the king had refused to accept these actions—to go the way of the three estates, the parliamentary way— because the disposal of these things had "been trusted wholly with our predecessors and us." That is, they were beyond the competence of Parliament, not even "proper to your debates." The result of this odd conflation of logics was to employ the omnicompetence of Parliament to deny the omnicompetence of Parliament. The *Answer* was forced to close its circle of double-talk by insisting upon the veto afforded to the royal estate. That brought back the notion of parliamentary omnicompetence—providing Parliament did nothing. If it acted, by means of the royal assent, it broke the back of the ancient constitution that had, by constant practice "since there were kings of this kingdom," proscribed the way of the three estates in matters of the "regal authority."[19]

This was hardly a promising beginning for the "classic" statement of the balanced constitution. The celebrated extended description of it, which followed shortly upon this most perplexing initial excursion, was more direct in its equivocations but no more prepared to resolve them. The major discussion was imbedded in a rejection of the fourth of the Nineteen Propositions, the one that would have placed the raising of the king's children under parliamentary control. Once again the *Answer* deployed a phrasing of equality to make a point about an unjust inequality, for this proposition would have denied to the king rights not questioned of the meanest of his subjects. On any fair reading, it accomplished the job—the *Answer* was not about to destroy the least tittle of the king's right. But on the same fair reading it will be seen that the *Answer* had to change the meaning of words in midpassage and to come down, by turns, on opposite sides of equivocations in order to get the scheme of the three estates of king, Lords, and Commons to say what the authors wished it to say.

The fourth demand was so outrageous that it became an emblem for the rest, especial proof that all the "demands" were "too much in style, not only of equals, but of conquerors." But Charles would not accede to them even "in a parliamentary way." That was the crucial point; even though the king legally could go the way of "three" (as it had been put in earlier excursus) to join with the other two estates to divest himself of his rights, he refused to do it. He refused for his own sake as for his subjects', for that would destroy by peaceful, legal revolution the "equal, happy, well-poised and never-enough commended constitution of the government of this kingdom." And it was a kingdom; to accede to the demands would make the king a duke of Venice, the kingdom "a republic."[20]

This was the moment of appearance of the celebrated passage. To the language of estates as it had been seen so far, an important, necessary, but potentially misleading element was added: the classical-humanist terminology of constitutions in terms of the One, the Few, the Many and their combinations. That idiom had entered England during the great flurry of mid-Tudor humanism, when it was sometimes naturalized by labeling as estates the English manifestations of the One, the Few, and the Many. By the first years of the English reign of James, the language had been identified fairly thoroughly with presbyterianism, and it disappeared with the decline of English presbyterian agitation, only to be revived by the latter-day presbyterians and independents of the late 1630s and 1640. For reasons we have briefly mentioned, royalists without presbyterian instincts had found mixed government convenient to use for their extreme-case analysis of a king laid beneath the level of the other two estates.[21]

But let the *Answer* speak for itself:

> There being three kinds of government amongst men, absolute monarchy, aristocracy and democracy, and all these having their particular conveniences and inconveniencies, the experience and wisdom of your ancestors hath so molded this [the "constitution of the government of this kingdom"] out of a mixture of these, as to give to this kingdom (as far as human prudence can provide) the conveniencies of all three, without the inconveniencies of any one, as long as the balance hangs even between the three estates, and they run jointly on in their proper channel.[22]

There was already more than a hint of divergent directions. Here was the language of classical republicanism, the mixture of the three kinds of rule, but it was used to support a denial that England was a republic. Moreover, the language of leveling, and of measurement of the even balance, was conjoined to a notion of function and incommensurability, the "proper channel."

Of course, these cross-purposes presumably were hidden from the authors, and they went on to complete the point by an enumeration of the virtues and defects of each of the three "estates." Absolute monarchy could lead to tyranny, aristocracy to "faction and division," democracy to "tumults, violence and licentiousness"—precisely what had been earlier laid to the Commons' charge.[23] The virtue of monarchy was unity "under one head" to resist foreign invasion and domestic insurrection, the "good of aristocracy" was the "conjunction of counsel in the ablest persons . . . for the public benefit." To democracy belonged "liberty, and the courage and industry which liberty begets." The analysis was conventional enough, from the republican perspective. The most remarkable feature was the identification of military virtue ("courage") with the Commons. Although this was a republican commonplace with deep resonances in English thought, the aristocracy was left with remarkably little to do, to give counsel without giving valor, to advise a king but not lead the country in feats of arms.[24] Whatever might be the facts of the peerage's influence in 1642, here and elsewhere the *Answer* regarded the second "estate" not so much as James Harrington's Crassus but as Lepidus.[25]

The specification of the virtues of each form was also a specification of function. This function was further elaborated in the ensuing passage, which surveyed the "proper channel" of each estate, moving swiftly from an equality of shared function to a discrimination and specialization. "In this kingdom the laws are jointly made" by the king, the "House of Peers, and by a House of Commons chosen by the people." All three had "free votes," but (the *Answer* said "and") all had "particular privileges." The king's were "intended" to bridle the "great ones" in their "division and faction," and the "people" from their infernal trinity of tumults, violence, and licentiousness. These powers, in short the prerogative, were the "government . . . , power of treaties of war and peace, of making peers, of choosing officers and councilors for state, judges for law, commanders for forts and castles, giving commissions for raising men . . . , benefit of confiscations, power of pardoning, and some more of the like kind." Every one of the named powers except the confiscations was an object of parliamentary interest or control in the Nineteen Propositions; all of them thus were denied by the logic, at once republican and monarchic, of the king's particular privileges. The *Answer* had done the job.[26]

Curiously, however, the *Answer* had turned about-face on a key word in the discussion. "The government" was trusted to the king. The government was the old medieval *gubernaculum* (as distinguished from *jurisdictio*, which was conjoint) and the modern executive power.[27] Government was thus something less than the whole political enterprise; earlier, however, the *Answer* had set out to describe "the constitution of the government" of the kingdom, a phrase that could only mean in its context the entire political structure. The shift in meaning was significant. Two very distinct ways of viewing "this kind of regulated monarchy"[28] were engaged, one that took for its leitmotiv the joint activity of legislation and republican theory, the other one that stressed, as the *Answer* had just stressed, the king's functionally distinct and superior position over the rest of the realm, the people and the magnates.

A brief description of the particular rights of the other two estates followed. The House of Commons had the prime responsibility to see that the king's "high and perpetual power" would not be used against "those for whose good he hath it." At a time when the Parliament was claiming to function as a supreme council as well as a court, and not only in the Nineteen Propositions, the *Answer* allowed the Commons the initiative in taxation and the right of impeachment but not—according to the restricted sense of the word— "any share in government, or the choosing of them that should govern." Again, the House of Lords came in a passive third: it had the judicatory power (with respect to impeachments) and was "an excellent screen and bank between the prince and people, to assist each against any encroachments of the other." The *Answer* then recounted how Charles's "willing" consent to the Triennial Act and the bill to prevent the present Parliament from being dissolved without its own consent made the power of the two houses "more than sufficient" to prevent tyranny.[29]

Kept within their "proper" channels, then, each estate regulated the others: the republican theory of balance, applied to a monarchy, created the homeostatic paradise. The "encroaching of one of these estates upon the power of the other" destroyed it; for that reason Charles could not consent to the demands in the parliamentary way, for it would take the monarchical function out of the One's control, leaving the king with "at most a joint government": again, the "government" resided with the king. In the first of several stages of predicted collapse, the "councilors (or rather . . . guardians)" called for by the demand to control appointments to the privy council would turn on the king as a mere equal to them, indulge in their characteristic vice of "divisions," and finally turn on the people, as "now so much their inferiors" who were but lately of a "nearer degree." Aristocratic usurpation, however, would provoke popular resistance and "infallibly beget yet greater changes."[30]

Further frights would attend the popular revolution. "The church" and the "second estate" (seen as essentially on a par, at least on the next rung to be demolished) would "follow the fate of the first." The scenario of the Nineteen Propositions would be repeated, this time with the peers receiving "like propositions." "All power being vested in the House of Commons," the need for secrecy and expedition would cause "affairs of state" to devolve upon "some close committee." At last the "common people," who in the present and near future had to be "flattered" and countenanced "in all their wild humors," would discover the secret of state that "all this was done by them, but not for them, grow weary of journey-work, and set up for themselves." They would "devour that estate which had devoured the rest" in a riot of "parity and independence" that would see the end of "all rights and properties, all distinctions of families and merit." England would descend from its "splendid . . . form of government" (in the first, general sense) into the "dark equal chaos of confusion," a Jack Cade or Wat Tyler atop it all.[31]

The problem with this discussion was that it was inconsistent with all that preceded it. In devouring the House of Commons, the "common people" were not destroying anything remotely resembling a democracy, by the usual terminology of the day or by the *Answer*'s own internal referents. The democracy, the third "social" estate, was characterized by plebeian vices and by the citizen virtues of industry and courage; suddenly, however, that same estate had been capable of the wholly unplebeian act of the close committee—faction by another name—and had to fear the abolition of the distinction of family and merit as well as property. If the second description hewed much closer to the facts, it did so only by drawing away from the theory. The authors of the *Answer* could not abide by their own scheme of estates any more than they could employ consistently one definition of government.

In both of these inconsistencies, the *Answer* aligned itself with predominant opinion. As Edward VI had learned for his copybook, as Sir Thomas Smith had reiterated in *De republica Anglorum,* as Sir Thomas Aston said again in 1641, the gentry of England was its minor nobility. Gentlemen may have been made cheaply in England, and the notion of minor nobility had little or no legal underpinning, but it was simply incompatible both with Continental practice and the necessity of local leadership that there be no lesser nobility, armigerous in both senses.[32]

The other inconsistency was more fundamental. A republican language had been used to argue the case against a republic. Moreover, the strictly egalitarian implications of calling the king an estate were at odds with the notion of function and ownership—the proper channel—by which the estates were distinguished and the king placed in a category sufficiently distinct that it was hard to see in what respect he could be called equal. While both the king and the two houses had means to protect themselves or their own interests from the others, only the king had the means to protect himself and the others. He had, in short, the "government" as that word was used in the midst of the discourse on the constitution to mean the prerogative or executive power or *gubernaculum,* not as it was at the beginning and end of the discourse to mean the entire political frame, in accord with both the republican motif and the stress on the equality of the estates that had been more or less encrypted within it.

This equivocation was necessary to preserve the king's right, to reject the "government"-grasping Nineteen Propositions, and to state the facts as they then stood. When the republican language was braced by the astringency of the facts, it became a façade for a more fundamental anatomy of the constitution. It was bipartite; it was that of king with his subjects and the king alone, the *dominium politicum et regale* of Sir John Fortescue. The "republican" three estates of the *Answer,* on the face of it a shadow language to make the *dominium politicum* the centerpiece of the whole, was in reality a successful yet equivocal way of asserting the continuing independence of the *dominium regale.*

It was ingenious; it was also dangerous. The too-clever parts of the *Answer* were attempts to conform the *dominium regale* to the worst-case analysis of the denial of "free vote" in terms of estates. That style of argument had been deployed successfully in an earlier part of the *Answer;* it had had a short but vigorous career in the months immediately preceding the *Answer;* [33] it was also the locus of the only other occasion of the use of the language of the three estates of king, Lords, and Commons by the king's official spokesmen in the ongoing war of words.[34] The interior of the celebrated passage had done the job, but a great many books are judged by their covers. Charles's opponents had a vested interest in taking the *Answer* on its face, and so began the great debate over coordination, as Weston and Greenberg have called it, in the civil war and after.[35] Most though not all of the royalist writers felt as Hyde had. Of these Sir Roger Twysden is especially apposite. He could quote with approval Giovanni Francesco Biondi's description of England as a "ben constituita aristo-democratica monarchia," but he also insisted that his three estates were the bishops, lay nobility, and the commons.[36]

✳

Manifestly Falkland and Culpeper had not caused either the king's or the law's part of the sky to fall. Their definition of estates, so worrisome to Hyde, had not proven to be antimonarchical, as Hyde had feared. It was invoked to allow them to say with justice, as had the barons at Merton in 1236, that they did not wish the law changed: "Nolumus leges Angliae mutari."[37] Hyde, however, was a holist, and much, indeed most, of his fear about the *Answer*'s definition of estates rotated about the exclusion of the bishops. Even the antimonarchism was a reflection of the episcopal exclusion, in Hyde's view; it also will be remembered that Hyde discreetly kept his precise reservations about the *Answer* to himself because he knew that Charles was "jealous" of the affections of Falkland and Culpeper to the church.

Here, arguably, Hyde's worries were better founded.[38] Hyde had built the bishops into the fabric of the ancient constitution, and (at least in his *History* and *Life*) the latter into the fabric of heaven, the divine plan. Not that Hyde thought the bishops' position was *jure divino* in the Laudian sense: rather, the bishops had done the Lord's work of peacekeeping and harmonizing, as had the monarchy. Falkland and Culpeper were not opposed to bishops; indeed, both were in favor of them. But they did not share Hyde's holistic perspective, a perspective that was also Charles's. Falkland was an adiaphorist informed by a thoroughly Christian skepticism; Culpeper was a *politique*. Hyde loved episcopacy for the reason it left Falkland indifferent: it was a political institution. He loved it for a reason no true *politique* could fathom: its politics encouraged the virtues, the good order, learning, and decency, that God intended for man. Falkland and Culpeper were content to see the bishops, late of the House of Lords, as peers in point of right, historically part of the *Answer*'s second estate.[39] This formula allowed a great many things to be implied about the tumults, but none of them to be said. That could preserve silence on the all-but-impossible issue of whether the exclusion of the bishops was truly a part of the reform program.

Hyde's own declarations, quite as much as the *Answer*, had maintained that eerie silence. But the *Answer*'s adversion to the estates of king, Lords, and Commons seemed to Hyde to pour salt on the royalists' own wound. And as much as he knew that Falkland and Culpeper had not intended it, he could not rest. In his resistance Hyde took his stand with Richard Bancroft, whose "never enough lamented death" had stilled his attempt to extinguish "all that fire in England which had been kindled at Geneva," with Launcelot Andrewes and John Overall, "who understood and loved the church."[40] These men, as will be seen, were the great expositors of the importance of Hyde's own view of the constitution. But how they and their king, as Hyde and his, had come to their views is a story that, in its first development, brings us far from the *Answer to the xix propositions*.

2
The Idea of the
Estates of the Realm

Terrible fates can befall a community: tyranny, chaos, loss of favor among the gods. Men blame themselves for these misfortunes and seek to prevent them by a vigilant defense. One such defense is to be found in the community's self-evident truths, propositions seemingly demonstrated by their mere assertion. They are its nonnegotiable facts; change them and the world is upside down. As the perils change, so do the truths, albeit in no predictable fashion. Few sights in the history of ideas are so fascinating as the changing of the guard. The story of the making of the *Answer to the xix propositions* is one such tale.

Self-evident truths can never be upset by the evidence; the world, not the truth, is at fault. Nor can they be proven—certainly not scientifically; scientific truths demand the possibility of disproof. Self-evident truths, indeed, actually are diminished in status when held to standards of verifiability reserved for more doubtful matters. Evidence or authority adduced in behalf of an axiom is less a proof than a celebration, and it is not the proposition but the witness that is commended. For all this, self-evident truths come and go or, often enough, come and go and come again. Remembered and forgotten rather than proven or disproven, they displace others and are displaced themselves.

The doctrine or version of the estates of the realm in the *Answer,* and similar antecedent formulations going back to the sixteenth century, ran up against such a self-evident truth. The king, Lords, and Commons of these statements deviated from another division of the community, too obvious to be gainsaid without peril. This division was also tripartite, but in it the three orders or estates—the *oratores, bellatores,* and *laboratores* familiar to medievalists and others—were placed under a king who was distinct from and superior to the three groups. Arguably this scheme was in a declining phase in sixteenth- and seventeenth-century England, indeed in a state of decomposition. Yet England, as will be seen, was not the whole terrain of action, even for England. There was Europe and, above all, Scotland, and there the traditional three estates had maintained their grip. And in England itself the hoary scheme had met certain needs so well as to make it difficult to abandon. The matter can be put the other way around: to renounce the traditional triad of those who pray, fight, and work was potentially to attack the order memorialized by the scheme and so to arouse it from hibernation or even a sleep otherwise unto death. For fifty years before the *Answer*, as recently as two years before the *Answer*, a variant of the triad of those who pray, fight, and work had been deployed to attack the division of the estates into king, Lords, and Commons. The historian of affairs, the historian of misery must note that the attack was not always justified. But the historian of ideas does not dwell on the merits of the case except to record the sometimes awesome power of the preconceived and the self-evident. Such notions do not need evidence, yet they create it. To abjure is also to conjure.

The notion of the tripartite community of priests, warriors, and toilers has come under intense scrutiny during the past twenty years, especially by French medievalists associated with Georges Duby and Jacques Le Goff.[1] These scholars have directed an almost dialectically Hegelian effort to occupy the interstices between two opposing responses to the truism of the three estates. One view took the traditional triad pretty much at face value, making it as much a commonplace of the textbooks as of the medieval world, a convenient shorthand for a doubtless more complex but not counterfactual reality. A more self-consciously scientific history smirked at the crudity of the scheme. More variegated and nuanced contemporary descriptions and the ambiguities of local and shifting usage and practice were paraded as proof that the older view was caricature, not fact. This sociological approach treated the complexities rather than the reductions as "reality." In this way, the variety and the open-endedness—hence, even if accidently, the freedom—of much medieval life was celebrated.

The French historians simply have conceded both positions and gone on from there. The tripartite scheme was obviously important to many of those who adverted to it; it was also clumsy as sociological description. Because some of the earliest representations of the three estates came from men with a practical interest in being right—a king and political clergymen—one question arises, although it can be asked in two forms. Why were they so blind? Why were we so blind as to miss their own preoccupations?

Duby, Le Goff, Jean Batany, and others within this school begin their answers with a frank admission that they come to the problem, if not to its solution, through the work of Georges Dumézil, whose own approach has been to see the medieval three estates as a particular manifestation of an idea vastly larger in its compass of space and time, a manifestation of an Indo-European "ideology" of the three "functions" pursued by Dumézil and his own students for over forty years.[2]

Dumézil argued that the "tripartition" of the functions of prayer and judgment, war, and toil is an element common on one level or another to all Indo-European societies but to them alone; like the languages of the Indo-European family, trifunctionality was speciated from an original genus. Aboriginal trifunctionality may or may not have been linked to a presumed objective social structure; Dumézil has pursued trifunctionality only as a stylization or ideology that can be recovered through the residues preserved by the discrete Indo-European peoples.

These remains are not identical in form, substance, or intensity. In some cases, particularly among the Greeks and the Romans, trifunctionality had nearly disappeared by historic times, being preserved only scantily in myths and legends and subconscious thought structures. The Germans, Scandinavians, and Celts preserved a rather larger mythological residue, permitting fairly direct and full reconstructions of the aboriginal tripartition. Among the Vedics and the Persians such reconstructions were matched by an overt this-worldly social vocabulary. The familiar orders or castes of Indian Aryans are a well-known example—brahmans (priests), kshatriyas (warriors), vaisyas (merchants and craftsmen).[3] In a similar vein, Caesar described the Celts. There were the Druids (with their preference for a synodal organization, a point of no mean interest to this study), the *equites,* and the third genus, the *plebs,* voiceless, debt-ridden, and all but slaves.[4] Dumézil's research has made Caesar's observations all the more remarkable, for it is quite clear that trifunctionality or tripartition long had ceased to organize either the Roman or the Greek mentality. Caesar was not reporting something entirely cognate to his own social world.

But the problem has been to get from the three functions to the three estates, to use the words of Jean Batany's pioneering Dumézilian manifesto.[5] One must leap from Caesar to Alfred of Wessex (d. 899), the first medieval European known to have used the figure of the three orders as actual social description. One must move from pagan myth residues of the Celts and Scandinavians, whose trifunctional ideology is recovered by a process not radically different in its interpretative texture from psychoanalysis, to the overt, purposeful—self-evident—dicta of Alfred and, about a century later, of worried Anglo-Saxon and French clerics. Still more difficulties attend the interposition of new membranes, nontrifunctional and even non-Indo-European, through which the ancient tripartite idea must pass. There is a thin but tenacious membrane, for the early Middle Ages, of Roman civilization, a thicker one of the Latin language, which had to be adapted, indeed twisted, to provide words for the idea. And most of all, trifunctionality had to pass through the Semitic and Hellenistic filters of the Scriptures.

Inevitably, then, the revival or reappearance of trifunctionality in Western European thought was no mere rehash or repetition but a creative act. Some attempt has been made to find a connective tissue linking ancient and ninth-century Celtic trifunctionality and to use the latter as a means to explain the appearance of the three estates in Anglo-Saxon England.[6] But the Celtic and the Anglo-Saxon formulations are so different in texture that even a whole series of such missing links will not suffice by itself to explain why and how Alfred and the others came so to express themselves; there is an uncloseable gap between a story with trifunctional characters and a constitutional theory. Here, for an odd reason, the French scholarship is extremely suggestive. For it is also true that the English recovery of trifunctionality preceded the French, by more than a century in Alfred's case, by a crucial two decades in a more sustained outburst of the figure around the year 1000—decades marked by close contact between English and French leaders and a certain symmetry of concerns among those who employed the figure. Duby, especially, has sought to preserve for his French subjects an integrity and originality of vision not well measured by terms such as English "influence," and if this is correct for the French it is surely more true with respect to the English and a supposed Celtic influence.[7]

For Duby and an Italian scholar, Ottavia Niccoli, the crucial word to describe the revival of trifunctionality is "imagination."[8] A folk memory becomes pertinent, becomes a structure for the musings of men who are both scholars and public men. The actual and an ideal fuse but not necessarily very well: self-evident truth is being created by being remembered or, perhaps, misremembered. Of Dumézil's tripartite ideology Duby says, "ordinarily it remains latent, unformulated; only rarely is it brought out into the open in the shape of imperious statements as to the proper ideal of society."[9]

But there was such an emergence in medieval Europe, and it is first to be noticed in England, in the late ninth century and again a hundred years later. Never was there a more English idea, unless it was a British one, with all due respect to Dumézil's framework. There is, first, a gloss by Alfred upon a passage he translated from Boethius's *De consolatione philosophiae*. The scholar-king wrote that he was not interested in wealth and power for their own sake. But Alfred insisted that he could not, no more than another man, perform his "craft" without "tools" and "material." A king needed his land "fully manned." He needed "men who pray [gebedmen], and soldiers [fyrdmen] and workmen [weorcmen]."[10]

That is all Alfred said on the three estates. It is enough: three brotherhoods or fellowships (geferscipe) under a king, for the use of a king in his mission of rule. Alfred's homely figure might seduce us into believing that it was a reflection rather than a structuring of social reality. But that would be wrong; this is the realm, too, of imagining; Alfred's England was renowned for a blurring of the line separating those who fought and those who worked. The Anglo-Saxon army could not have existed in the form it did in a world so rigid as those of functional brotherhoods. Yet Alfred, an administrative genius in a crisis of invasion, glimpsed the successful performance of function to lie in a distinction, at least a specification of orders. Like many, perhaps most, of the early formulations of the estates, his was as much or more a creation or imagination of the facts as a statement of them.

The suspicion that Alfred's strongly royalist view of the three orders was linked to a crisis mentality is reinforced by similar patterns revealed in the statements made by two clerics a little more than a century later. Renewed Danish invasions and a sense that internal discipline was crumbling provoked reflections that placed the three orders, in their later common Latin forms, within a Christian framework of good and evil and the divine plan. Aelfric, abbot of Eversham, used the figure three times (once in a letter to Wulfstan), and one of these statements is all but restated by Wulfstan. As Aelfric had it (a seventeenth-century translation is peculiarly appropriate to this study),

> The throne is founded upon these three [columns or] pillars: *laboratores, bellatores, oratores. Laboratores* are plowmen and husbandmen, whose only is the charge to procure us whereon to maintain life. *Oratores* be they who

gain us unto God, . . . and the service of God, as a spiritual labor, is only their charge for the behoof of us all. *Bellatores* are such as defend our cities and land, by force of arms withstanding an enemy that goes about to subdue us. . . . [The knight] is the minister of God; in his own place set, to work revenge upon evil doers. These be the three pillars . . . that uphold the chair of estate; and down that falls, if one of them be decayed; whereby the other become unserviceable.[11]

And Wulfstan: "Every just throne stands on three props [stapelum], that stands perfectly right. One is *Oratores*, and the other is *Laboratores*, and the third is *Bellatores*." Wulfstan defines each, then continues: "On these three props shall every throne stand with justice among Christian people. And if any of them become weakened, soon the throne wavers; and if any of them fail entirely, then the throne falls down, and that will be the entire ruin of the people."[12]

Aelfric's context is eschatological. His royal throne comes into play as he meditates upon the evil only too apparent in the sixth and last age. It is important to note the mutuality of the three orders, which is seen also in Wulfstan's formulation. But more important, because prior, is the distinction of men. Each group has its "only" charge. Another of Aelfric's discussions of the estates was similarly poised and similarly if specially pointed: the passage occurred as an appendix to a discussion of the Maccabees (the parallels to England were too obvious even for statement), but it was a warning to spiritual men to keep to their prayers, not don the warrior's arms.[13]

Altogether the most remarkable element of these two nearly identical formulations is the furniture. Like Alfred's use of craft and tools, Aelfric's and Wulfstan's image of the throne is forced, though here it is the image itself rather than the orders that have received most of the violence. Just what is it that the abbot and archbishop see? A throne on a tricolumnar base? That would be an odd arrangement, one hard to square with Aelfric's geometry of collapse. A three-legged throne? That perhaps is how the passage was remembered in the seventeenth century, indeed within weeks of the *Answer*.[14] But thrones (king-stools)—whether chairs or the more common fold-stool—had four legs.[15] Nothing could more neatly demonstrate the artificiality, that is, the cunning and purposefulness, of the reference to the three orders in England around the year 1000.

About a generation later similar figures, similarly brief and employed for similar purposes, were remembered and invented—imagined—in northern France. In the heart of Francia the Carolingian dominion was nearly in a state of political collapse, and two Carolingian bishops found tripartition useful for a purpose that routinely has been described as "reactionary": to restore a supposedly ideal, supposedly abandoned or threatened social order. Le Goff indeed has described their mentality as a social fear bordering on "panic."[16]

In 1024, Gerald of Cambrai was reported to have said that "since the beginning, mankind has been divided into three parts, among men of prayer, farmers, and men of war; . . . each is the concern of both the others." The words occurred in a panegyric of Gerald known to have been commissioned by the bishop himself. Duby's careful exegesis of the passage in its several contexts demonstrated that the trifunctional figure served two purposes dear to the heart of Gerald, a bishop and a scion of the Carolingian house. One was to shore up royal authority by making it absolute master of the sword, which otherwise was wildly and cruelly wielded by an almost obscene knighthood. The other was to reassert the authority of the bishops in the face of challenges posed by heretics and by the egalitarian implications of the Peace of God movements that were rife in time of heightened eschatological expectation. "Various perverse leveling policies" and the anarchy of the warriors could be attacked by showing the basic inequality of the world from the beginning (along with the mutuality and charity that are the necessary complements of divine inequality) and by subordinating both the clergy and the warriors to their supreme heads, the bishops and the king. Interestingly, in light of the English story of the later sixteenth century and the seventeenth century, the clergy and the bishops were all but identified in this first Continental statement.[17]

A few years later Adalbero of Laon, another bishop of princely stock, provided another of these terse dicta: "Triple then is the house of God which is thought to be one: on earth, some pray, others fight, still others work; which three are joined together and may not be torn asunder; so that on the function of each the works of the others rest, each in turn assisting all."[18] Claude Carozzi's analysis of this passage in the *Carmen ad Robertum* is a remarkable demonstration of the purposes served by and the mechanism by which "la vieille idéologie indo-européenne" became a Christian and European doctrine.[19] Like Gerald, Adalbero took for granted that the sword is or ought to be wielded by the king, the other men of war being merely his ministers; similarly he saw the bishops as the possessors of the power of prayer, all others being their delegates. But Adalbero's king was also *sacerdos*, charged with maintaining a proper distinction among the kinds of men; only he, with the sword, had the power to do so. Yet the confusion of orders was precisely the problem. The *Carmen* also was bothered with the outbreak of heresy, often itself linked with a confusion of orders. But the real villains for Adalbero were the monks, particularly those influenced by Cluny. On the one hand, they would set themselves apart from the bishops and secular clergy, make themselves a distinct and superior sort of men. On the other, they would disturbingly draw the warriors to them and away from the discipline of the king, "monkify" them into crusaders. This theme, Duby has demonstrated, is important not only to Adalbero but to much of the subsequent medieval career of the three orders: the figure flourished where episcopacy sought to combat the would-be independence of the monks and where bishops and king were in substantial accord.[20]

Carozzi demonstrates that the trifunctional figure served to reconcile and superimpose several bipartite oppositions, of which the distinctions between nobles and serfs and clergy-bishops and monks are the most significant. The antithesis between nobles and serfs was between the beautiful and the ugly; they were both animals, however, and subsumption of the nobles under the *rex-sacerdos* served to keep them beautiful, powerful, and yet tame. The danger posed by a distinct order of monks was neatly eliminated by placing them under the bishops. The monstrosity of monk-knights was averted by the distinct orders of those who pray and those who fight. That, for Adalbero, was the "house of God."

The results of these painful researches into the origins of the orders of those who pray, fight, and work seem just a bit surprising to the French historians who have undertaken them. Is it that the three estates appear from the beginning in France to be invoked in the name of counterreform, in resistance to chiliastic and antinomian vapors exuded by would-be holy laymen and would-be militant monks, in the threat they posed to the traditional and sacred loci of power? English historians might be less surprised. They have heard it before, in their training, and later, in the flow of time: "No bishop, no king."

The prima facie absurd attempts to compass heretics and reformers, so automatic to the French bishops, bring to mind the wild charges of anabaptism and Munsterian fanaticism laid at presbyterians and "puritans" of a later age. Who were these heretics of the early eleventh century in France? There was a certain Leutard, who, upon a nocturnal vision of bees entering his private parts, gave up his wife and became a prophet. There was the largely well-to-do group of men and women with their homemade gnosticism in Orléans in 1022, spiritual adepts infused directly with the Holy Spirit. There was a more hard-headed crew in Liège and Arras, whose rejection of the sacraments of the church, which they shared with the mystics of Orléans, was linked to social righteousness—un-Catholic workers, so to speak.[21] What had these to do with the orthodox, Cluniac reformers? The leaders of this international movement had sensitive noses for power that led them to the locally powerful laity, particularly those amenable to a different logic of the sword that owed little to princes, much to their local influence, and most to God. Once again, English historians need little prompting. How could the sturdy lay puritans and the orthodox men of "gifts" of the later sixteenth century and the seventeenth century be brought together with the Familists, with the deranged Leutards of their own period, John Hacket and Edmund Copinger, with John of Leyden? The English historian knows that James did it; he recalls litanies of abuse from court clerics along these lines. He does not believe it, yet somehow he recognizes a certain type or style of thought, even a structure. If he persists in his comparisons, he sees in these monks and knights the spirit of others more familiar to him. He sees presbyterian clergymen and their lay allies, men living in two worlds at once, the City of God and the City of Man; he sees the court and—if these laymen could make the world over in their image—the godly, disciplined country. Of course, the historian knows better than to allow his mind to wander.

In such circumstances did the three orders make their reappearance in Europe. The tripartite figure was not always put to identical purposes: Le Goff, in particular, has stressed its utility in asserting a creative, honorable role for toil.[22] Nor did it have a continuous prominence in European thought. On Duby's reckoning, the scheme all but disappeared from French thought after the early eleventh-century outburst, though it returned to "stay" in the middle of the twelfth. "The hiatus corresponds to the collapse of the monarchical state." By contrast, in England there was "no eclipse, at least no protracted one."[23] In early twelfth-century England the trifunctional scheme was employed repeatedly, sometimes with some eccentricity. Eadmer of Canterbury's *ordines* of *orantes, agricultores,* and *defensores* (1115) were explained by means of a strange barnyard comparison between them and sheep, cattle, and dogs.[24] More significant perhaps, certainly more edifying, is the report and manuscript illustration of a trifunctional nightmare Henry I had in 1130; Henry was attacked in turn by rustics, knights, and clergy, each with their proper tools.[25]

From this time forward the three orders became a European commonplace, a generalized, inescapable part of the culture. In the fourteenth century English preachers treated the three orders as a commonplace; so did John Wyclif and Sir John Oldcastle.[26] No doubt specialized researches will reveal a nuanced picture for England; this writer is struck by the oddity, for example, that the idea was rampant in Lollard circles, while Reginald Pecock, a remarkable opponent of the Lollards, hewed determinedly to a bipartite distinction of clergy and laity, even when tripartition clearly would have made some of his points better.[27] Yet in the main, no doubt, in England as elsewhere the prime purpose of the three estates under the king was reactionary, though not necessarily in a pejorative sense. It upheld order, distinction, inequality; it urged a return to the virtues rather than a restructuring of society as a remedy for social ills. Much of its character can be glimpsed in the way it handled the anomaly of the merchant: God made the three estates but the "Devil made the burghers and usurers" went one fourteenth-century sermon.[28]

If England was the source of the infection, in the twelfth century as well as before the Conquest, it was quite late in manifesting one symptom of the disease. Modern research rather convincingly has revealed that the "afforced council" that came to be known as Parliament was not considered a meeting of the estates, let alone three of them, at least until late in the fourteenth century or, more likely, early in the fifteenth. This critical fact—that the English Parliament took root without significant reference to a system of estates—is of enormous importance for the story that follows.

The same fact also has a historiographical bearing, for the debates and then the orthodoxies inspired by the *Answer* from the seventeenth to the nineteenth centuries did their share to shape scholarly opinion even well into the twentieth. By the later eighteenth century, it took a career heretic like David Hume to point out that the then-orthodox triad of king, Lords, and Commons was a seventeenth-century novelty—a style that, though "implied in many institutions, no former king of England would have used, and no subject would have been permitted to use."[29] Hume's judgment is not wide of the mark.

In a sense, the reconstitution of the traditional estates into the pre-modern constitution was one of the tasks Bishop Stubbs set for himself in the nineteenth century. His pages on the early history of the figure of the *oratores*, *bellatores*, and *laboratores* remain useful summaries, and his attempt to view the English Parliament from the days of Edward I forward as an assembly of the three correlative estates of the lords spiritual, lords temporal, and the Commons, was, if anything, the opposite of the insularity with which he often is taxed.[30]

But Stubbs's attempt to find the three estates enshrined as a constitutional principle in the English Parliament from the Model Parliament of 1295 forward has been roundly and decisively rejected on two grounds. First is the point of mere fact: for some considerable time thereafter, parliaments had various memberships; the meeting of 1295 (or 1265) provided no model. Second, and far more significantly, it has been argued that to focus upon the constituent elements, rather than the function, of early parliaments is to ask precisely the wrong, because unhistorical, question. The membership of Parliament raised no points of principle. According to this view, stated most vigorously by H. G. Richardson and G. O. Sayles, parliaments were specialized meetings of the king's council, called primarily to do justice; their "afforced" or beefed-up membership reflected function, not a preconceived notion of status-based representation.[31]

But Richardson and Sayles did not concern themselves otherwise than to correct prevailing misconceptions about the early history of Parliament. Albert Frederick Pollard, by contrast, had a more far-reaching purpose: to read elements of sixteenth-century constitutional and political ideas out of the history, in the main, of the fourteenth and early fifteenth century. Pollard viewed the non-status-based curial English Parliament as essentially and irrevocably determined, for sixteenth-century purposes, by practices and habits of thought well in place before the middle years of the fifteenth century, a period that Pollard regarded as an inconsequential anomaly.

Pollard's dazzling *Evolution of Parliament* argued that it was a "myth" to consider Parliament as an assembly of estates.[32] The connection between "blood nobility" and the right to summons in the House of Lords (or what came to be called such) was a "fiction." Indeed, "Parliament, so far from being a system of three estates, is the very negation of the whole idea." This was a fortunate circumstance, in Pollard's own surprisingly insular view, because it rejected the notion that there were "three states," not one, each "entitled to veto national progress." England thus avoided the horrors of a political system linked to the estates: the "dilemma of stagnation or revolution," a "representative system founded on class distinctions" —in a word, France.[33]

To call Parliament a "negation" of an idea that was not, on Pollard's own reckoning, asserted until the fifteenth century was not very helpful. But parliaments in England never could be subsumed well or completely to a system of estates on the French model; this is not to say that it was not done, but only that it could not be done without forcing some of the facts out of the model and forcing others to fit. There was, for example, the truth, approachable from several directions, that peerage and nobility were not coincident categories in England: blood right did not guarantee a personal summons and the ranks of those called noble were far greater than the dozens or scores of men who received personal writs of summons. The right of the bishops and abbots at least could be seen as an expression of their civil position—their baronial rank—rather than their spiritual function (though this was and remained a vexed question); certainly the bishops and abbots did not possess a veto or a separate cameral position that neatly would have mirrored a distinct *status*. Moreover, in a point stressed particularly by Helen Cam, the election of knights and burgesses was an expression of locality, not class; the House of Commons, when it came to exist, was not a "house of routuriers" but of "communities."[34] Only such a view could account for the presence of gentry within the Commons in the fourteenth and fifteenth centuries as in the sixteenth, and not only in the shrieval seats. Finally, as Frederic William Maitland has remarked, English law developed in response to the claims of tenure, not personal status; there was little but custom and local recognition behind a claim to nobility or the rejection of it.

But what of the three estates of the preachers and social theorists? Pollard knew it was the "prevalent theory"; with some contempt he remarked that "we are told" that they were the clergy, the nobility, and the commons.[35] If the three orders existed, they were not important. Pollard made much, though ultimately with little success, of the ambiguities and equivocations of the word "estate" in English, particularly as seen in the phrase, "the estate of the king." Pollard also tried to establish that use of the concept of estates to describe Parliament, when it did occur, was far from uniform. In 1401 Parliament was likened to a trinity of three estates, not those of medieval tradition but of the *Answer:* king, Lords, Commons. The *Modus tenendi parliamentum* knew of six *gradus*, one of which was the king.

William Thirning in 1399 spoke of five estates, one of which—"bachelors and commons"—was divided "by north" and "by south."[36]

Other aberrant usages can be added to Pollard's file. In 1433, John Stafford, bishop of Bath and Wells, defined the "triplex regni status" as the "prelati, proceres, et magnati"; the "milities, armigere, et mercatores"; and "in populo, cultores, artifices, et vulgares." The latter group, though an estate of the realm, was not included in the Parliament.[37] In 1483 in a draft sermon (later revised in accordance with the conventional enumeration of the estates) John Russell, bishop of London, made the three "parts" to be king, Lords, and Commons.[38] On Pollard's reckoning, the traditional view was an alien notion unneeded for parliamentary purposes before the Treaty of Troyes of 1421, when for the purposes of uniformity in sanctioning classes the English Parliament was described in terms close to those of French Estates-General. From that time forward, it came "slowly and doubtingly" into use in England.[39]

The assault of Maitland and Pollard upon Stubbs threw historical studies into something of an uproar. In 1924, an innocent, nonhistorian reviewer for the *Times Literary Supplement* thought he had got the matter right in criticizing a book for making the estates out to be king, Lords, and Commons. Stubbs had done his work, it would seem, but Pollard quickly turned to the letters column to insist that there was no error, at least if the Rolls of Parliament, Lord Burghley, Bulstrode Whitelocke, and Charles Fox were evidence. Within a week, Sir Frederick Pollock (then at work on his edition of John Selden's *Table talk*) argued back that the traditional anatomy of lords spiritual, lords temporal, and Commons had the preponderance of authority behind it; George Greenwood similarly argued that the view Pollard preferred among the aberrants (king, Lords, Commons) was essentially a doctrine of the "popular lawyers" of the seventeenth century. The hapless reviewer was left to hope that the Institute of Historical Research would "get the question definitely settled and the right interpretation, whatever it is, accepted by everybody."[40]

Had Pollard gone too far? The full answer had to wait a decade and came in a massive rebuttal of Pollard's view for the fifteenth century by Stanley Bertram Chrimes. Chrimes was a neo-Stubbsian who, while rejecting Stubbs's view that the "three estates theory" (as Chrimes called it) was in place in 1295 or for some time thereafter, asserted vigorously that it came into play decisively in the early fifteenth century and became constitutional orthodoxy well before 1485. If the origins of Parliament lay apart from a system of estates, its later fourteenth- and fifteenth-century development was inexplicable without such a system. Chrimes demonstrated that Pollard had, in effect, created greater ambiguity about the term "estate" than in fact existed. Smoothly and decisively he showed that Pollard's "estate" of the king was a mirage, a confusion of two discrete senses of a word, which context normally kept apart. Chrimes also reasserted, as best he could as matters stood in 1936, the dominance of the traditional estates as a scheme of social analysis in the fifteenth century, usefully adverting to a recent literary study that showed the continuing grip of the traditional scheme upon the fifteenth- and sixteenth-century mind.[41]

Chrimes's main task was to demonstrate that the traditional social categories were brought into play in institutional theory and practice in the fifteenth century. His primary analytic tool was a tabulation of the sanctioning clauses to statutes from the accession of Richard II to 1 Henry VI. The examination revealed "gradual consolidation" in the formula of assent from heterogenous and apparently indifferent constructions until 1429, when the appearance of the lords spiritual and temporal and the Commons, but no others, became the standard, the phrase "by authority of Parliament" being added consistently (with only two exceptions) after 1444.[42] Paralleling this process was a first stage of rather vague bandying about of the "estates of the realm" at the end of the fourteenth century and a second stage of increasingly confident assertions of the three traditional estates thereafter.[43] The process was already to be seen in 1404, well before the Treaty of Troyes. As Henry Beaufort, bishop of Lincoln and Winchester, put it in 1404:

> each realm resembles the body of a man, in which the right side resembles the holy church, the left side the temporality, and the other members resemble the commonalty of the realm. Wherefore, our lord the king wishes to have the advice, counsel, and general assent of all the estates of his realm, and for this he has summoned his present Parliament.[44]

In 1428, the "assent of the three estates," apart from the king, was noted in an important document defining the powers of the protector.[45] From this time forward the documentation is considerable. Against an overwhelming body of contrary evidence the notion that the three estates came only "slowly and doubtingly" into use will not stand up.[46] Bishop Russell corrected his lapse of 1483 in the sermon he actually delivered; only once, then, in 1401, was the king ever included among the three estates, and the bishops were never left out from distinct and separate mention, save for Bishop Stafford's usage in 1433. Whatever may have been the case in the record and process concerning Richard II in 1399, the three estates, traditionally defined in their parliamentary forms as lords spiritual, lords temporal, and Commons, played an unambiguous role in the records surrounding the accession of Richard III. Bertie Wilkinson, who felt impelled to challenge Chrimes's view about the meaning of the "estates" in 1399, is nevertheless in no doubt about the general fifteenth-century view of Parliament as an assembly of estates.[47] In Chrimes's view and Wilkinson's, Parliament was not simply an assembly of estates in the fifteenth century, but it was not less than one, and if problems remained about the nature of the connection between the Commons and the commons, about nobility and peerage, about the precise position of the bishops, they were not so great as to prevent the traditional enumeration of the estates, in its parliamentary form, from becoming the standard.

*

Fifteenth-century reliance upon the traditional three estates provided a bedrock of usage by which later writers, especially of the seventeenth century, could gauge their own views. Whether one liked it or not, fifteenth-century practice rendered the enumeration of the estates found in the *Answer* at odds with the greatest part of the visible evidence. When antiquarian interests and skills developed late in the sixteenth century and early in the seventeenth, when also the fifteenth century had become antique, fifteenth-century usage made it appear that alternative views of the estates were varieties of special pleading, less scholarship than politics. There were politics and passions on both sides of what became briefly a burning question late in the sixteenth and early in the seventeenth century.[48] But when the storm had calmed, it seemed to most learned people that a fact, not an opinion, was involved.

But an antiquarian response was not of much interest to the mid-Tudor humanists, however much the later antiquarianism was the offspring of humanist learning. Before the revival of interest in the question of the estates, there was one more phase, a bland indifference to the whole business, an interval when the fifteenth-century pattern was not so much denied as ignored, irrelevant both to the problems and the intellectual predilections of mid-Tudor Englishmen.

Geoffrey Elton made this case in a major study, *"The Body of the Whole Realm": Parliament and Representation in Medieval and Tudor England,* an attempt in an odd way to assert Pollardian truths for the sixteenth century against the assault by scholars of the fifteenth century upon Pollard's delving into their territory. It was perhaps not quite an accident that Pollard showed an ill-disguised sympathy for enumerations of the estates that included the king, even as he attacked the whole notion itself; Elton has set himself the same task, in effect, in rescuing the sixteenth-century constitution (especially that of the mid-sixteenth century) from the implications of the fifteenth century.

Elton conceded to the fifteenth-century consensus, much as Chrimes (if not Wilkinson) conceded to the consensus on the curial, nonrepresentational origins of parliaments. The concept of the three estates under and apart from the king was at least the "theoretical" position in the fifteenth century. Despite his own doubts about the practical significance of all the talk, in particular about the prospect of reconciling the House of Commons with the "Nährstand," Elton agreed that it was "obvious" to fifteenth-century observers that "Parliament consisted of the lords spiritual, the lords temporal, and the Commons."[49] Around 1530, however, a shift in usage came to express a distinct sense of the institution, one that had the effect of reducing the three-estates conception into insignificance. Whereas the fifteenth century saw the king as distinct from Parliament (king and Parliament), mid-Tudor sensibility tended to see the king as part of Parliament (king-in-Parliament).[50] The word "estate" was not used often (it may have been deliberately avoided) by Elton's sources, certainly not used by Elton himself. The mid-Tudor stress was on a partnership of king, Lords, and Commons, each equally a "part" of the Parliament. Probably it was a lawyer's caution that led James Dyer, for example, so to speak in law French; the less said about the details the better.[51] In this way, the "ghost of Fortescue and the middle ages was laid to rest."[52]

Fortescue was not so easily dismissed, any more than the fifteenth century was; the new antiquarian impulse gathering strength in the later sixteenth century would take care of that.[53] The heyday of the mid-Tudor pattern was short, although like all else it left its legacy. Established around 1530, the easygoing mid-Tudor humanist idealism was under pressure less than sixty years later. Its vocabulary sometimes had been put to more radical purposes than those for which it had been called into play; more consistently, it came to be associated with the hot-headed protestantism that Henry VIII hated as much as he hated anything. Unsurprisingly, when this next pivoting of the seesaw occurred, the old, the Dumézilian, the fifteenth-century vision of the estates was remembered. The mantle of Alfred and Aelfric, perhaps even more the mantle of Adalbero and Gerald, descended upon James VI and I and Richard Bancroft. Before that occurred, mid-Tudor humanism gave England a brief, innocent flirtation with the constitutional scheme employed in the *Answer to the xix propositions.*

3
The Sixteenth Century: Mixed Government and the Estates to the Rise of the Presbyterian Movement

Much of the current interest in the *Answer to the xix propositions* and its place in English political thought stems from an illuminating book by Corinne Comstock Weston, *English Constitutional Theory and the House of Lords, 1556–1832*.[1] Weston settled upon the *Answer* as the seminal document it certainly is, and she uncovered its place in constitutional thought from the 1640s through the nineteenth century. She showed that long after the *Answer* itself was all but forgotten its categories and thought patterns continued to control thinking about the English constitutional structure.

When Weston turned her attention to the matter of the *Answer*'s origins, however, the results were rather less successful. Hers was a pioneering study. Like other pioneers, she had the courage to get lost, and she did so. Her entire interpretive structure was based on false premises and ultimately upon false understandings of the facts. She was not aware that the language of mixed government by the estates had been employed widely by opposition theorists during the Short Parliament and the first year or so of the Long Parliament—that is, that it had been current for two years before the publication of the *Answer*. Nescience led her to mistake the originality of the *Answer*: whereas she thought the *Answer* was, in the context of the mid-seventeenth century, the originator of its own doctrines, in truth its originality lay in its adoption of modes of thought identified with the opposition. Second, and connected with the first point, she did not know that a key though tacit assumption of the *Answer*—that the bishops were not an estate—had been declared a treasonable doctrine (for Scotland) by Charles I in 1640, and that in so declaring he was parroting an opinion dear to his father and one shared (in a more muted form) by Queen Elizabeth.

Weston was aware of the almost total absence of expressed notions of mixed government earlier in the seventeenth century and was puzzled by it (as had been R. W. K. Hinton before her and J. G. A. Pocock afterward).[2] But she could offer no reason for it. Yet some reason had to be offered, because, as she did know, there had been some exploration of the idea of mixed government in Tudor England.

Indeed, in her search for origins, Weston had to latch onto the Tudor period if there were to be any origins at all. This approach led her into a number of predicaments. Working with several fairly well-known and accessible writers, she tried to find in them a "firm foundation" for the *Answer.*[3] Such a firm foundation presumably would establish: (1) that there was a clear if not altogether complete set of Tudor notions upon which the *Answer* could have built; (2) that these notions were common enough to be accessible to the *Answer*'s authors; and (3) that these notions were acceptable for use by a king to plead his own case. In each task she failed. The writers she used were either far less clear than she wished them to be or tinged with a radicalism that was as unacceptable in 1642 as it had been during the sixteenth century. And given these limitations, some of which she recognized, by way of qualification, there simply was not enough evidence to provide the firm foundation for which she was searching. Weston seemed to have conceded this point when she added to her slim evidentiary corpus some additional material created ex nihilo: "there was probably much unrecorded talk about mixed government."[4] Had she succeeded in her quest, the situation would have been even more confusing, for then her firm foundation would have supported a nonexistent ground floor (the early seventeenth century) with the *Answer* somehow levitating above it.

It is to be remembered that Weston's study was a pathfinding effort; her difficulties were those of an able scholar struggling to make sense of limited and refractory evidence. If nothing else, she inspired other scholars to probe further, and since the publication of her book a certain amount of new evidence has come in.[5] Yet it remains true that mixed government disappeared in the early seventeenth century, and that basic fact is as puzzling as it ever has been. Recently, in a book written jointly with Janelle Renfrow Greenberg, Weston has offered a new solution. Perhaps by giving more weight to some of her earlier scruples, Weston now has dispensed with the "firm foundation." The new study of the *Answer* and its influence, *Subjects and Sovereigns,* argues "that the political ideas of Tudor Englishmen were not prototypes of the parliamentarian ideology of the 1640s," parliamentarian ideology being what opposition theorists extracted from the *Answer*, which was more than many royalists wanted but really no less than the *Answer* stated. In a related vein, though she now recognizes that the *Answer* had some consanguinity with the earlier statements of the opposition in 1640–1642 and that these statements raised the thorny matter of the estates of the realm, Weston dismisses such antecedents as unimportant: "it was not until the publication of Charles I's *Answer to the Nineteen Propositions* that the membership of the three estates became inextricably linked to theories of kingship and hence an explosive issue, engaging widespread interest and penetrating seventeenth-century political thought."[6] It will be demonstrated that it is precisely in the sixteenth and very early seventeenth century that "membership of the three estates became inextricably linked to theories of kingship and hence an explosive issue, engaging widespread interest." Weston clearly enough, though quite accidentally it appears, stated the problem and gave exactly the wrong answer. That is why she now argues that the *Answer* was all but sui generis.

The task, then, is to show that Weston was wrong the first time and wrong the second, despite the fact that she seemingly holds an opinion now diametrically opposite to the first. That her first interpretation was wrong will be indicated by the following examination of the Tudor evidence concerning mixed government by the estates of the realm before the rise of the presbyterian movement. That she was wrong in her second interpretation will be shown in due course.

Mixed government by the three estates of king, Lords, and Commons: it is a cumbersome phrase. Why should such stress be laid upon it? It was, to be sure, in terms of these "estates" that Charles and his advisers described the constitution in June 1642. The expression, then, is accurate. But is it not an idle pedantry? So perhaps it seemed to Weston in *English Constitutional Theory and the House of Lords*; she devoted no more than a footnote and a brief textual remark to the business of estates.[7] She recognized that the enumeration of estates in the *Answer* was not the traditional one. But because the scheme used by the *Answer* was not entirely unknown in earlier English history, because indeed it was to be found occasionally in the Tudor evidence known to her, Weston simply let the matter rest.

There is an excellent rationale for ignoring the *Answer*'s seemingly gratuitous glossing of the classical-humanist terminology of the One, the

Few, and the Many as "estates." From the point of view of "pure" classical-humanist political theory, "estate" is an irrelevancy, even a barbarism. What is more, with respect to the future significance of the *Answer*—twenty and more years down the road—the use of "estate" to gloss monarchy, aristocracy, and democracy seems to be neither here nor there.[8] The constituents of the balance have to be called something, one supposes, and it does not seem to matter much what they are called. To look forward or—perhaps to say essentially the same thing—to look with secular eyes upon the English constitution is to be suitably indifferent to the business of estates. "Mixed government" will do, maybe with a remark or two that a polemical edge is to be found in calling the king an estate.

But this facile treatment ignores the most significant point about the *Answer*. It was not entirely a secular document, and it reversed a long-standing royal insistence that the traditional enumeration did matter. Charles had reiterated this point as recently as 1640.[9] The insistence was concerned intimately with the fate of the bishops in two kingdoms, England and Scotland—which was what led Charles to declare, as had his father earlier, that it was treason to assert that the bishops were not an estate of the realm. And, as indicated, Hyde's distress over the implied exclusion of the bishops from their due place as an estate of the realm was that it was quite as damaging as the *Answer*'s overt description of the king as an estate. It considerably simplifies the situation to accept Hyde's remarks at face value.

To appreciate the force of the point, we must anticipate our story a bit and allow an assertion that will be proved later: there was nothing intrinsically or essentially radical about the use of classical political theory to describe the English constitution. Sometimes it was radical; sometimes it was not. Most tellingly, on at least two occasions before 1642, it was strongly royalist. In Arthur Hall's painfully public outburst in 1581 and in the discrete ruminations in 1611 of Thomas Egerton, Lord Ellesmere, consideration of the English constitution in terms of the three classically defined "estates" of king, Lords, and Commons was employed to do exactly what the celebrated portion of the *Answer* was designed to do, namely smash the pretensions and expose the excesses of the Commons in order to preserve the power of the prince.[10] Thus whatever was wrong with mixed government by the estates—and James and Charles thought it wrong—was extrinsic to the notion in its pure, classical form. That extrinsic element was presbyterianism, which (in England) embraced the theory of mixed government as a way of settling another set of concerns—concerns having to do with the bishops and royal supremacy in causes ecclesiastical. Presbyterianism tainted mixed government in the eyes of James VI and I and his son.

Earlier sallies into the domestication of classical-humanist political thought sometimes revised the enumeration of the estates without really intending to say anything decisive about the place of the bishops or the clergy in the body politic. They were, one might say, accidentally secular. Perhaps the first significant penetration of classical-republican conceptions came and went without ever being noticed as such. This entry occurred with the introduction of the Thomistic *regimene* into English thought by Sir John Fortescue.[11] Had Fortescue understood Thomas as Thomas understood himself, elements of classical sensibility might have entered English political consciousness with Fortescue's famous adaptation of Thomistic thought, the notion of the *dominium politicum et regale*. But Fortescue did not ponder upon the republicanism of Thomas. Far from being a statement of the constituents of the body politic, Fortescue's *dominium politicum et regale* was a legalist notion, a formula used to describe two channels of royal authority. To simplify things somewhat, the *dominium regale* was the prerogative or area in which the king could act absolutely, in the sense that he could act "from himself" alone. The *dominium politicum* was not, in Fortescue's hands, an expression of the Aristotelian "polity" as it had been in part for Thomas; rather, it was primarily and simply the other channel of royal authority, in which the king was bound to act according to certain modalities and not otherwise. The boundaries of the two forms of rule were established by a law that was above both; the law established one area in which the king was bound by law to act within the law and another in which the king by law was "absolved" from law—an area of discretion, of free will, almost of "executive privilege." So while Fortescue is rightfully a source of the idea of limited royal government, he was not a proponent of mixed government properly so called. Fortescue's mixture was of laws, not men; his fundamental distinction was bipartite rather than tripartite; the idea of the three traditional estates could be cozily nestled (as it was in the fifteenth century) within a part of the territory of the *dominium politicum*, the part accorded to the Parliament.

A better beginning for the introduction of classical terminology into English political thought can be found in Thomas Elyot's *The boke named the governour* (1531).[12] Elyot was in no sense a proponent of mixed government. He enters the story because he saw the English language as deficient in political vocabulary and sought consciously to remedy the defect by the importation of foreign words. Part of the exercise, as he saw it, was to introduce into English the classical and humanist vocabulary of the three pure forms of government. (Employment of these words remained self-conscious even in the early seventeenth century: almost every Tudor and early Stuart expositor of mixed government assumed that his readers would need help with these "hard words.")[13] Thus Elyot began his book, largely a manual on the education of competent and virtuous rulers, with two chapters of definition. In the first he fought a valiant but losing battle with his beloved English in trying to halt the well-advanced practice of translating *respublica* as "common weal." Elyot preferred "public weal" because "public took his beginning of people: which in Latin is *Populus*: in which word is contained all the inhabitants of a realm or city, of what estate or condition so ever they be." "Common," however, was to be associated with *plebs*, which "in English is called the commonalty, which signifieth only the multitude, wherein be contained the base and vulgar inhabitants." With similar care, he defined aristocracy and democracy in his second chapter and distinguished both from sovereign rule by a single person.[14]

Elyot's intuitions were correct. There was a marked looseness in the use of all these exotic words and notions in the early sixteenth century. A case in point is Thomas Starkey's *Dialogue between Cardinal Pole and Thomas Lupset* (ca. 1535), a work that originally formed a part, though a weak one, of Weston's original body of Tudor evidence for mixed government. It is true that Starkey reported Reginald Pole to have said that "the most wise men, considering the nature of princes, yea, and the nature of man as it is indeed, affirm a mixed state to be of all other the best and most convenient to conserve the whole out of tyranny."[15] To realize this happy mixed state, Starkey had Pole argue that Parliament should repose its "counsel and authority" when not in session in a fourteen-member council. It would nominate another council, the king's "proper" (hence, privy) council, which was to advise the king directly.[16]

These suggestions are retrogressive or visionary, depending on one's point of view. In one sense they look backward to the Ordainers and the Appellants, baronial king-yoking councils that knew nothing of mixed government by the estates and much of baronial insistence that the king was only one of the peers. Indeed, inasmuch as the king had direct control of the appointments of the first council and of the second by a route scarcely less so, and inasmuch as the basic function of the council was but to "advise," the plan looks in some ways less ambitious than the thirteenth- and fourteenth-century attempts. On the other hand, Starkey's rendition of Pole presumes the continuity of the concept, if not the actual existence, of the Parliament. The parliamentary council would serve as a legal watchdog and *in extremis* could summon a parliament. It would have an interest in the *arcana imperii*: leagues and confederations, wars and peace. It would subject the king to permanent counsel, to law and advice, will he or will he not. This anticipated some of the projects of the Long Parliament in 1640–1642: the Triennial Act, the revival of the *custos regni*, the Nineteen Propositions.

But was there a clear, consistent social vision to differentiate this "mixed state" from a limited one? Was there a connection between the social and the institutional orders? Let us look closely at the composition of the two councils. Starkey presented two slightly differing versions, one somewhat before and one immediately after his remarks on the virtues of the mixed state.

Extra-sessional parliamentary council: King's "proper" council:

First Version

4 great lay peers	2 bishops
2 bishops (London and	4 lords
Canterbury)	4 men (spiritual and temporal)
4 chief judges	learned in law and politics
4 citizens of London	

Second Version

Chief Constable	2 doctors in divinity
Lord Marshall	2 doctors in civil law
Lord Steward	2 doctors [*sic*] in common law
Lord Chamberlain	4 nobles
4 chief judges	
4 citizens	
2 bishops (London and	
Canterbury)	

The composition of the extra-sessional council does not conform to any of the prevailing social anatomies. Churchmen, lay peers, and commoners there were, but the proportions and the details do not match the traditional view of the three estates, or of aristocracy and democracy. Moreover, this council (according to the second, expanded version) in which Parliament should repose its "counsel and authority" was largely composed of men who owed their membership to an appointment to office by the king. The great peers did not represent the nobility; they were appointed by the king. The clerical component is no easier to construe as representative. The omission of the archbishop of York militates against it; and again, appointment lay with the king. So too the chief judges were members ex officio, their office being a royal appointment. The four citizens of London were the only members whose appointment *might* not lie with the king, but clearly there is no right to infer that they represented the commons; in 1535, London was not yet in a position to speak for the "citizens" or even the merchants of England, let alone the commons. And it is odd to assume that London would be given a choice of its contingent to the council if the other groups were not.

But the social ambiguity of the council is irrelevant, for the council was formed according to different principles—which, one suspects, owe more to Starkey than to Pole. The council was to stand in for Parliament when Parliament was out of session; but in the early sixteenth century that function could be accomplished only by resort to people normally in or near London. If it is assumed that the great officials spent much of their time at court, unlike most peers, then all the members of the council were found between Fulham and Lambeth. Moreover, the virtue of the extrasessional council seems to reside in the professional or official expertise of its members as much as anything else. It is confirmed by the composition of the "proper" council, which according to the more developed version was preponderantly a body of specialists.

In no sense, then, was the Starkey/Pole mixed state an institutional mixture of the social elements of the realm, either of the three traditional estates or of the Few and the Many. Rather, it was an institutional arrangement to ensure that the king was advised by officers of state and consultants. It was to that principle that both king and Parliament were to submit; the "mixed state" turns out to be a bureaucrat's idea of Utopia.

*

If, as Weston claimed, it were "but a step" from the limited constitutionalism of Fortescue to the classical mixed constitution, Starkey did not take it.[17] Perhaps "in retrospect nothing seems more natural," but it was not until 1547 that anything remotely like that step was taken.[18] This was an important moment because it was the first occasion in the Tudor record that the estates were defined as king, Lords, and Commons (and only the third known instance in English history, the others having been in 1483 in a draft sermon later corrected to accord with the traditional view, and in 1401). Weston has yet to notice it.

By November of 1547 Stephen Gardiner, bishop of Winchester, already had crossed the line that separated acceptable from dangerous dissent against the further reform of the church undertaken by Protector Somerset. Since late September, this holdout against further reformation had been confined to the Fleet, largely to restrict him from communicating with his more vocal supporters. They were hoping to use the lower house as a vehicle to protest the Visitation Articles and Homilies of 1547, the leading edge of the reformers' program. Gardiner had no prospect of influencing his fellow bishops, and his hopes lay in a claim that the protector, his council, and the bishops could not outlaw things permitted under the Henrician statutes. Only an act of Parliament could repeal an act of Parliament.

Gardiner, a wily man, pursued this point with Somerset in a letter that was part of a running argument between the two over the respective roles of faith and charity in justification before Christ. Gardiner informed Somerset that the proper relation of faith and charity was that of coordination which

> may be well resembled in the making of laws in this Parliament, when the acts be passed by the three estates, which be all three present and do somewhat to gather and concur to the perfecting of the law; wherein we may not say that any one estate only made the law, or that any one estate excludeth the other in the office of making the law.

The king's assent does not exclude the "other two estates" — "there is none estate only that maketh the law."[19]

Gardiner was stating an obvious fact, that it takes king, Lords, and Commons to make an act of Parliament. His position is incontestable, the epitome of conventionality. But he selected an indirect means of expression. The figure of faith and charity is strained and the reference to estates is peculiar. The direct evidence will not yield an explanation, and perhaps there is none. Some ancillary points, however, suggest a possibility. Gardiner himself was later the author of an untitled manuscript accurately dubbed by its modern editor as a "Machiavellian treatise." In that treatise, which was in considerable measure a set of Machiavellian reflections upon English history, Gardiner showed himself fully conversant with political analysis in terms of the One, the Few, and the Many (king, "barons," "people," as Gardiner had it).[20] Nor was Machiavellian insight something that was only accessible when Gardiner went abroad. A close ally of Somerset, William Thomas, Clerk of the Council, proposed about 1549 a full course of study in Machiavellian politics for the education of the young Edward VI. Thomas claimed, disingenuously, that his study questions came from "divers authors," but in truth they were cribbed, often *seriatim*, from the chapter headings of *The prince* and *The discourses*.[21] It may be, then, that elements of classical political theory underlay Gardiner's too-subtle formulation. All in all, it is at least suggestive for the future that the first Tudor attempt at viewing Parliament in terms of the estates of king, Lords, and Commons came at a perilous and troubled moment, by a man moving rapidly toward the political fringes. But Gardiner's target was the protector, who stood for the king. Gardiner was no friend to the compliant Edwardian bishops; equally unquestionably, he was a friend of order, rank, and degree and to the conservative instincts that eventually took him back to Rome.[22]

The connection between the revised estates and classical mixed government is a likely inference in Gardiner, but it is no more than that. It was shortly to become less a matter of inference than assumption. The pace of domestication quickened in the days of Queen Mary and, not surprisingly, it was in those days that mixed government by the revised estates migrated to the radical end of the political spectrum. Though, as indicated, mixed government was not intrinsically radical, neither was it intrinsically conservative. The later presbyterians who found it useful knew mixed government in part for the service it did for committed protestants during the Catholic interlude. A remarkable instance is *A shorte treatise of politike power* (1556) by John Ponet, Gardiner's successor at Winchester.[23] *A shorte treatise* is remembered largely as an argument in favor of the right of tyrannicide; it is important to see that Ponet's theory of mixed government and his doctrine of tyrannicide (which certainly would be no commendation of the book in Elizabeth's England) grew from the same root. Ponet located the origins of government in God's postdiluvian injunction to Noah, "Whoso sheddeth man's blood, by man shall his blood be shed."[24] "By this ordinance and law he instituteth politic power and giveth authority to men to make more laws."[25] Tyrannicide is the divinely ordained consequence of a tyrant's violation of the terms of his tenure, mixed government the result of God's decision to leave the form of the state to "the discretion of the people." Ponet described the possible choices: government by one king or judge, by "many of the best sort," by "people of the lowest sort," or by "the king, nobility, and the people all together." Immediately, and revealingly, he repeated himself in the language of classical governance, defining the first three choices as monarchy, aristocracy, and democracy and the last as "a mixed state: which men by long continuance have judged to be the best" and most durable. Rather vaguely, Ponet went on to locate the focus of mixed government in the institutional arrangements of various countries, pointing to the diets in Germany and the "parliaments" in England and France.[26]

The judgment of Weston that Ponet's thought "reflected that of Tudor England" is not acceptable.[27] Ponet's thought obviously did not, given its doctrine of private tyrannicide and given also its ranting against the nobility as bitter as any in the sixteenth century.[28] Yet it was not antiepiscopal, either. Ponet was a bishop when he went into exile and so described himself cryptically, on the title page of *A short treatise*, "D.I.P.B.R.W.": Dr. John Ponet, bishop of Rochester and Winchester.

✳

Ponet's thought is not the firm foundation for mixed government, at least for the mixed government of the *Answer.* Another of the Marian exiles provides an equally challenging case, albeit for very different reasons, and his, too, has been claimed as the very soul of Tudor constitutionality.[29] John Aylmer's *An harborowe for faithfull and trewe subiectes* (1559) is a part of the shaky foundation for later mixed government, a part of the process by which Tudor Englishmen familiarized themselves with a strange and alluring vocabulary of politics; but it was, as its author seemed to confess, more wishful thinking and polemical exaggeration than a fair statement of fact.

An harborowe was a rebuttal of a most notorious and well-read pasquil of his own party, John Knox's anti-Marian diatribe, *The first blast of the trumpet against the monstrous regiment of women.* Trying to reassure Knox and other misogynists that the new queen, Elizabeth, posed no threat to her country, Aylmer cataloged the many virtues of the young monarch. Then, as a kind of throwaway line, he argued that even if Elizabeth were not as he described her she could do little harm because of the nature of the English constitution. "Where mixed rulers be," a marginal note ran, "women's government can not be dangerous."[30] How Aylmer squared the thought with the reasons for his own exile is an interesting question. But it was only the beginning of a whole series of desperate shifts to make the best of a bad case.

England, Aylmer said, was not "a mere monarchy, as some for lack of consideration think [a revealing admission], nor a mere oligarchy, nor democracy, but a rule mixed of all these."[31] Each of the three pure forms was defined in the margin. In the mixed state, "each one of these have or should have like authority."[32] As the double verb indicates, Aylmer hedged between a description and a wish. The only evidence Aylmer possibly could adduce for his contention of "like authority" was the Parliament, "wherein you shall find these three estates: the king or queen, which representeth the monarchy; the noble men, which be the aristocracy; and the burgesses and knights the democracy." Aylmer then took a wild leap: Parliament was not the "image" of a mixed state "but the thing in deed."[33] That is, the Parliament—which was a very occasional institution in Tudor England, as Aylmer well knew—was virtually the entire government in England.

Aylmer's description has received the imprimatur of Geoffrey Elton, who quoted it as a fair statement of Tudor constitutional arrangements in his influential collection, *The Tudor Constitution*. But Elton severely edited *An harborowe* to suppress many of the difficulties in Aylmer's scheme, notably Aylmer's own reservations. Before Aylmer's words become constitutional scripture, some of the problems need examination. Not least among them are the many signals that Aylmer was less sure about the mixed government of Tudor England than were some of his modern expositors. First, Aylmer's description of England is based on a tendentious and possibly ironic comparison with Sparta. The Spartan constitution, as Aylmer himself admitted, did not have a properly monarchical component at all. It was essentially a mixture of aristocracy and democracy, Aylmer indicated, and if England were like "Lacedemonia the noblest and best city governed that ever was," it had no real monarch at all.[34] That, of course, was not true, as Aylmer himself repeatedly recognized. Moreover, according to Aristotle, a notable defect of the Spartan constitution was precisely that it proved incapable of controlling its women; if Aylmer knew of this supposed flaw, he must have had his tongue in his cheek from the beginning.[35]

Indeed, Aylmer goes on to describe or wish—the ambiguity persists—England into the Spartan mold. As he says, "In like manner, *if* the Parliament use their privileges: the king can ordain nothing without them."[36] Aylmer then adds that "if" the king acts alone, he is to be blamed as a usurper, and the rest for their "folly" for permitting it. Had it happened? Had English fact run counter to radical classical theory? Is that the meaning of the two "ifs"? Aylmer's view is clear from his own words: "in my judgment those that in King Henry VIII's days, would not grant him, that his proclamations should have the force of a statute, were good fathers of the country, and worthy commendation in defending their liberty."[37] Aylmer's remark is not, as Elton has suggested, a reference to moderates who sought (successfully) to have the Act of Proclamations reduced in "scope and weight"[38] but rather to those who would not have had any such act at all: it was precisely the purpose of the Act of Proclamations that proclamations should have the "force" of statutes—as the act put it, that proclamations would be "obeyed, observed, and kept as though they were made by act of Parliament."[39] Aylmer immediately compares his vanquished Henrician patriots with the cowardly, and quite real, Marian Parliament: "Would God that court of late days, had feared no more the fierceness of a woman, then they did the displeasure of such a man."[40] Practice, Aylmer tells us unambiguously, belies theory.

Much of Aylmer's subsequent discussion hews closer to the actual constitutional line. But one startling assertion-cum-wish does not. Again, the "if": "If she judged offenses according to her wisdom, and not by limitation of statutes and laws: *if she might alone dispose of war and peace*: if in short she were a mere monarch, and not a mixed ruler" there might be more to fear. "But the state being as it is or ought to be (if men were worth their ears) I can see no cause of fear."[41] As Aylmer well knew, and as the next reign amply discovered, the disposition of war and peace did in fact belong to the monarch alone; that is, to prince and council, not to prince-in-Parliament. The "ifs" and the "ought to be" and his view of the Spartan constitution, where war and peace— "policy" —was a conjoint responsibility, leave little room for doubt.

Aylmer, like Ponet and Gardiner before him, is an important figure in the story of the reception of classical mixed government in Tudor England. He explored mixed government, the revision of the estates, the compression of all government into the *dominium politicum*, the parliamentary way. Aylmer's tract was influential, precisely in the right place, for the second part of our story: Martin Marprelate remembered the Aylmer who would have "our Parliament to overrule Her Majesty, and not to yield an inch unto her of their privileges."[42] As has been shown, Aylmer was not so sure those privileges really existed. His reservations, his counterfactuality, his possible irony warn against taking his views as a Tudor commonplace. Elton and

Weston were wrong to claim so much for him. Equally, in relegating him and Ponet to mere footnote qualifications in her new argument, Weston has fallen into the opposite error.[43] Aylmer was a king yoker, if a half-hearted and possibly ironical one. There is one direction we cannot take: whatever might have been Aylmer's intentions toward monarchy, there was nothing profoundly anticlerical or antiepiscopal in his doctrine of estates. None should be expected from that committed, devout, but moderate exile who was on his way to becoming Elizabeth's bishop of London.[44]

Gardiner, Ponet, and Aylmer shared one characteristic besides their predilection for odd formulations of the English constitution: at the time of their statements they were on the political fringe. It might be argued, from their cases, that resort to mixed government and estates-revision was a property of those on the outside and of those writing in times of acute instability. Later Tudor and early Stuart mixed government and estates-revision, after the rise of presbyterianism, had a similar texture, though with a significant difference. The earlier Tudor figures seem more to reflect instability than seek to cause it; later on, the languages we have been examining themselves became destabilizing elements and were used as programs to change the facts. They were not the poses of essentially conservative men or the gasp of a man like Ponet, tottering on the brink of the madness of uncontrollable hatreds, but programmatic schemes of hard-headed radicals out to create a stir.

*

Two early Elizabethan writers, Sir Thomas Smith and John Hooker, provide an intermediate stage. Both wrote early in the reign of Elizabeth, when the memory of Marian troubles was still fresh and when the Elizabethan regime did not possess the stability it later acquired. Smith's exploration of mixed government and Hooker's similar exercise in the revision of the estates may well be carry-overs from the earlier mentality. But both men shared a devotion to the facts, to scholarship and accuracy, that is not evident in the highly charged statements of Gardiner, Ponet, and Aylmer, and this detachment drove Smith and Hooker to far more cautious positions. Writing in the 1560s and early 1570s, the two men shared something else: they brought the period of early exploration of mixed government and estates-revision to a close. There was little further development of these themes in England for about twenty years, until presbyterianism and Scotland began to bear heavily on the shape of English constitutional thought.

Smith's *De republica Anglorum* was written in 1565, repeatedly revised, and printed finally in 1583. Circulated widely in manuscript before printing, and in its tenth edition in 1640, it is altogether a delightful book in its genre. But consistency is not among its virtues or its purposes, and what it means has long puzzled scholars. Smith's modern editor, Alston, argued persuasively that Smith had primarily a juridical conception of Parliament—that is, that Parliament was a court of law and, like the other courts of law in England, it was an expression of the royal will.[45] R. W. K. Hinton took an utterly contrary line, arguing that Smith had twin, linked notions of parliamentary sovereignty and mixed government.[46] J. W. Allen, despite a more balanced treatment, finally concluded that Smith was "by far" the most important exponent of "the view of England as a mixed monarchy."[47] Weston is especially instructive. She approvingly quoted these words of Allen's in her first book and reversed herself in the second, pointing out that Smith viewed the king as the "fountain of [Parliament's] power" and that the laws gave the king "both an absolute power and a royal power regulated by laws."[48] That is, Smith was a theorist within the tradition of Fortescue's *dominium politicum et regale*, although Weston does not quite so put it. Her second view, and Alston's, are closer to the mark, but neither view will do by itself.

These interpretive discords arise from the book itself. Smith says a great many things, some of them contradictory, many of them simply divergent and unreconciled. Some of the muddle is a result of the patchwork composition of the book. But Smith was an able writer and, had consistency been more pressing than his other purposes, no doubt he would have troubled to put matters right. These other aims often have not been held in view by Smith's expositors, who struggle against Smith's own preoccupations to find a systematic treatise that was never intended to be.[49] Smith's first purpose was realism, a determination not to write "in that sort" as Plato or "Sir Thomas More's *Utopia*" of "feigned commonwealths such as never was nor never shall be," but of England as it "standeth and is governed at this day the xxviii of March *Anno* 1565."[50] The second purpose, neither in opposition to nor in tension with the first, was encomium—quite as much as Fortescue's master work, *De republica Anglorum* is *de laudibus legum Angliae*. Smith celebrated the facts, as did Fortescue; what Fortescue's editor and student, Stanley Bertram Chrimes, says of him is as accurately said of Smith: his views "are in no sense utopian—

they simply reflect the facts."[51] Smith's third purpose was frankly (though not explicitly) semantic experimentation.[52] Like Elyot he was out to enrich the political vocabulary of his countrymen; Smith, a civil lawyer and professor of Greek who was also fond of the nativist social description of William Harrison, tossed out a great many varieties of social and constitutional terminology, a wordsmith's display of his wares.

Smith began his book in a way that no longer should be surprising: with a definition of monarchy, aristocracy, and democracy. After a discussion of the meaning of justice in light of these three terms, he dropped them.[53] He then moved to the conception of the One, the Few, and the Many by "they which have more methodically and more distinctly and perfectly written upon them." This is the Aristotelian sexpartite scheme of a good and an "evil" form of the One, the Few, the Many. Again, a discussion of justice was called for, now in the framework of the sexpartite scheme, but Smith soon terminated it because it seemed to endorse a right of rebellion or resistance to evil rule.[54] As far as the private subject was concerned, the six forms were irrelevant. Smith moved on to a new distinction between simple and mixed forms of government. Here he concluded that while in reality constitutions are often mixed they were denominated by the part "which is more and overruleth the other always or for the most part."[55] Inexplicably, after he shifted to a tortured discussion of various kinds of monarchy—tyranny, hereditary kingship, absolute but untyrannical kingship, dictatorship in the Roman sense, and "royal power regulate by laws"—Smith simply gave up.[56] What mattered was England, and all that had passed were red herrings: "I do not understand that our nation hath any other general authority . . . neither aristocratical, nor democratical, but only the royal and kingly majesty."[57] It turns out that England is a monarchy by history, by the nature of the people, by current practice.

In fact, nowhere in *De republica Anglorum* did Smith actually say that England was a mixed monarchy.[58] Hinton had to "suppose" it, Weston (when she so argued) to "infer" it. The inference is not implausible, but Smith did not draw it and he provided no clue as to what way it might be mixed, whether England was a monarchy tempered with aristocracy and democracy or with aristocracy alone.

Soon Smith was off on another word chase when he set out to describe the social composition of England and the relationships, if any, the social vocabularies bore to the institutional order. He began this discussion with a consideration as to whether bondmen, soldiers (a "host"), or women properly could be considered part of the commonwealth. The bondmen were excluded because they did not share in the commonweal; the soldiers could only "abusively" be described as members; women were members only if they had titles in their own right.[59] Then Smith offered a wide range of social distinctions drawn from Greek, Latin, and French and chose none.[60] He emerged with a quadripartite distinction he lifted from William Harrison's *The Description of England*: the nobility, itself divided into *major* ("lords," that is peers) and *minor* (gentlemen of several ranks); citizens and burgesses; yeomen; "the fourth sort of men which do not rule" —wage-workers, poor husbandmen, traders without land, copyholders, and "all artificers."[61]

Smith did not seek to assimilate the classical constitutional terminology with the social categories he introduced. He did not identify the nobility or the upper part of it with aristocracy; nor did he consider the implications for classical terminology of the "fourth sort," especially in respect to his later claims that an act of Parliament embodied the assent of the meanest person of the realm. If anything, he undercut the constitutional significance of his and Harrison's quadripartite social terminology when he sheared the lower nobility completely away from the higher, to make it conform to the structure of the Parliament. He drew an analogy to make the point. The Romans

> seemed to make but two orders, that is of the Senate and of the people of Rome, and so in the name of the people they contained *equites* and *plebem*: so when we in England do say the lords and the commons, the knights, esquires and other gentlemen, with the citizens, burgesses and yeoman be accounted to make the commons.[62]

If there were in England any mixture of monarchy, aristocracy, and democracy, it could be found only by splitting English institutions or English social categories; the classical scheme was not reflected by them.

That is not all. In his detailed exposition of Parliament in book 2 of *De republica Anglorum*, Smith shifted his usages and conceptions. The Parliament now was supposed to embody "every man's consent" either "in person or by procuration and attorneys."[63] That does not sit well against the earlier "fourth sort." Nor does it account for the clergy, of whom, to this point, scarcely a word had been said. Then, suddenly and forcefully, Smith repaired the omission. In Parliament, he said, the prince, the barony, the commons, and—the phraseology is important—"the bishops for the clergy" come together.[64] Smith here did not endorse the alternate formulation that the bishops sat only by right of their baronies. A casual phrase, from book 1 before the passage borrowed from Harrison, explicates exactly what Smith meant: "the word *populus* doth signify, the whole body and the three estates of the common wealth," which in that context was clearly distinguished from single persons.[65] Thus, on top of all else, Smith adhered to the traditional enumeration of the estates. Given that, diametrically opposed interpretations of his analysis are possible. When William Harrison borrowed from Smith his description of Parliament to "requite" the "like borrowage he hath used toward me," he concluded that the Parliament consisted of "the three estates, that is, the nobility, clergy and laity."[66] When William Lambarde cribbed with a few minor changes the selfsame passage, he concluded that the three "estates" were the king, the Lords, and the Commons.[67]

Realism and semantics carried Smith to this point. When he embarked upon his description of the powers of king and Parliament, encomium joined the others. Smith now entered, with what may be called Fortescuean circularity, into a celebration of the mystery of the facts, a celebration of the mysterious "et" of the *dominium politicum et regale*. Parliament was the "most high and absolute power of the realm of England." It could make and change the laws. But the king, who was part of Parliament, "doth distribute his authority and power" to the rest of the body politic.[68] It was the king-in-Parliament that was "most absolute" —even, perhaps, to the defining of the prerogative inasmuch as the prerogative was law.[69] That would seem to make Smith a parliamentary supremacist. Yet the prince was also "absolute" by "himself." And Smith's listing of the king's absolute powers was full indeed: war and peace, treaties, control of the privy council, sole control of martial law "in the field," control of money "by proclamation only," the gift of all spiritual and temporal office, the monopoly of justice, wardship and marriage of those who hold lands of him as tenants-in-chief, and the dispensing power, by which the king could dispense with the application of the statutes of his "most absolute" Parliament.[70]

Small wonder, then, that Smith has befuddled his expositors. His enormous popularity, his influence upon and contact with other Tudor political writers, disseminated widely the classical political terminology with which he began his book. That he failed to exploit his own essays into classical categories should tell two things. First, if he were the greatest exponent of mixed government of his day, he did not know it. But, second, the same fact-centered care that led him away from error, the same acuity that kept him from confusing "is" with "ought," gave more credibility and respectability to the classical language than it otherwise possessed. Additionally, Smith's laudatory statements of what a king alone and what a Parliament could do, in the tradition of Fortescue, were incapable of resolution into distinct competitive spheres that expositors and consistency prefer. Both are part of a mystery of constitutionality, a "binity" that, like the first two persons of the Trinity, is a mystery of coevality and consubstantiality: make one or other prior or superior and there is error. The law functioned as a kind of Holy Spirit for Smith; it was neither above the king alone and king-in-Parliament nor below them, but another distinct expression of the underlying oneness of them both.[71] And that, when it worked, was how it worked in England, which was more often than not. And because it was true, Smith could get away with it and communicate to others the fullness of one without derogating from the other. Others, of course, were often less at ease with the facts: they wanted to change, to simplify things, to be heretics of various sorts. Only a Smith could touch them all. His was a gospel for all people.

✳

John Hooker's *Order and usage of the keeping of a parlement in England* was a more pedestrian book, but in many ways it was not so very different.[72] It too was extremely influential; it too was careful to get things right; it too reflected the humanist energies that had driven Smith. Like *De republica Anglorum*, the *Order and usage* hedged its bets; and again like *De republica Anglorum*, it gave, albeit accidentally, a kind of authority to disparate views that only a careful, indeed overbalanced treatment could. Its importance lies not in the naturalizing of classical terms but in its exploration of another problem often associated with it, that of the estates of the realm.

Hooker's *Order and usage* was written and published in 1572. Its author, the chamberlain of Exeter, was a man with close ties to his city and to the committedly protestant, nearly puritan, lay culture that gave its spirit to much of the political order in Elizabethan England. Hooker was a Parliament man, a backbencher with antiquarian interests that ultimately issued in the *Order and usage*. But Hooker also was linked closely with the clergy of Exeter. He was a friend of several bishops and future bishops of the church, some of whom had sponsored his education; a gesture of his continuing affection for them, after his *Order and usage,* was another work, a catalog of the bishops of Exeter.[73]

Hooker received a fine classical education: like Smith he was a civil lawyer and a humanist. Hooker reveals an easy familiarity with many of the sources of classical constitutional thought, refers admiringly to Spartan and Roman republicanism, and seems to have read Polybius.[74] But his substantial humanism was less overt than Smith's: it was implicit. Much of its force was directed to purposes of no interest at all to Smith. Hooker was an antiquarian whose understanding of the Parliament was strongly colored though not controlled by that strange and troubled document he did so much to publicize, the *Modus tenendi parliamentum*.[75]

It is worth noting at the outset, given what follows, that Hooker was no antimonarchist. He often had a high conception of Parliament, but he could reach no less high for the king, "God's anointed being the head and chief of the whole realm and upon whom the government and estates thereof do wholly and only depend: . . . without this his authority: no Parliament can properly be summoned or assembled."[76] When Hooker, taking a cue from the *Modus*, called the king an estate of the Parliament, we cannot conclude that his intentions were hostile.

The *Modus*, a text of which Hooker included in his own, is a document that will enter the story at several points ahead. Hooker was not the first of his generation to exploit it, but he was its prime popularizer; when, as editor of Raphael Holinshed's *Chronicles*, he inserted his *Order and usage* into the 1587 edition, the *Modus* went with it. The *Modus* was a treatise of the early fourteenth century, fanciful enough in its own day. In no sense pertinent to this study did it correspond to the practice of Parliament as it then stood, nor did it claim to. The *Modus* flew higher, claiming to present the ancient laws of the kingdom before the Norman Conquest. The enthusiastic, sometimes uncritical Saxonism of the later sixteenth century, which Hooker shared, took the *Modus* at its word. It presented the ancient constitution.

The *Modus* said nothing about the three estates. It did speak of six degrees (*gradus*) necessarily to be summoned to a Parliament: the king, the barons and earls, the bishops, the clerical proctors, the knights, and the citizens and burgesses.[77] The *Modus* went on to assert, in what the seventeenth-century lawyer William Prynne not mistakenly called its "strange leveling clauses,"[78] that in matters of taxation the voice of two knights outweighed that of an earl, two proctors that of a bishop. If the bishops and barons were summoned but did not attend, the business of the Parliament could continue. There were parliaments, asserted the *Modus*, before there were barons. So long as the king agreed with the commons—the proctors, the knights, and the citizens and burgesses—the business of the Parliament could be done.[79]

Thus far the *Modus*; now as to what Hooker did with it. The proctors were long gone, and Hooker, who was interested in Parliament "in these days," was prepared to allow the *Modus* to serve as guide, not as master.[80] Thus the king became an "estate," as he had been in the *Modus* a degree, a *gradus*. Following the *Modus* in its assertion that the bishops sat in Parliament by right of their baronies, not their spiritual functions per se (it is to be remembered that the *Modus* did insist upon the proctors, the representatives of the lower clergy), the bishops and the barons formed one estate in the House of Lords. Finally, the knights and citizens and burgesses, shorn of their fellowship with the erstwhile clerical proctors, formed an estate of their own, the House of Commons.[81]

So there were three estates in Parliament. One of these estates included the bishops, but not insofar as they constituted a distinct order or estate in the commonwealth. Hooker in this fashion did much to publicize this alternative enumeration of the estates of the realm and to garb it with the supposed antiquity of the *Modus*. But, oddly, for Hooker there were also four estates. This friend of the bishops was uncomfortable, it seems, at leaving them in their spiritual guise out in the cold. Accordingly, he described the bishops and proctors of the lower clergy as forming conjointly an estate—and, when Hooker thought about it, he saw not only four estates (kings, nobles, commons, clergy) but three houses (upper, lower, and convocation, which last Hooker took quite as seriously as the others.)[82]

Like Smith, Hooker wanted to keep his cake and eat it. He wanted to cover the facts as he understood them: the laity's fact, for which there was abundant and better precedent than the *Modus*, that the bishops sat in the Lords by virtue of their baronies; the clergy's fact and the world's fact, according to centuries of cultural tradition, that if that were all the clergy had in England it was not enough. So too with Hooker's comfort in calling the king an estate: he meant no harm by it. That had not always been true, and it was not to remain true. But like Smith, Hooker shared with a wide public a vocabulary that was acceptable as long as it was in his hands.

The vocabulary did move outward. It has been noted that William Lambarde, the foremost of the Saxon antiquarians not in orders, glossed Smith's passage on Parliament—as Smith would not and Harrison did not—as being about the three estates of king, Lords, Commons. Lambarde knew the *Modus*, "an ancient written treatise . . . to be seen in many hands," and he knew the *Order and usage*.[83] Lambarde did not trouble himself with Hooker's alternative four estates and three houses, but again there is little question of hostility to either king or bishops or clergy. Lambarde wrote after Arthur Hall, and more than a note of indignation at Hall can be detected in Lambarde's *Archeion*.[84] But Lambarde, writing in the laudatory or celebratory mode that he shared with Smith and Hooker, did not treat politics as a zero-sum game in which the estates, however defined, rose or fell at each other's expense. Nor could Lambarde, another committed puritan, entertain antiepiscopacy; his nomenclature was not designed to exclude the bishops from Parliament.

By these routes among others, the *Modus* moved into the seventeenth century. We shall see it again, but when it returns it no longer will be quite so naive. In 1585, Burghley himself spoke of the king, Lords, and Commons as the three estates.[85] Five years later, such talk in Parliament likely would have cost even Burghley his job.[86]

These early essays in the domestication of the classical-humanist constitutional terminology and of the revision of the estates share some common features, though not always with a clear pattern. First in importance is the frank recognition that the language of the One, the Few, the Many was unfamiliar to English readers. Even into the seventeenth century the words continued to be exotic. Monarchy as a simple synonym for kingship was familiar, but in its precise and technical sense of rule by the One it was as alien as the technical meanings of the other two terms. Second, many of those who used these terms did so to advance the notion, if not the cause, of political balance and mixture. Although it recently has been denied, the notion of coordination of power was not wholly alien to the thinking of Tudor Englishmen. Not all of its implications were worked out, as they would be in the 1640s, and there were also inconsistencies with the "facts," with contemporary practice and common ways of conceptualization. But to say that something is incomplete or inconsistent is not to say that it does not exist at all; by that standard the *Answer* would have to be dismissed as no testimony to mixed government, because of the hold upon it of Bractonian and Fortescuean habits of thought. It also should be clear from Smith and Hooker that as precision in description increased, classical terminology or revision of the estates grew less single-minded either in politics or in language. Yet even as Smith and Hooker unintentionally revealed the limitations of mixed government and estates-revision by their honest failures of consistency, they gave in that very failure a certain political and intellectual respectability to these ways of thought that, in the hands of Gardiner, Ponet, and Aylmer, had drifted toward irresponsibility. Burghley and Lambarde could not have thought as they did had these men been their sole precedents for the pattern.

Ponet did not use "estate," but he would not have objected to it, having described mankind in terms of the One, the Few, the Many with no reservations. Gardiner used "estates" and we have to suspect that he knew its implications for classical theory in 1547, beause he certainly did later and because Machiavelli, to take only the leading case, was apparently in vogue at court at about the same time. Aylmer did yoke "estates" and classical terms. Were these three the only witnesses it would seem that the linkage had something to do with debasing the power of kings, that it reflected, however obscurely, a desire to change facts by changing the meaning of words, in this case the burden of meaning of the traditional idea of the three estates of the realm or of Parliament under a king.

This is a shaky foundation, not so strong as Weston wished it to be in her first book and not so weak as she insists in her second. To put it another way, it is a foundation not for the *Answer* but for two generations of opposition to that very style of thought, the subject of the next three chapters. On the other hand, Smith, Hooker, and Lambarde could entertain the language without entertaining radical conclusions. A certain naiveté was yet possible for Englishmen brought up in the political world of the early and mid-sixteenth century. They were not out to humble monarchy but to exalt the community of the realm. Either of Weston's views can be supported with some of the facts but not all of them. And there is nothing in the surviving evidence we have surveyed to suggest that classical political language, or the revision of the estates with which it was associated, was used to deflate the position of the clergy or the bishops. Such king yoking as there was did not involve as well an assault upon the bishops.

Aylmer, Ponet, and Gardiner took some perilous steps into the linguistic unknown. Hooker and Smith perhaps sensed the peril and retreated. But none of these figures, by his words alone, generated a controversy as such. None was made to suffer for them. As words qua words, these were not as they were soon to become, in Bancroft's phrase, dangerous positions. Much of the concrete politics of these writers could be expressed in terms of the *dominium politicum et regale,* which had no ecclesiology inherent in it and which could be used and abused to express a wide range of both conventional and extreme points of view. Indeed the older language did these things so well that is is fair to ask why the new styles were employed at all. There can be no single commanding answer. The lure of humanism and linguistic experimentation is surely a good part of the story—it is perhaps not a coincidence that Aylmer was Lady Jane Grey's tutor in Greek, that Smith taught Greek at Oxford, that Hooker was expert in the language. This side of things is perhaps also highlighted by the fact that of the figures we have considered only Lambarde had any real training in the common law. Smith was a civilian admirer of it, Hooker was also a civilian, and the rest were churchmen.

Yet there is another side. Smith and Hooker were disinterested in the outcome of their linguistic forays; they modified their words to conform with the facts. No such thing can be said of Ponet and Gardiner, and Aylmer came close to modifying the facts to conform with the words. These three were out to change the world, not very radically in Gardiner's case, more so with Ponet and with Aylmer, who seemed to be aware of what he was doing. As befits a weak foundation, there is here a weak indication of an irreducible nonconformity in search of a voice. It would not be worth the notice save that it was the way of the future.

The interpretation of the earlier Tudor evidence offered here accords well with the only Tudor critique of the new turn of phrase made before presbyterianism changed its meaning. This was the work of Arthur Hall, an irrepressible eccentric who shared with the other figures considered here a flair for the nuances of language and an expertise in Greek.[87] In 1579 Hall published *An Admonition by the Father of F. A.*, in which he took on the mixed constitution of king, Lords, and Commons.[88] Hall understood each of these "estates" as a manifestation of the appropriate classical form. Because of the imperfections of each, he went on, the three estates had been combined. In this description of the present constitution, the encomiastic vein of Smith and Fortescue was perverted into a cloying and saccharine paean to the Commons, the manifest insincerity of which was revealed by Hall's perverse description of the electorate. It included "the artificer, the beggar . . . all of those sorts." But Hall's real point was historical. All this excellent wisdom was due solely to the grace of kings. The House of Commons, in particular, existed only because kings had seen fit to permit it. If there were councils or moots among the Anglo-Saxons, the Commons was no part of them. Since Canute, moreover, the realm had been held by right of conquest. The Commons in Parliament did not exist until 20 Henry III; its right to consent to legislation, in Hall's mind the point of the exercise, was a mere, relatively recent extension of the royal will.[89]

In 1581 Hall was roundly attacked in the lower house for his tirade, which ultimately cost him his liberty. His guardian, none other than Burghley, barely could contain the assault, a task rendered the more difficult by the fact that Hall's argument and personal style were as far removed from the accommodating manner of Burghley as ever could be. Hall was forced to recant. The point that bothered the Commons was the assault upon its antiquity. Remarkably, when Hall betook himself to the bar to acknowledge the antiquity of the Commons, he did so by repeatedly calling the queen "the head" of the whole realm and distinguishing her from "the three estates of the realm, *as they are called.*"[90] Hall, of course, was correct in his assertion that the Commons was not an immemorial component of Parliament, and it is fascinating that when he was forced to change his facts he changed his vocabulary. He was not about to let his enemies have it both ways.

One more point: having said as much as he did about the motives and pretensions of the Commons, Hall surely would not have flinched from an attack upon or notice of the bad ecclesiology of his opponents, had he seen one. There can be little question, however, as to Hall's own attitude toward ecclesiastical authority, for he was a crypto-Catholic. Nor is there any question about his enemies: his prime tormentor was Thomas Norton, a near presbyterian.[91] The year of Hall's chastisement was indeed a turning point in the fortunes of mixed government by the estates. But the turn was made in Scotland, and neither Hall nor Norton knew of it.

4
Presbyterianism and the Estates, ca. 1580–1603

Mixed government by the estates of the realm, upon the advent of presbyterianism in Scotland and England, took on meaning that had been absent, ambiguous, or latent before. Had Weston been aware of this transformation when she made her first statement on the origins of the *Answer*, she would have had the evidence of firm foundations in the Tudor period that she was seeking. There was, however, a critical difference: advocacy of a revised version of the estates was treason in Scotland and sedition, at the least, in England. Demonstration of this further dimension reveals the incorrectness of Weston's recently revised view that Tudor ideas "were not prototypes of the parliamentary ideology of the 1640s." In fact the Tudor antecedents are clear, and it was not the *Answer* they inspired but rather the opposition language of 1640–1642—which the *Answer* mimicked and turned on its head. The same story also solves the mystery of the evidentiary lacuna of the early seventeenth century. James had several long and difficult chapters in his career as James VI that moved him, as James I, to will out of existence the concept of mixed government by the estates of the realm. By 1606 he had made it in England an idea non grata.

The explorations of mixed government and the revised anatomy of the estates before the onset of presbyterianism were political in orientation: they had little or nothing to say of religion or ecclesiology. Moreover, their politics were neither monolithic nor always even clear. Yet it can be seen that these resorts to mixed government were directed to determining the roles of king, nobility, and commons and that they explicitly or tacitly took the structure of Parliament as their model. They caught part—though only part—of the temper of Tudor politics, a temper that Elton describes in terms of partnership and of placing Parliament in the center of the political process.[1]

But as presbyterianism spread, as it adopted the language of mixed government in England and of revision of the estates in both England and Scotland, and as reaction to it in both kingdoms mounted, the entire situation changed. The very texture of discourse changed, becoming controversial not merely on the level of doctrine—for that always had been a possibility and sometimes a fact—but also and more fundamentally on the level of the meaning of words. Vocabulary itself became the battleground. A new element was introduced: a concern about the word "estate" as it reflected an ongoing argument about the fate of the bishops and the clergy. With that concern came a tipping of the balanced, but quivering, scales of prepresbyterian explorations of mixed government by the estates—a tipping toward radicalism, both political and religious. In Aristotelian terminology, what before had been "accidents" of mixed government and the estates became "essences," at least in the thinking of presbyterianism's most bitter opponents and of some of its defenders. Both of those extremes were "wrong" in the sense that there was no inherent radicalism in the language of mixed government by the estates. Contingencies, however, made it seem otherwise, as the bitter practicality of the issue became manifest. Out of the caldron of bad temper and hostility and fear came a great many things, few of them salutary for either England or Scotland. One of them is what James really meant when he said, at Hampton Court in 1604, "No bishop, no king."

In the 1570s the first wave of presbyterianism in England explored the possibilities of mixed government in the service of the presbyterian cause. The thought patterns are revealing, both in terms of what the early presbyterian theorists did and in terms of what they did not. For Thomas Cartwright and Walter Travers, the two leading English presbyterian theoreticians of the time, the vocabulary of mixed government was useful in two distinct but related ways. Mixed government provided a supplementary vocabulary of church governance; it also provided for civil governance in a most curious fashion: an analogy was turned back upon itself.

For Cartwright and Travers, presbyterian polity was essentially and primarily a scriptural matter. Presbyterianism was the pattern of the apostolic and primitive church, so they claimed; its basic categories (pastor, doctor, elder, and deacon) were taken—wrenched, their opponents often said—from Scripture. Derived in this way, presbyterianism claimed explicit divine sanction. Episcopalians at this early point did not claim so much, preferring to regard church polity as, in itself, an *adiaphoron* (a matter indifferent) subject to the rules of reason and prudence. Later—the first signs may be detected in Richard Bancroft's sermon at Paul's Cross in 1589[2]—episcopalians divided among themselves on the matter. Some still adhered to the adiaphorist line, whereas others moved more aggressively, first to the position that episcopacy was at least divinely allowed as a godly form of governance, and later to the fully confrontational position that episcopacy had the exclusive divine right that presbyterians claimed for their own scheme.

That side of the struggle between presbyterians and episcopalians, crucial in the 1590s, is relevant to the 1570s only insofar as it sheds light upon the status of the supplementary language of church polity employed by Cartwright and Travers and later English presbyterians. They claimed that that supplementary language, the language of mixed government, also possessed divine right. In actuality, by any honest reckoning the application of the terms of mixed government to Scripture is only an analogy or an interpretation, for there is no mixed government in the Bible. But when the analogy was made, when mixed government for the church was invested with divine right, and when the analogy was turned back upon the state, presbyterians entered into an Alice-in-Wonderland world in which, it would seem, sounds were to be judged only by their echoes.

Travers was the simpler of the two. In the church, he maintained, Christ commended the power of the keys to an assembly of elders. This, like every other presbyterian proposition, was at least in principle a conclusion drawn from Scripture, but Travers used a secular vocabulary to describe that assembly:

> as Lacedemon had an assembly of elders, Athens a high court named Areopagus, Rome a Senate, and finally, every kingdom and commonwealth a council whose authority is chief and sovereign in all affairs, and by whom the rest of the society are governed, so likewise the church hath an assembly of elders.

Travers did not have a parliament in mind; this body was instead a supposedly aristocratic governing council of the church, composed solely of pastors and doctors. Travers was responding to the charge that presbyterianism tended toward democracy or popularity, and he made it clear that his supreme body "whose authority is chief and sovereign in all affairs" excluded all but rulers. In this sense Travers was avowedly aristocratic, at least within his own terms of reference. On the other hand, the church as a whole was a mixture of the One, the Few, the Many, even though in that mixture the Few were preponderant. Christ was the head, the One: if one looked beyond to the human agents of the divine purpose the church was "rather theocracy." There was democracy, too, in the consent of "the people" in "matters of great weight."[3]

Therefore, the church had a mixed government, one that unquestionably excluded royal supremacy. In this way, if in no other, mixed church government by divine right impinged upon the civil constitution, inasmuch as the Elizabethan royal supremacy (though perhaps not the Henrician) was established by, and was a part of, the civil constitution.[4] Beyond this point, Travers became hazy about the character of the civil state. He did not call it a mixed government, but he showed something less than devotion to monarchy when he wrote of the synods of "any one whole kingdom, free state, or commonwealth" and when he stated that in monarchical, aristocratic, and popular states all power lay originally in the people, who of their "free will" chose magistrates to rule over them.

The little that Travers lacked, Cartwright supplied. The church, Cartwright wrote,

> is governed with that kind of government which the philosophers that write of the best commonwealths affirm to be best. For, in respect of Christ the head, it is a monarchy; and in respect of the ancients and pastors that govern in common and with like authority amongst themselves, it is an aristocracy, or the rule of the best men; and, in respect that the people are not secluded, but have their interest in church-matters, it is a democracy, or a popular estate.

Again the analogy from civil governance, invested with divine right; now, more clearly, the conclusion:

> An image whereof appeareth also in the policy of this realm; for as, in respect of the queen her majesty, it is a monarchy; so, in respect of her most honorable council, it is an aristocracy, and, having regard to the Parliament, which is assembled of all estates, it is a democracy.

The parallel was fortunate, in Cartwright's view, because the government of the church was prescriptive. In a piece of high presbyterian cant that long was remembered, Cartwright wrote that the civil constitution ought to match the ecclesiastical, "even as the hangings to the house." Civil government thus was relegated to a species of interior decoration. Yet, to extend the metaphor, the architect had cribbed his plans from the decorator: he had built according to the classical-republican theory of mixed government.[5]

No aspect of Cartwright's ploy was lost on John Whitgift, the archbishop of Canterbury and Cartwright's archopponent. He caught instantly the implications of the "hangings" and the "house": on Cartwright's principles, "no government of any commonwealth ought to be monarchical." To fight his way through mixed government, Whitgift used the analysis of the school of sovereignty, of those like Aristotle and Jean Bodin who believed that one of the three elements must be supreme lest the constitution collapse. Parts could be mixed, Whitgift argued; in England "all the states" could be "represented" in Parliament, yet one "ruleth and beareth the greatest sway." In England, this was the prince. The constitution, despite admixtures, was monarchical, for even in Parliament the "judgment, confirmation, and determination" lay with the prince.[6]

Cartwright and Travers shared a radical politics. It is true that much of the presbyterian laity had more conservative and more monarchical instincts, but that is beside the point. Cartwright and Travers were not typical of this phase of the presbyterian movement; rather, they led it.[7] Like leaders of other movements that combine the broadly based with the esoteric, they had followings that varied with what they had to say. In adopting the language of mixed government they resolved, for themselves and no doubt for Whitgift, the latent ambiguity that had characterized the earlier Tudor usages. Mixed government meant a denial of the royal supremacy; it also meant a church-state-church hall of mirrors in which, either in Travers's stumbling manner or in Cartwright's bold formulation, the civil constitution was less monarchical than others thought. That was Whitgift's opinion, and he was not wrong.

But Cartwright, Travers, and Whitgift shared a silence. For all that the abolition of bishops was the negative program of presbyterianism, none of the three raised the matter of whether the bishops were an estate.[8] None drew upon the linkage that had been forged, though crudely, in the earlier period between mixed government and the revised version of the estates. Quite as Cartwright could speak of Parliament as composed of all estates, so could Whitgift, neither pausing to question what was meant. In the 1570s, even the archpresbyterians and their opponents failed to realize what Hall and Norton, more understandably, failed to realize in 1581 but what Hyde realized in 1641: that mixed government and the revision of the estates went together and bore inseparably upon king and bishops. Surely this is no accidental omission. If Cartwright and Travers had known, they would not have hesitated to make the point; even had they not, an expert inference hunter like the archbishop somehow would have found it, if only he had known that he should.

✳

In the early 1570s, while Travers and Cartwright were at work in England, the kirk of Scotland was not yet the battleground for dogmatic and doctrinaire presbyterianism it was soon to become. If, as recently has been argued, the kirk before the Melvillean era was more determinedly "reformed" than recent orthodoxy allows, it remains true that there was as yet no frontal root-and-branch assault upon episcopacy.[9] The General Assembly indeed represented the whole kirk, but its existence posed no threat to the existence of diocesan episcopacy. As for civil government, Scotland's unicameral Parliament had been routinely and uncontentiously considered an assembly of the three traditional estates under the king. The first estate was that of the bishops (and the abbots before their removal) who sat, it was never gainsaid, *pro clero,* for the clergy. The second was the nobility; for some purposes in the Scottish Parliament, the nobility was divided into higher and lower groups, the barons and the lairds or shire commissioners. The third estate was composed of the commissioners of the burghs. The system was ancient, and though the tripartite scheme did not correspond very well with certain features of Scottish social arrangements, nobody seems to have noticed or cared. Moreover, in contrast to England, Scotland had produced no exploration of alternative enumerations, and it had a far different, far closer structural and functional relationship of the estates of the realm to institutional reality and habits of thought.

But then things began to change rapidly, both in the religious realm and in the political. With Andrew Melville's return to Scotland in 1574, and most likely as a result of it, presbyterianism grew increasingly combative. Melville had been educated in Scottish and French universities and then had gone to Geneva, where he imbibed the doctrines of the radical reformer Theodore Beza. Upon returning to become principal of the

University of Glasgow in 1574, Melville quickly became the leader of the presbyterian movement in Scotland. Moreover, he and his adherents gained a great deal of influence over the more moderate protestant reformers in the kirk. But presbyterianism posed a fundamental constitutional problem, because by universal agreement the bishops represented the spiritual estate in Parliament, and because by all-but-universal agreement the spiritual estate had to be represented. Melville provided a solution in the form of his two-kingdom theory.[10] Church and state, he declared should have nothing to do with one another institutionally; the king and other great personages should have no special voice in the kirk corresponding to their positions in the state, and the clergy and elders (the officers of presbyterian polity) should have nothing to do with the state. Melville's proposed solution appealed to the most extreme and doctrinaire presbyterians, but the moderates found it unpalatable and conservatives found it appalling. Even so, Melville and his friends temporarily had their way. The moderates agreed wholeheartedly with Melville's proposal, set forth in his *Second book of discipline* (1578), that presbyterianism be the form of government within the kirk; what they would not swallow was the counterpart idea that there be no ecclesiastical representation in Parliament. Yet without thinking through the implications of what they were doing, they joined the Melvillians in the General Assembly and had the *Second book* adopted in its entirety. By April 1581 the ambiguities disappeared. The General Assembly at Glasgow actually provided an official translation from a spiritual to a more political vocabulary of church government: the earlier condemnation of the unscriptural episcopal "office" was intended, the General Assembly now declared, "to condemn the whole estate of bishops as they now are in Scotland."[11]

*

The timing of the translation was not accidental. By the late 1570s, while the kirk was still speaking of "office," conservative elements at court had discovered in presbyterianism a specifically political menace: the abolition, so it was understood, of the estate of bishops. As early perhaps as April 1576 and certainly by 1578, the Lord Chancellor of Scotland, Glamis, wrote to Theodore Beza that bishops were to be retained in Scotland because they were a necessary constraint upon the habits and stubbornness of the people and because the bishops were by the long usage of the laws and ageless custom a third estate of the realm. To change the system would be to throw the commonwealth into peril.[12]

Beza's reply, first printed in 1580, was at once combative and, on the crucial matter for this study, strangely deferential. Beza responded vigorously to the social argument and like all presbyterians refused to allow bishops a civil function. But the Genevan pastor did not directly attack the argument regarding the three estates, and he carefully provided for some clerical participation in politics.[13] At a time when polemic and counterpolemic proceeded line-by-line and phrase-by-phrase, Beza's silence about the estates was tantamount to a concession.

Wittingly or not, Glamis had targeted his defense perfectly. Had Beza felt free to confront the bishops' rights directly on the ground of the chancellor's assertion—that bishops or the clergy were an estate—it is likely that Beza's reply would have had international repercussions. But he did not, and the tardiness in publishing a reply (assuming that the letter was drafted as early as 1576) further reduced the effectiveness of Beza's counter. The estate argument would remain an effective part of the episcopal and royal armory, to be revived in 1581 in a much more telling and immediate forum for Scottish affairs.

To this story we shall turn shortly. But the episode could have resulted differently, and a slight examination of the situation among Francophone Calvinists will suggest how this turn of events might have come about. Beza, in fact, found the three traditionally defined estates crucial for his political theory in *De jure magistratuum*. The estates were the whole community apart from the king; Beza's clericalism and own sense of history would not allow him to depart from the traditional enumeration. Doubtless, the indirection of his 1580 response to Glamis reflected his earlier commitment, in the French context, to a clerical estate.[14] However, Beza's outlook was not shared by other leading theoreticians of the Huguenot cause. The three great testaments of Huguenot sensibility to appear shortly after the massacre of 1572 took surprisingly divergent tacks on the crucial question of the composition of the estates in France—crucial because so much of monarchomach theory hung upon the role accorded to "the estates" however defined, and because some thinkers, unlike Beza, perceived difficulties (apparently religious as well as political) with the traditional enumeration. François Hotman's *Francogallia* and the pseudonymous *Reveille-matin des françois* took issue with the clerical claim to be an estate, platitude though it was. Hotman, indeed, defined his estates as king, nobles, and representatives of the towns, using classical terminology as a lead-in. He professed to find these three estates embedded in the farthest reaches of the Francogallian polity. Thus, clerical representation was a Romish usurpation. Though a great scholar, Hotman could not quite manage to pull off this most tendentious reading of the evidence. In the critical passage of the second edition, Hotman rather lamely justified his monumental reordering of the facts on the grounds that he was revising an earlier heterodox enumeration of Claude de Seyssel and that his own classically defined enumeration was "*commodius*," an almost apologetic reason.[15] The *Reveille-matin* agreed with Hotman in the exclusion of the clergy but advanced a still different scheme: nobles, magistrates, townsmen.[16]

Such disparate formulations might suggest that laicizing and clericalist mentalities were at least potentially divisive among Huguenots, quite as they proved to be among Scottish and English presbyterians. Hotman's doctrine, in particular, shows that the presbyterian–mixed government nexus (which we shall see established in England in the later 1580s) was not solely an English phenomenon, just as Claude de Seyssel's earlier experimentations suggest a capacity, before the Reformation in France, for innocent adaptions of classical theory in France, like those we have seen in England before the later 1580s.[17] However, the disagreement among Huguenots about the estates was not fundamental in France. Short of a protestant but episcopal regime in France, there is no reason why it should have been. Even as Hotman's revisions of *Francogallia* tended to lay ever greater emphasis upon the place of the estates and, by consequence, his own version of them, others refused to follow his lead. Beza was not alone; the *Vindiciae contra tyrannos* (1579) adhered to the traditional enumeration of the estates.[18]

Had Hotman's perspective been dominant, Beza might have rejected Glamis's argument from estates altogether; had Glamis consulted with Hotman rather than Beza, the lawyer-historian's arguments directly might have influenced Scottish presbyterian thought. But neither occurred, and in October 1581 the same argument about bishops as an estate was advanced on behalf of the young king, James VI, by his cousin and confident, Esmé Stuart, sieur d'Aubigny, whom he made duke of Lennox. In that month Lennox, a near-Catholic who regarded Melville as a virtual anti-Christ, brought the question of ecclesiastical representation before the General Assembly. James Melville, Andrew's nephew, had no doubt about Lennox's motives: "the duke of Lennox, by Guisian counsel and direction, not daring [to] put at religion plainly, pressed the restoring of the estate of bishops." The General Assembly set a committee to study the matter. Its conclusions, which were adopted unanimously, were not entirely satisfactory either to the "court," from whence the project stemmed, or to the Melvillians.[19] On the one hand, the need for the presence of the spiritual estate in Parliament was accepted in direct contravention of the Melvillian principle that ministers should not have civil employment; the kirk needed men in Parliament "to discharge the kirk's duty." On the other hand, they were not to be bishops, but commissioners appointed by the General Assembly "from time to time," that is, as need be. This compromise was not implemented.[20]

As James Melville later described the episode, it was the beginning of a long story, as if the ploy of Lennox and the later conduct of James were different aspects of the same subject.

> At that time it was a pity to see so well a brought up prince till his bairnhood was past, to be so miserably corrupted in the entress of his springal age, both with sinistrous and false information . . . and with evil and most dangerous grounds and principles in government of kirk and common-weal. Then was he made to think worst of the best men that ever served in this kirk and country; to think the whole manner of reformation of religion to have been done by a privy faction, turbulently and treasonably.[21]

The observation may have been hindsight, but it was not incorrect. As Gordon Donaldson has written, in the context of Elizabeth's warning to James in 1592 of a "sect" in both kingdoms "as would have no kings but a presbytery," James did not need to be lectured on the point, having been aware of it "from almost his earliest awakening to political consciousness."[22] If his attitude needed reinforcement, reinforcement was soon to come. In 1582 James was kidnapped by a band of earls and held captive in Ruthven Castle for a year. The motives of the Ruthven band had nothing to do with presbyterianism, but its members were anti-Lennox protestants and the radical presbyterians supported their action. When James was rescued a year later, his mind was sealed.

In 1584 the king reiterated the necessity of the spiritual estate. The preceding three years had seen the partial establishment of presbyterianism, through the commitment to implement the Melvillian *Second book of discipline* and through the actual creation of some presbyteries. In the main, inasmuch as the General Assembly could not abolish episcopacy outright (it could not abolish a title not in its own gift, and it could not seize the lands and revenues of the bishops), presbyterian strategy was to bypass episcopacy rather than confront it directly. But in those areas of the country where presbyterianism was only partly implemented or even merely a paper scheme, episcopal authority continued, including the control of presentments to benefices. Had not the Ruthven interlude with its presbyterian overtones given a new motive to the royal resolve, it is possible that an accommodation of sorts might have been worked out.

But James had been delivered from the Ruthven lords by the Lennox faction and had first taken refuge in the castle of the archbishop of Saint Andrews, Patrick Adamson. James reacted to both his past perils and his new freedom in the Black Acts of 1584. One of them turned into law the suggestion that Lennox had made in 1581. To put it another way, it took a *stylus curiae* and turned it into constitutional doctrine.[23] The preamble of the third of the Black Acts, "anent the authority of the three estates of Parliament," identified the maintenance of the three traditional estates with maintenance of an order both ancient and godly.

> The king's majesty considering the honor and authority of his supreme court of Parliament continued past all memory of man unto their days as constitute upon the free votes of the three estates of this ancient kingdom, by whom the same under God ever has been upheld, rebellious and traiterous subjects punished, the good and faithful preserved and maintained, and the laws and acts of Parliament (by which all men are governed) made and established. . . .[24]

So it began. But in recent years, that authority had been impugned, "at least some curiously travailing to have introduced some innovation." The king, however, had insisted that the "honor authority and dignity of the said three estates" should remain "according to the ancient and lovable custom observed in time bygone without any alteration or diminution." Therefore it was established that none of the king's subjects was "to impugn" the three estates or to "seek or procure . . . diminution of the power and authority of the same three estates or any of them." The next five words were the most important: "under the pain of treason."

Because this act had important consequences, both in the long run and in the short, it is instructive to see what it meant in the context of 1584. First, it had nothing to do with mixed government as that had been understood in Tudor England. Quite as sixteenth-century Englishmen before the rise of presbyterianism employed mixed government and the revision of the estates of the realm to make political points and conducted their religious and ecclesiastical arguments in different modes, so the Scottish argument about the estates in 1581 and 1584 was conducted without regard to the theory of mixed government. In several ways, the Scottish argument about the estates was political, but Scottish monarchism and antimonarchism were expressed in different ways. The amalgamation of the revision of the estates, mixed government, and the attack upon episcopacy was an English response that was not prefigured, although it was crucially shaped, by Scottish occurrences.

Second, the most startling aspect of the act "anent . . . the three estates" is the resemblance it bears to the habits of thought surveyed in Chapter 2. Nothing in the sixteenth-century English evidence so far surveyed is remotely like it. No one in England had seen fit to defend the traditional accountancy of the estates against the machinations of Gardiner, Ponet, and Aylmer. The reticence of Smith and Hooker, the smirk of Arthur Hall at the three estates "as they are called," may have reflected the skepticism of an uneasy conscience, but, with the possible exception of Hall, such malaise was inarticulate. But this act, which reflected the views of James and his friends of the day, called into play the hoary logic of the three orders. "Under God," the three estates had maintained the public order; conversely, the failure to maintain them individually and severally in their "own integrity" would destroy the realm and was therefore justly punishable as a treason.

This kind of reflection was far more common in Scotland than in England. The defections of the estates was a usual theme of Scottish moral criticism, the stock of countless sermons. In Tudor England, by contrast, though the great statements of order theory had done somewhat similar duty, the categories of duty were more variegated, the divisions were more gradual, the overlaps (such as between the roles of father, teacher, magistrate, king) were more numerous. Tudor Englishmen were taught to know their place, but they were told rather less single-mindedly what their place was. Nevertheless, it had not been treason until 1584 in Scotland to attack or "impugn" the scheme of the estates.

That was new and menacing. It was also practical. James had linked the fate of the bishops, the attacked estate, to the fate of Parliament in two ways. On the one hand, the integrity and repute of a fundamental institution could be used to shore up the position of episcopacy; what James lacked the authority (or the reason) to call heresy, he might yet call treason. On the other hand, Parliament was an institution that, unlike the General Assembly, James had some hope of controlling. Opposition-centered historiography tends to slight the Scottish Parliament because it was not a very effective vehicle for the expression of opposition politics, short of coup or revolution. But that is exactly why the institution was important, at least to James. Apart from the court itself, it was probably the most effective instrument he had, in large measure because of the support he could expect from the bishops. What the General Assembly did, James could seldom undo, but he could provide an alternative to that response by working through Parliament. No Parliament, no bishops; no bishops, no Parliament.

The third of the Black Acts was part of a program to give to James something like the English royal supremacy.[25] An exchange of 1585 between James and some presbyterian ministers made this intention clear. In a survey of the Black Acts, they fell upon the act "anent . . . the three estates" cautiously but revealingly. They were far from attacking the principle of the "liberty of the three estates," which was "lovable and ancient." Yet the act was "obscure." It ought not to be used to support bishops; rather, the representation of the kirk ought to be at the ministers' own disposal, according to the law of God. Ministers and elders should be sent from the kirk as commissioners, just as the burghs sent commissioners.[26] James's reply disposed of the supposed ambiguity. James made it utterly clear that the logic of spiritual representation meant one thing only to him. Quite as his presbyterian opponents had done, he thought the issue of the spiritual presence a pretense to revive episcopacy: the act, wrote the king, was "so reasonable and necessary, that it needeth no declaration nor explication, except only this, that my bishops, which are one of the three estates, shall have power, as far as God's word and example of the primitive kirk will permit, and not according to that man of sin's abominable abuses and corruptions. But I can not enough wonder where you find that rule, or example, either in God's word, or any other reformed kirk, that some ministers, by commission of the rest, ought to be one of the estates in Parliament."[27] To deny the bishops, "my bishops," was treason.

*

Only after the passage of the Black Acts did the Scottish argument about the estates enter England. It came with the numerous presbyterian exiles who fled from the wrath and the uncertainties of the newly combative James and of the earl of Arran, the ruthless leader of what might be called the counterrevolutionary coup d'état that had restored the king. The exiles included many of the leaders of the party, including both of the Melvilles. Their stay had two effects. First, they entered into sustained conversations with leading English presbyterians. Second, they accidentally revealed more of themselves to their English enemies than they had intended. The Scots had gone to England, rather than to the Continent, because the English puritans and near-puritans who controlled policy toward Scotland had, by their own actions, encouraged the Scots to hold a warmer view of England than the facts warranted. But the most concrete result of the emigration for both countries was that the English episcopal authorities were enabled to prepare a fuller dossier upon them than they might have otherwise.[28] In this task they were aided considerably by Patrick Adamson, who had come to England around Christmas of 1583 to try to break the puritan hold on Scottish policy and to open up a new channel to the English bishops and the queen.[29]

Only after the penetration of the Scots did the new mixed government appear in England, in which republicanism or parliamentary supremacy was bound up with attempts to eliminate episcopacy. The first indication of the new order came in 1587, in three speeches that Job Throckmorton delivered in the Commons. Together, the speeches formed a single cohesive political-religious program. The first, a plea for the parliamentary execution of Mary Stuart, canvassed the possibility that Mary's death could be accomplished by the action of princes alone. But, Throckmorton continued, there was no need to "sail so far" because there was "redress enough at home." He went on:

> why, I pray you let me ask you one question: may not one write upon the doors of this house Quid non so the thing be warrantable by the law of God? . . . under warrant of God's law what may not this house do? I mean the three estates of the land. To deny the power of this house, you know is treason . . . the thing is lawful to be done, and this house hath absolute power to do it.[30]

Throckmorton was up to something. He conflated the power of the Commons with that of the Parliament and gave either or both "absolute" power; and he, too, dabbled in the definition of treason. In his second speech he went on to define the three estates. The occasion was a proposal known as Cope's Bell and Book, a desperate presbyterian scheme for the voidance of all existing ecclesiastical legislation by bill and the substitution for it of the Geneva prayer book with its appended presbyterian scheme of discipline. Throckmorton pushed this ploy by urging the superior competence of the "three estates of the land" over the bishops, the "grave fathers," in a frightful pun.[31] The third speech—an attack upon the claims of the "imp of Scotland," James, to the English throne—sent Throckmorton into hiding to escape the Tower.[32]

Throckmorton also was implicated in the production of a series of presbyterian tracts that appeared from October 1588 into 1589, all under one variety or another of the pseudonym Martin Marprelate. Martin employed the double analogy variety of mixed government theory. The church was a mixture of Christ, the monarch; the elders, an aristocracy; and the people, the democratic component. The "civil government of our kingdom" was likewise a mixture of the monarchy of "Her Majesty's person," the aristocracy of the "higher house of Parliament, or rather at the council table: democractical in the body of the commons of the lower house of Parliament." If Martin and Throckmorton were indeed the same person, Throckmorton's "estates" and Martin's mixed government (with no mention of estates) would be variants of the same idea. And Throckmorton's authorship of the Marprelate tracts, always the likeliest possibility, has been vigorously and, it is to be hoped, decisively reargued by Leland Carlson.[33] An additional strong indication of the identity of Martin and Throckmorton can be derived from a close reading of Martin's remarks, which establishes, at the least, that mixed government and the revised estates were stand-ins for each other. But Martin wrote these words in response to an enormously successful anti-Martinist work by Thomas Cooper, the bishop of Winchester. Cooper's book, like the writings of Richard Bancroft, provides the key to Martin's meaning. Both were English responses to the menace posed by the language of Scottish presbyterianism, a threat that Martin/Throckmorton had begun to put into practice.

*

Throckmorton and Martin (to speak of them as distinct figures) perceived the importance of mixed government for presbyterianism. So had Cartwright and, less clearly, Travers; but whereas Cartwright and Travers did not latch onto estates as a critical term of connection, it appears possible that Throckmorton did. They were not alone. Richard Bancroft, Whitgift's former chaplain and the future bishop of London and archbishop of Canterbury, and Thomas Cooper were also at work, seeking to discover the import of recent Scottish events upon the English presbyterians. Both men figured importantly in the story in 1588–1589 and in the story as it unfolded thereafter.

Bancroft made up his mind about English presbyterianism in 1588–1589. He never changed it, so it makes sense to follow his ideas *en bloc* from 1588 to 1593. Bancroft's development is instructive. Late in 1583 he began compiling an antipresbyterian dossier, which he continued into 1585. Much of the contents of this notebook appeared in his later works, sometimes word for word. This early gathering of materials was in the main Bancroft's own attempt to develop the insights of Whitgift. At first he had no sense that presbyterianism held any view at all on the question of the estates of the realm. Perhaps as a groping step of sensitization, even as a kind of intuition, Bancroft called the four parochial offices of presbyterianism (pastor, doctor, elder, deacon) "estates." Casually and conventionally he used "estate" in still another common sense, in calling the whole church the "ecclesiastical estate."[34] But in February 1589, at his famous sermon at Paul's Cross, Bancroft added the new motif to his repertoire, a repertoire that otherwise had not changed notably since 1584–1585.

In his sermon Bancroft recited recent Scottish history to an English audience as a warning of the perils it held for the English. His avowed source was *A declaration of the king's majesty's intention and meaning,* a tract Patrick Adamson had written, with James's approval, to justify the passage of the Black Acts.[35] The *Declaration* had been printed in London in 1585; the 1587 edition of Holinshed's *Chronicles* disseminated it to a wide public. It was rich in the idiom of estates in which the Scottish struggle had been conducted. Bancroft collated it into his earlier reflections of 1584–1585, upon which he drew in his sermon. The Scottish presbyterians, he told his auditors, "erected by their own authority their ecclesiastical senates" and by so usurping traditional episcopal jurisdiction "did alter the laws at their own pleasures, without the knowledge and approbation, either of the king or the state." He added, "they likewise took upon them to discharge the estate of bishops, and to declare the same to be unlawful." Because James knew that he must "either discharge himself of the crown, or the ministry of that form of government," the king by act of Parliament "overthrew their presbyteries, and restored the bishops again to their places." There was a considerable problem with Bancroft's analysis, true as it was. Since the *Declaration,* James had done an about-face. He had accepted the act of annexation of 1587, which stripped the bishoprics of their revenues and brought episcopacy in Scotland as low as it had ever been. Bancroft tried to sweep the reversal aside: "The king . . . is not altered. *Ictus piscator sapit.* His crown and their sovereignty will not agree together."[36] Bancroft was nearly as apothegmatic as James at Hampton Court.

In 1593, Bancroft published two large books in which he pursued the theme further. This time, the "scottizing" of the English presbyterians was the theme itself, not an illustration, as it had been earlier, of the dangers of the presbyterian mentality. *Daungerous positions and proceedings, published and practised within this iland of Brytaine, under pretence of reformation, and for the presbiteriall discipline* was notable from its first words; Bancroft, in his own way, was already thinking in terms of the most intimate of relations of Scots and English. Presbyterianism was a British problem. Bancroft had little doubt of where the problem began; his hated running titles told the tale— "Scottish Genevating," "English Genevating," and "English Scottizing." His references to the problem of the estates were significant. Rehearsing the story he had told in his Paul's Cross sermon, adding much on Anglo-Scottish connections, and tacking on a properly horrifying account of the presbyterian turnaround in Scotland, Bancroft turned to a prediction:

> So as now it may be daily expected, when these godly brethren, for a full conclusion of their attempts, will take upon them, (as their masters did in Scotland) to discharge the estate of bishops, and to direct their commissioners to her most excellent Majesty . . . under the pain of excommunication, to appoint no bishops hereafter, because they have concluded that state to be unlawful.[37]

The theme was reprised in Bancroft's second work, *Pretended holy discipline,* which was an examination of the contradictions of Calvinism. Here the "overthrow" of "the state of bishops" was depicted as a design of international Calvinism, whose éminence grise was not the eponymous master but Theodore Beza. Bancroft sought to establish the hypocrisy of those who "greatly grudged at" the place of bishops in the English House of Lords and the Scottish Parliament. They proposed that clerical commissioners who were to be selected in some other way than by royal appointment would take the place of cast-off bishops, either to advise like the legal officials in the House of Lords or to vote. Like a parallel proposal that Bancroft discovered in the confiscated papers of the English presbyterian John Field—a proposal to employ commissioners as a kind of presbyterian high commission—these schemes would permit presbyterians to seize the authority that they, on two-kingdom principles, disallowed in their opponents. These were temporary expedients to be given up when the work was accomplished.[38]

Bancroft saw far into the Scottish designs. He did not, however, directly engage the civil politics of "estate" as such; he did not in his own works connect it with the civil constitution except (as was common) to see the two spheres exerting a sympathy, a gravitational pull on each other. But Bancroft tellingly explored the sources of presbyterian political vocabulary in a slightly different vein, one that explored the analogical thinking that from the start had been a feature of English presbyterian politics. He gave an account of the origin of presbyterianism in Geneva, an account that was designed to spare Calvin most of the blame, heap it on Beza, and cut through the claims of presbyterians that their church government arose from apostolic practice and scriptural injunction. Instead, Bancroft argued, it came about because of the political temper of the Genevans. Calvin, he said, only adopted presbyterianism as an expedient. The civil structure in Geneva would allow of nothing more monarchical. The unruly Genevans having cast off "their monarchy" of episcopal rule in favor of a "popular state," Calvin resorted to presbytery as an ecclesiastical counterpart of "their Senate." Growing warm, Bancroft insisted that the point must be understood "in some overt sort," because presbyterians forever urged going back to apostolic times. The present age, alas, was one that "crieth out: the first institution, the first institution, every thing must be brought back to the first institution." Yet the presbyterians shared another feature of the times: the "cantoning" of kingdoms (that is, their transformation into Helvetic republics) was in many men's mouths, and "travelers" remarked "what a notable thing it is to live in Venice."[39] If Bancroft did not look further into English mixed government, it may have been that he did not believe it could exist. To judge from his marginalia, his tutor in politics was Bodin. After Bancroft's onslaught it became de rigueur among episcopal apologists to make the same point. As Richard Hooker had it, "hereupon we hold that God's clergy are a state, which hath been and will be, as long as there is a church upon earth."[40]

The gap in Bancroft's analysis—the lack of a direct connection between "estate" and the civil constitution—was closed at least somewhat by Thomas Cooper. Whatever Cooper lacked was filled in by a process of mutually reinforcing inference involving Cooper, Martin, and the privy council. Cooper's remarks on the business of estates generated a considerable body of replies and, brief as they were, they were the key texts in this phase in the English argument over mixed government and the estates. They were profoundly disturbing and therefore helped to advance the flow of ideas.

Cooper's basic insight was that the civil constitution would be threatened directly by the abolition of the episcopal estate; he also employed the sympathetic or analogical argument. If the two are put together—which is what his opposite numbers on the presbyterian side seem to have done—Cooper is seen to have come within a hair's breadth of establishing that the abolition of the episcopal estate was an act of overthrow, of revolution in the civil constitution. He began by taking on the challenge of "estates," not in Scotland, but in England. This approach is notable for a reason other than that he merely carried Bancroft's analysis home. It may have been only an oversight on Bancroft's part, but his Paul's Cross sermon, which was directed at Martin, only analogically related the Scottish happenings to his main theme. Cooper, also replying to Martin at an early stage in the controversy, assumed that the matter of the estates was an English concern and attacked Martin by means of it, even though Martin had not actually used the word himself in a significant context and, indeed, would never do so.

Cooper's crucial point was that "the laws of England to this day, have stood by the authority of the three estates: which to alter now, by leaving out the one, may happily [i.e., perhaps] seem a matter of [more] weight, then all men do judge it."[41] If, he continued, "there were no more than this one thing . . . the alteration of the the state by all the laws of this realm," it would be dangerous, even "by offering to do it." It is not difficult to see what Cooper meant, given the universal assumption, not always remembered today, that every state was a corporation, quite as the least guild in the kingdom was also a corporation, a body politic. The terms body politic and corporation were interchangeable. Cooper's position was that the elimination of one of the three estates would cast into doubt all of the kingdom's laws made by the prince and the three estates, because to eliminate the estate of bishops would be to dissolve the corporation called the kingdom of England. The old laws would become acts of a different body politic. Cooper, in short, was hinting at how Martin, with a single false step (calling for the abolition of the estate of bishops), could be charged with treason. No lawyer in his sanity would have argued such a case; it would have threatened a good many more than Martin; by a generous construction, it could have been used even against so arch an antipresbyterian as Bishop Bilson. But, as an episcopally inspired proclamation against Martin made clear, it was in such terms or in terms close to them that Martin's enemies were thinking. As it turned out, Marprelate prosecutions were made under 23 Eliz. c. 2, which defined seditious writing as a felony.[42]

Cooper later moved to the analogical and sympathetic argument, and as he did so the relatively common arguments he had been using changed character slightly. They were no longer scare tactics alone, though that they certainly were, but statements that could not help but be linked to an act of formal revolution, the dissolution of the body politic. Cooper's words were carefully chosen and psychologically insightful. The presbyterians' "whole drift" was to bring church government to the condition of a democracy or aristocracy.

> The principles and reasons whereof, if they be made once by experience familiar in the minds of the common people, and . . . [if] they have the sense and feeling of them, it is greatly to be feared, that they will very easily transfer the same to government of the common weal. For by the same reasons, they shall be induced to think that they have injury, if they have not as much to do in civil matters, as they have in matters of the church, seeing they also touch their commodity and benefit temporally, as the other doeth spiritually.[43]

As Cooper had it later on in the *Admonition,* nobles and gentlemen had best beware that the argument from original parity be transferred from the bishops and the clergy "to other states also . . . which yet seem not to be touched." If the "next house is on fire," it was best to watch the sparks.[44]

Cooper said not a word about mixed government. But, by linking the fate of the bishops to the fate of the other "estates," he brought the loose ends closer together. Very gingerly, Martin Marprelate picked them up.

✳

Martin did not use the word "estate" in his passage on mixed government; Throckmorton argued for a parliamentary supremacy by means of "estates" and to make a point against the bishops, but he did not resort to mixed government. Unless Martin and Throckmorton were the same, the connection will not quite reveal itself; even if they were, a slight doubt might remain as to whether Martin/Throckmorton grasped the connection himself. If he did, however, an important point would be established: the linkage that had eluded all the prepresbyterian political argument would have been made by, and because of, the twist in terminology Scottish events had forced on England.

A scrupulous reading of Martin's work reveals that Martin viewed the two languages of mixed government and the revised enumeration of the estates (king, Lords, and Commons) as essentially interchangeable and, what is more, part of a specifically presbyterian political-religious outlook. Incidentally, the same reading makes it highly unlikely that John Penry was Martin. The method, simply, is to establish the sources behind Martin's words, the passages from other books that provided the springboard for his own thoughts. On two occasions, when Martin overtly operated on one level—either that of estates or that of mixed government—tacitly he was responding to sources operating on the other.

Martin's disquisition on mixed government in *Hay any worke for Cooper* (1588[1589]) was immediately preceded by twelve lines of comment upon two passages in Cooper's book, both of which had to do with estates and not, ostensibly, with the mixed government that Martin himself thought was the apex of that line of thought. The two passages were separated by a few pages in Cooper's text, but Martin brought them together in his own reflections. In the first, Martin replied to Cooper's charge of "inconvenience"—that is, of the consequences to follow if one of the estates, the bishops, were removed. Martin argued back that men would indeed be ruled by such a mutated government, contrary to Cooper's position that the laws would be called into doubt, and the more so because they now would be obeying God rather than man—the "Pope's law and his canons"—which in Martin's view were the sole underpinnings of episcopacy. Thus Martin denied Cooper's assertion; thus the bishops were not an estate.[45]

Martin immediately amplified his position: "The laws of England have been made when there was never a bishop in Parliament as in the first year of Her Majesty. And this reason as all the rest may serve to maintain popery as well as the hierarchy of bishops." The first sentence referred to the making of the Act of Supremacy in spite of the refusal of the leftover Marian bishops to give their assent; the remark served to demonstrate that the bishops lacked a veto and were, by that logic, no estate. The clear inference was that the House of Lords was an estate, or a manifestation of one, the council, in a different form. The second sentence rammed home the point: Cooper's reason of "inconvenience" would have prevented the return to protestantism; the estate of bishops was incompatible with England as it stood.[46]

Martin turned a few pages in the *Admonition*. First he denied Cooper's charge that the church was popular (Cooper had hedged his bet—aristocratic or democratic) and then Cooper's consequence that the state would change in sympathy with the church. He denied it by arguing that both were already mixed governments. He did not, it will be recalled once again, use the word "estate," but obviously he was led to the point by having arrived at two necessary and prior propositions, both derived from consideration of Cooper's terminology: the bishops were not an estate, the House of Lords was. That is why there was no "alteration of the civil state."[47]

If this interpretation is rejected, several difficulties arise. One is that Martin's remarks about mixed government become gratuitous and intrusive in the logic of their appearance. Another is that Martin had company: another radical presbyterian later constructed a theory of mixed government by the estates of king, Lords, and Commons out of these same two passages of Thomas Cooper.[48] A third difficulty is that Martin did the same thing in reverse in an earlier squib, *O read ouer D. John Bridges* [the Epitome].

In this second instance of the identification of estates-revision and mixed government, Martin had in front of him, by his own testimony, the only passage available to him (apart from Arthur Hall) that spoke of mixed government by the three "estates" of king, Lords, and Commons. That passage, of course, was John Aylmer's analysis of the constitution in *An harborowe*. Martin came to it as he grew bored with the ponderous Bridges and turned to mock Aylmer, whom he regarded, revealingly but incorrectly, as a defector from Martin's own presbyterian cause, a "carnal" hypocrite who once pretended a hostility to bishops as "a snare to catch a bishopric."[49] Aylmer, it was true, had earlier criticized the bishops of his day for their wealth, worldliness, and civil rank; but he had called only for their reform, not their abolition.[50] Martin insisted, nonetheless, that Aylmer had opposed their "calling" and "usurping" of civil office—in one other, unused word, their estate. In Martin's mind, Aylmer's supposed antiepiscopacy had to have been linked to his earlier constitutional views. Aylmer's translation to the episcopate had "cooled" his "courage for in those days . . . you would have our Parliament to overrule Her Majesty."[51]

Martin's reference was to Aylmer's praise of those who had resisted Henry's Act of Proclamations, a passage that followed out of Aylmer's description of English government as a mixture of the three classical forms, which Aylmer had glossed as estates. In transcribing Aylmer, Martin went back to three words ("In like manner") that had closed out the analogy with Sparta, words that unmistakably adverted to Aylmer's earlier forwarding of the power of the three estates over the power of a single person. This time, at least, the bishop had not been carnal; "brother John" had "spoken many things worthy the noting," especially by "Parliament men," who could use them in "putting down lord bishops" even "against their king's and queen's mind."[52] In this way, it can be seen, Martin began with an attack upon the estate of bishops (here the "calling" and civil office), moved to torture the bishop of London with his own youthful words about the supremacy of the three estates (so called by Aylmer) over the prince alone, and moved back again to the use of parliamentary supremacy over the prerogative to urge a parliamentary abolition of episcopacy. So automatically did Martin do this that he found it hard to believe that the Aylmer of "those days" did not do the like.

Thus Martin had estates on his mind when he sprang into mixed government, and he had mixed government before his eyes when he used *An harborowe* to attack bishops. Doing without "estate," he did what his alter ego did with "estate" in his parliamentary speeches in 1587: assert the supremacy of the Parliament over bishops and prerogative. In each instance one element of the complete notion was omitted. In Throckmorton's speeches it was the mixed government. In the passage on mixed government in *Hay any worke for Cooper* it was "estate," although Martin was staring at the word. In the Epitome, which linked parliamentary supremacy to the pulling down of bishops, it was the mixed government of Aylmer's text. The other prime candidate for authorship of the Marprelate tracts, John Penry, could not have done what Martin did. Altogether less clever than Throckmorton, Penry replied to Cooper's warning about the legal perils of abolishing an estate by replying that there were only two estates, the nobility and the commons.[53] Partly by the exclusion of Penry, partly by the identity of the doctrine, Throckmorton and Martin appear to be the same man.

One can only guess why Martin was so guarded about his full opinion— if indeed he was at all, for the identity of mixed government and the denial of the estate of bishops may have been too obvious to bother to state. Perhaps, however, Martin/Throckmorton felt that "estate" led too closely upon the heels of the Throckmorton of 1587. It also may have been something else, a feeling that the full doctrine was intrinsically subversive, in the sense that Cooper had put his finger upon at about the same time: to abolish the estate of bishops was formal revolution, an act that destroyed the body politic that then existed.

Interestingly, the word from which Martin shied—estate—is the one word that crops up menacingly in the proclamation "Ordering Destruction of Marprelate Publications"[54] issued on 13 February 1589, five days after Bancroft's sermon at Paul's Cross, after Cooper's *Admonition* had been written, and after the publication of only the first two of the Marprelate pamphlets, the Epistle and the Epitome of *O read ouer D. John Bridges*. The proclamation reviewed the "schismatical, seditious, fantastical" output of the secret press, which had attacked both church and state and had ridiculed the bishops themselves "beyond the bounds of all good humanity." It went on in a more specific way to isolate Martin's most dangerous views. The pamphlets tended "by their scope" to encourage the destruction of the government of the church, "the abridging, or rather . . . the overthrow, of her highness' lawful prerogative allowed by God's law and established by the law of the realm, and consequently to reserve, dissolve, and set at liberty the present government of the church," and the dissolution of "the estate of prelacy, being one of the three ancient estates of the realm under her highness, whereof Her Majesty mindeth to have such a reverend regard as to their places in the church and commonwealth pertaineth."

Clearly an episcopally motivated attempt to commit the whole council to its cause (no easy proposition), the proclamation never once suggested that Martin's presbyterianism per se was intolerable. That would not have passed the council; there are some words late in the proclamation that seem to be a counterattempt to protect university disputation, to protect acceptable dissent. Martin had to be gotten at in other ways. One way was through his denial of the royal supremacy, "the abridging, or rather . . . the overthrow" of the prerogative. But that was a cumbersome and unusual phrase, and it is not implausible that it was based on Martin's warm endorsement of Aylmer's cheerleading for those who had hindered Henry's Act of Proclamations; like most presbyterians in England, Martin elsewhere paid lip service to the royal supremacy and was ever vigilant in looking for proof that somehow the bishops were opposed to it. Another oddity is that, while Martin never used the word estate, the proclamation, making the connection that Bancroft had just failed to make in his sermon at Paul's Cross and that Cooper did make in his *Admonition*, accused him of destroying "the ancient estate" of the bishops, immediately after it accused him of slighting the prerogative. Perhaps the proclamation alighted upon the same reasoning that may have served Cooper and Martin. Perhaps it was simply assumed that Martin was Throckmorton.

Along with some of the lesser participants, Throckmorton faced legal difficulties in the aftermath of the Marprelate episode; Penry, though he died for his views, was never formally accused of writing the Martinist tracts. Throckmorton, however, was indicted by a Warwick grand jury in the summer of 1590 for "making" the Marprelate books. None of the legal paper of the indictment or its continuation at Westminster in the Easter term of 1591 survives, it seems; a second-hand but reliable report had it that Throckmorton/Martin had "declaimed against . . . ancient orders confirmed by all antiquity," a phrase that probably means, as Carlson has suggested, the estate of bishops.[55] Thus the net was closed about Throckmorton who, as Martin, never used the word "estate" in a significant context.[56]

In 1592, with the presbyterian movement on the wane in England, two books appeared and continued the skirmishing over the estates. Richard Schilders, the Middelburg printer of puritans, published *A petition delivered to her most excellent maiestie,* a tract largely designed to prove that the Martinists and other radical puritans did not fall under the penalties of 25 Eliz. c. 2. Pollard and Redgrave attribute the work to Henry Barrow, clearly an error, and Carlson has suggested that Throckmorton was the author. Unfortunately, this convenient hypothesis is a weak and quite unnecessary part of Carlson's case, and it is probably wisest to assume that *A petition* came from another pen, but one that shared the presbyterian–mixed government outlook.[57]

A petition argued that defamation of the bishops did not fall under the statute because bishops as bishops were no part of the queen's "body politic." The author distinguished between the body politic "of the realm" and the body politic "of her majesty." The latter comprised the queen's officers. The bishops were among these, to be sure, but their spiritual function ("jurisdiction") was contrary to Scripture; once again, presbyterians simply preferred to obey God rather than man and regarded it as a sufficient reply to all objections. The body politic "of the realm" consisted of "the three states of the Parliament," which were the queen, the Lords, and the Commons. In an interesting exercise, the author tried to show that Wyclif, Chaucer, and William Langland were also against "the state of bishops" —part of a groping attempt to find a historical pedigree for the three estates of king, Lords, and Commons.[58]

Matthew Sutcliffe's reply, *An answere to a certaine libel supplicatorie, or rather diffamatory,* fought history with history. The exclusion of the bishops, he said, was contrary to the reckoning of this realm, and common speech, and acts of Parliament, . . . contrary to the use of the French, from whence we had the word . . . and contrary to the reckoning of all Christendom . . . yea contrary to Christianity." The Scots had three estates, and if the Romans had but two (Senate and people) it was because they were heathens. Sutcliffe also detected something more than hostility to bishops in the revised reckoning of the estates: "you make the prince that is head, equal with the parts, and make others as good as him: which is the endeavor of this libeller."[59]

In these ways, Scottish argument about the estates had become the English. Suddenly the estate of prelacy had become a fighting position, as it had been in Scotland, and the estate of bishops had become part of the ancient constitution. That is why even Burghley, who had casually defined the three estates as king, Lords, and Commons in 1585, would find that the doctrine had become a dangerous position. The irony of it, which Bancroft had tried to cover up in his Paul's Cross sermon, was that the estate of bishops, name and thing, recently had come under severe attack in James's Scotland. If the English, with a good deal of help from James, suddenly had discovered the three traditional estates were part of the ancient constitution, the Scots, with equal suddenness, were now not so sure.

✳

The change in Scotland began when a group of English puritans persuaded Elizabeth to set loose the Ruthven lords, who had fled to England. They returned to Scotland in December 1585 and forced James Stewart, earl of Arran, James's strong man, into retirement. This counter-coup was widely popular among many elements in Scotland, notably the presbyterian ministers who had fled to England and who now scampered back to Scotland with the alacrity with which they had left it. These groups did not entirely restore the status quo ante Arran. Scottish politics from 1586 well into the 1590s was beset by numerous and countervailing pressures, and James and his chancellor, Lord Maitland, were fairly successful at setting one interest against another; but this is also to say that the presbyterians had considerable room for maneuver, and if they did not get everything they wanted, they did get more each year.[60]

Helping the presbyterian cause considerably was a wholly artificial strain placed upon the relations between James and the English defenders of episcopacy. James had felt that Bancroft had cast aspersions upon the king's sincerity in his Paul's Cross sermon; in fact, Bancroft was trying only to rally James, insofar as he was addressing the king at all, but the puritans who managed English policy toward Scotland did their utter and temporarily successful best to misrepresent James to Bancroft and Bancroft to James. Adamson was exposed as an agent, of sorts, of Bancroft, largely through the efforts of the English ambassador, the puritan Robert Bowes. Adamson was forced to make an abject recantation to the General Assembly, and national pride, if nothing else, forced James to repudiate him.[61]

Episcopacy was never formally abolished in Scotland during the period of presbyterian ascendancy from 1586 to 1596. But presbyterianism made steady gains, so many that by the beginning of 1596 the presbyterian David Calderwood, who was never a man to compromise with even a whiff of prelacy, thought the kirk had "come to her perfection, and the greatest purity that she ever attained unto, both in doctrine and discipline."[62] Well before that year, as early as 1587, presbyterians had so triumphed that some thought the king no longer the same man he had been in 1585.

The act of Annexation of 1587 was the parliamentary manifestation of the growing power of the presbyterians. This act stripped the episcopal sees of most of their revenues and lands, confiscating them in the name of the crown. Titular bishops continued to sit, but, devoid of wealth and of authority (partly by constitutional measures within the kirk and partly simply be being ignored), they were a "mere façade."[63] The act said nothing about estates, but it was later understood to have been about them. In 1598 James wrote of the need for repeal of the "vile" act as the means for restoring the episcopal estate,[64] and an act of 1606 noted, correctly, that the Act of Annexation amounted to the "indirect abolishing" of the estate of bishops.[65]

A rather obscure act of the same 1587 Parliament, "anent the Parliament," seemed to contemplate what actually took place in the intervening years, that lay commendators of episcopal lands would be a large part of the estate of prelacy. It specified that no person "shall take upon him the function, office or place of all the three estates or of two of them" but only be a member of the estate "wherein he commonly professes himself to live and whereof he takes his style." The episcopal estate simply might die off, a prospect that was apparently approached from a different angle in the fines specified for unexcused absence from the Parliament: earls were to pay 300 pounds, lairds to pay 200, prelates only 100, and burgh commissioners 100 marks.[66] A bishop was to pay only a third more than the meanest member of the Parliament for nonattendance, while any laird was valued at twice the rate even of the archbishop of Saint Andrews. A draft of a plea from "some of the brethren" in 1589 to Elizabeth, urging her to take action against Bancroft, referred to episcopal partisans as "the ecclesiastical estate (*as they are called*)."[67]

In 1592 there was the first parliamentary recognition of the presbyterian system that had been replacing episcopacy, in the act "for abolishing of acts contrary the true religion."[68] It is curious that this same Parliament also adopted an important change in parliamentary style, in the enactment clauses of statutes and in the listing of the members of the Committee of the Articles. Until 1584 it had been a matter of indifference whether acts were established in the name of the "three estates" or "the estates." The terms were interchangeable. The acts of 1584 showed a predilection for the style of "three estates" in the enactment clause, a pattern that previously would have been regarded as indifferent and idiosyncratic. But in 1592 and continuously thereafter, almost all acts were issued in the name simply of "the estates." The uniformity of the new usage suggests a polemical intention, as if there had been a conscious reaction to the conceptual implications of 1584 and of the English manipulations of it. There were only a few exceptions to this pattern. A number of them had to do with confirmations of lands that had been earlier granted and recognized in parliamentary acts. In these cases, the enactment clauses spoke of the three estates. The exceptions indicate that something significant underlay the change in style. These private acts, drafted originally by private lawyers, were careful to use the "three estates" because the lawyers wanted to make absolutely sure that the original and the later acts were to be understood to have issued from the same authority, from the same body. That is to say, there was decidedly some doubt about the matter, at least in the minds of the lawyers. It is obvious that the lawyers' scruple bears a resemblance to the point that Cooper made in his *Admonition*: to change the estates was to change the body politic.[69]

Moreover, there was an overt change that corresponded to the subtleties of the enactment clauses. At the beginning of every Parliament, a managing committee, the Lords of the Articles, was established; it was composed of members of each of the estates, who were listed by name under the estate to which they belonged. Before 1592, the lairds and shire commissioners were listed under the heading of the nobility. The titled nobles had their names listed first, and the lairds were listed next as a group under a subheading. In 1592 however, they were given a separate and equal heading, along with the nobles and commissioners of the burghs and clergy (who were then mostly laymen anyway). Depending on how one looked at it, there were now either four estates in Scotland, or three without the bishops—nobles, lairds, and burgh commissioners, In 1606, the ambiguity was perceived, and in the 1630s, when the episcopal estate was formally abolished, it was stated plainly that there were three estates without the bishops.[70] James apparently caught the drift of this line of thought in 1598 and rejected it.[71]

James's behavior in 1586–1596 perplexed contemporaries and has perplexed historians since. Was he a hypocrite? Had he a change of heart, in fact several changes of them? Was he lying in wait from 1586 to 1596, ready to pounce again on the presbyterians as soon as the opportunity arose? His enemies of course gravitated, as suited their case, to the hostile answers, although these were not the same from one writer to the next. A simple answer might be that James was consistent when he was strong and inconsistent when he was weak; it only slightly complicates matters to add that much of James's strength, when he had it, came from consistency, and it tended to feed on itself. It is also pertinent that James had a remarkable need for contact with clergymen. He preferred to be a Constantine, a lay bishop; if that were not possible, he would be, with equal measures of discontent and desperation, a ruling elder.

Whatever the meaning of James's shifts and turns toward presbyterianism in the later 1580s and early 1590s, by 1596 the king had returned to his original form.[72] Necessity and opportunity conspired to force his hand. The perfection of the kirk had meant to James an endless presbyterian rodomontade of slights, insults, and humiliations. Andrew Melville's lecture to James on the king's position as "God's silly vassal," David Black's sermon in which all kings' children were called the Devil's brood, and the Edinburgh riot in December 1596, which saw a multitude whooped to a frenzy by a sermon against the Hamans of James's government, were only the most conspicuous occasions.[73] It was no longer a time for cat-and-mouse diplomacy with England; the succession had to be secured, and James had come to the conclusion that ambiguous dealing with the radicals was not the way to go about it. The complexion of the court also had changed. The moderation and bridge building of Maitland had died with the chancellor. A suspected Catholic, James Elphinstone, was on the rise.

As James sought to regain some control over the kirk, the issue of the clerical or episcopal estate resurfaced. As before, the question of clerical representation in Parliament combined or conflated a generally perceived need for clerical representation (which was rejected on principle only by the most doctrinaire presbyterians) with a very specific question of how the clerical representation was to be accomplished, on which James and most of the moderates could now only disagree. The single point of universal agreement, in fact, was that the existing arrangement was unsatisfactory. There were still a few surviving "bishops" about, stripped of their authority and their lands. Without intervention of some sort, their deaths would bring to an end the episcopal estate in Parliament, by any proper use of the term. On the other hand, the lay commendators of the old episcopal and abbatial lands also sat for the clerical estate, a situation repugnant to all but themselves.

James's first moves were extremely tentative. He already had been trying to use commissioners elected by the General Assembly as a means of control over that body; any device by which parity might be combated was better than none, and, in the practical sense, James could better influence a few than a multitude. The use of commissioners could be extended. A compromise proposal was floated in which individual presbyteries would nominate, but James would elect, commissioners to serve as the clerical estate in Parliament. The two groups of commissioners, though constitutionally distinct, nevertheless could have overlapped in membership; a measure of hierarchical discipline might have been restored. Surprisingly, these compromise proposals fell through, and it does not seem that the initiative in rejection came from the king.[74]

James pressed on without the kirk; understandably, his new project, which was considerably less conciliatory, reflected bitterness at his rebuff. An act of 1597 took the first step toward the revival of episcopacy in a meaningful form. It recognized James's right to appoint "actual preachers and ministers in the kirk," or "such other persons as shall be found apt and qualified to use and exercise the office and function of a minister or preacher," to presently vacant bishoprics, and to appoint such clergymen to any prelacies (including abbacies) that should fall vacant in the future. These royal appointees were to attend the Parliament and vote as "freely" as had prelates "at any time." The logic was the same as it had been earlier: prelates had "ever represented one of the estates of this realm." Their "privileges and freedoms" had "been from time to [time] renewed and confirmed"; they were now to have the rights they had "at any time of before."[75]

It is usual to minimize the importance of the act of 1597. First, the act established only "parliamentary bishops" who had no standing within or with regard to the existing structure of presbyteries and General Assembly. Their ability, therefore, to exercise traditional diocesan responsibilities of episcopacy was nil. Second, new bishops on this provision were not appointed until 1600, although it was also true that an aging Catholic holdout from the Reformation, who had never been formally deprived, was returned to his place in 1598. Moreover, the act served more to enrage than cow the General Assembly, whose practical control over the ministers was, if anything, enhanced by the provocation.

All this is true; but it is also incomplete. James had done what he could. Every position of the act was significant. There was to be a genuine clerical estate in Parliament—"actual preachers and ministers"—and if, as was clearly anticipated by the act, the presbyteries and General Assembly suspended or excommunicated those who accepted parliamentary pre-lacies, the "such other persons" passage authorized the king to go it alone. The careful distinction between prelacies then vacant and those to fall vacant was not simply lawyerly overdraftsmanship; there was a point to it, and a potentially divisive one at that. The currently vacant prelacies were ones then in the king's gift, prelacies that had not been commended to laymen. The others were in lay hands; the expectation had been that they would be heritable, but here, faintly, was the mention of another prospect, that the lands might be reunited, somehow, sometime, with the titles. Finally, and remarkably, not only was the logic of the ancient three estates invoked once again, not only was there an attempt to assert the existence of continuity with the past that recent events belied, but there was also an attempt to overleap the Reformation itself in justifying their function. Their privileges were to be as great as ever they had been, even in times of popery.

Once the deed was accomplished, presbyterians were quick to connect it with a continuous royal policy. It was at once something new and something old. One presbyterian denounced the scheme at the time as a Trojan horse; another said of the new bishop, "busk him as bonnily as you can," but you will still "see the horns of his miter."[76] It was clear even in England that James again had latched onto his beloved three estates. Robert Cecil's informants in Scotland, having explained the recent turn of events in the language of the three estates, were ordered to employ the same language to try to get through to James on another matter of deepening mutual interest, the succession: if James were not careful, Elizabeth might use her "three estates" in ways that would not favor James's hopes.[77]

By a General Assembly at Dundee, in March 1598, presbyterians had largely succeeded in breaking moderate sympathy for the scheme of clerical representation, so that James, borrowing a Melvillian expression, protested that he would not have either papistical or "anglican" bishops.[78]

But George Gledstanes, in arguing for clerical representation, was apparently in close touch with royal thinking when he "alleged that the whole subjects were divided in *tres ordines,* in respect of their living in the common weal, and, therefore, the kirk must be one estate."[79] Significantly, Gledstanes was attacked for this speech—which earlier had been the most uncontentious of platitudes in Scotland—on the ground that it was a political language inappropriate to the discussion of religion. Presbyterians in Scotland could sever the political and religious spheres quite as well as their English counterparts could link them.

But Gledstanes may have been hinting at the depth of commitment of the king to the doctrine of three estates. Already in his *Trew law of free monarchies,* James had made clear how the estates of the realm were, in his view, connected to constitutional forms. "The kings . . . in Scotland were before any estates or ranks of men within the same, before any Parliaments were holden, or laws made: and by them was the land distributed . . . states erected . . . and forms of government devised and established."[80] This supremacy of kings over the estates, which were royal creations, was a feature, James suggested rather imprudently, not only of Scotland but of England as well. And that supremacy was essential to a free (that is, sovereign) monarchy and is what distinguished it from the government of "elective kings, and [even more] of such sort of governors, as the dukes of Venice are, whose aristocratic and limited government, is nothing like to free monarchies; although the malice of some writers hath not been ashamed to mis-know any difference to be betwixt them."[81] The supremacy of the king over the estates was the opposite of those mixtures of monarchical and aristocratic authority, stemming from different first principles, that characterized the republic of Venice, a mixed government if there ever was one.

James returned to the theme in a different way in *Basilikon doron,* where he employed it as an organizing principle of a good part of the book. "The whole subjects of our country," he wrote to Prince Henry, "(by the ancient and fundamental policy of our kingdom) are divided into three estates."[82] Working the main vein of Scottish social criticism, he surveyed the vices of each estate. In a well-known passage, he accused the clergy, or some of them, of anarchic and democratic excess, of being even more lawless than the men of the Borders and Highlands. The remedy was the elevation of the godly and learned among the clergy to "bishoprics and benefices," which could be accomplished only by the repeal of "that vile act of annexation." Repeal would "re-establish the old institution of the three estates in

Parliament, which can no otherwise be done."[83] James was utterly serious about the three estates as the foundation of his monarchy; it was more than a cover story for the revival of episcopacy. He made a point of noting that the "small barons are but an inferior part of the nobility and of their estate." In so doing, James was running against an irreversible tide; but clearly he demonstrated that those changes of style that marked the assumption of the rank of estate by the shire commissioners meant nothing to him.[84] Order itself was predicated upon the existence of the three estates. The survival of monarchy depended upon their submission, the function of monarchy being to preserve them in their integrity.

In 1598 *Basilikon doron* was a secret book. Seven copies were printed quietly in February 1599.[85] But a copy fell into James Melville's hands and either he or an associate, John Dykes of Kilkenny, gathered out of it some "anglo-pisco-papistical" conclusions.[86] They were quite accurate. Among them were:

1. The office of a king is a mixed office, betwixt the civil and ecclesiastical estate.

2. The ruling of the kirk weal [cf. "common weal"] is no small part of the king's office.

7. Parity amongst the ministers can not agree with a monarchy.

8. The godly, learned, and modest men of the ministry should be preferred to bishoprics and benefices.

9. Without bishops the three estates in Parliament cannot be re-established. Therefore, bishops must be, and parity banished and put away.

10. They that preach against bishops should be punished with the rigor of the law.

13. For a preservative against [puritan] poison there must be bishops.

15. The ministers' quarrel was ever against the king, for no other cause but because he was king.

16. Parity is the mother of confusion, and enemy to unity, which is the mother of order.

17. The ministers think by time to draw the policy and civil government, by the example of the ecclesiastical, to the same parity.

Dykes brought these propositions into the Synod of Fife (September 1599) without indicating the source. Not surprisingly, the synod judged them "treasonable, seditious, and wicked."[87] Dykes was sought out under an order of the privy council, and he fled. One who was present at the synod, and who was well aware of the source of the "anglo-pisco-papistical" propositions, was George Gledstanes, whose usefulness to the king as an expositor of the three orders already has been noticed.[88]

✳

The struggle to place the parliamentary bishops within the framework of the kirk was a drawn-out affair. Moderates wanted to make them tolerable, by making them virtual agents of the ministry; the presbyterian hard-liners never gave up their opposition to the whole scheme; episcopalians fought to convert the parliamentary bishops into ruling bishops with proper endowments. Important steps along that road were taken only in 1606 and 1611. The immediate details are of no importance to this study. The pressure seemed irresistible that "the king must have one of his three estates."[89]

✳

Shortly after the Synod of Fife of February 1598 there was "a fearful eclipse."

> The whole face of the sun seemed to be covered and darkened. . . . The stars appeared in the firmament. Sea, land, and air was still, and strucken dead as it were. The ravens and fowls flocking together mourned exceedingly in their kind. Great multitudes of paddocks [frogs] ran together, making an uncouth and hideous noise; men and women were astonished, as if they day of judgment had been coming. . . . The like fearful darkness was never seen in this land.

David Calderwood had only one explanation for it: God's displeasure at "the estate of bishops."[90]

5
Dangerous Positions, 1603–1637

Constitutionally, James's accession to the English throne in March 1603 was merely a personal union of two distinct crowns in one man. To the dismay of both his Scottish and his English subjects, however, James VI and I was not content to let the matter so rest. What doubtless had long been in his mind now surfaced as his grandiose scheme for a full union of the two kingdoms into a single "Great Britain," with its strange terminology of North and South Britain (Scotland and England) and the Middle Shires (the old Borders). Questions more substantive than terminology were involved: matters of citizenship, of tenures, of conformity of laws, of rights of merchants, of rights of Scots to English offices.

One question that did not come up, officially, was that of union in religion. Part of the reason it did not come up officially was that it was not supposed to have been necessary to raise it. Supposedly, in religion the two kingdoms were already united. They were both protestant, they were both reformed. Conventional justifications of James's plans scarcely touched upon religious union, taking it, like common language, as a thing already accomplished, as a ground or motive for further union rather than an impediment to it.[1]

But more important is the fact that James would not let it be otherwise: the commissioners for union from both parliaments were not instructed to discuss ecclesiastical matters. This in itself was a statement of James's intentions regarding the religious aspects of union. If James sought any conformity of the two churches at all, it was conformity in acknowledging the royal supremacy (and as James understood it, the personal royal supremacy) in matters ecclesiastical. To enforce silence was precisely to enforce, in one important respect, the policy James sought to impose. In

97

any event, it soon became clear that the union of the two churches was very much a significant business to James, to his bishops in both churches, and to their opponents.

In church matters, perhaps more than in any other area, James I can only be understood as James VI, and vice versa. As king of Scotland, James had sought to bring the kirk into line with the English church as he chose to regard it and intended it to be; as king of Great Britain, he had no intention of letting that policy lapse, either by default or through inactivity in Scotland or by allowing in England those things that had so irritated him in Scotland. Thus the issues in Scotland—including the political-religious question of the estates of the realm—came south with James in 1603.

Like the other, more public aspects of union, the union of the churches began to be pursued a year after James's accession. The canons of 1604 enjoined English Christians to pray specifically for the churches of England, of Ireland, and—for the first time—of Scotland.[2] Given the virtual dominance of Bancroft in the church, the new addition was menacing; and the menace was compounded both by the English publication (and first large edition) of James's *Basilikon doron,* with its severity and its version of the three estates, and by the Hampton Court conference of 1604, with its famous royal dictum, "No bishop, no king."[3]

What was needed, if English puritans and presbyterians were to thwart James's designs, was a specifically English response from an eminently respectable source, to his high churchmanship and his ultraroyalism. Such a response was forthcoming in 1604 in the form of a book that refreshed the late Elizabethan debate over the three estates of the realm—showing that the concerns of the king and his episcopal friends were shared, *mutatis mutandis,* by his English opponents. The book was *An assertion for true and Christian church-policie,* its author William Stoughton.

A little is known about Stoughton. The first student to matriculate at Christ Church, so elected from the Westminster School in 1561, Stoughton took his Bachelor of Arts in 1565, a Master of Arts in 1568, and supplicated for his Bachelor of Civil Law in November 1571.[4] In 1575 he appeared in Leicestershire, perhaps as a client of the earl of Huntingdon and certainly as a friend and protector of radical puritans close to the earl, such as Thomas Wood and Anthony Gilby. Stoughton operated as a radical puritan "mole" within the Court of Arches, using his position as lay commissary to protect his friends in the parish of Groby, a puritan hotbed and a peculiar jurisdiction of the Court of Arches, from scrutiny by more rigorous elements inside the court.[5] According to a preface written by an unidentified descendant to a later edition of *An assertion,* Stoughton also wrote *An abstract of certaine acts of parlement* [1584],[6] a vigorous assault upon episcopal pretensions, including their civil functions, even their seats in Parliament.[7] In the Parliament of 1584–1585 (the only one for which he sat), Stoughton took a leading role in religious agitation. On 23 February 1585 he "offered . . . a certain supplication in parchment of certain abuses in the ministry within the county of Leicester, and also a note of certain articles in paper concerning some disorders in the bishop's ministry." Edward Lewkenor, a better-known puritan, offered a similar petition from east Sussex. Both were read by order of the house. Later, Stoughton was a member of the committee that brought in a failed bill "against excessive fees and taxations" in ecclesiastical courts.[8] From that point until the publication of his book in 1604, Stoughton drops from public view.

An assertion for true and Christian church-policie has received some notice as an attack upon church courts, and Brian Levack has called attention to it as evidence of that rarity, an English civilian of radical views; but it was more than a vitriolic attack upon the jurisdiction of the English bishops.[9] Stoughton's attacks upon abuses in church jurisdiction were harsh but they did not go beyond the limits of acceptable dissent; yet Stoughton apparently regarded the book as dangerous, for he had it published in the Netherlands by the Dutch printer of English radicals, Richard Schilders. Others seem to have held the same view. In certain copies of the book containing a signed preface to "the most worthy and Christian gentlemen, the apprentices and students of the Inns of Court," Stoughton's name was "defaced and deleted."[10]

Both the significance and the danger of *An assertion* lay in Stoughton's unrepentant and unbending Elizabethan presbyterianism. At a time when presbyterianism was being cast off rapidly in favor of quiescence and moderation and the search for personal spirituality, Stoughton grimly revived an old controversy, that of 1589 between Thomas Cooper and his opponents, notably Martin Marprelate.[11] That controversy, as has been seen, was in good part an Englishing of the Scottish argument over the estates of the realm. Now, for the benefit of the Scottish king of England, Stoughton insisted on bringing the argument, buried during half a generation of repression, to new life.

Stoughton in fact had written the book when Elizabeth was still queen and when Thomas Cooper's *Admonition* was still news. His incomplete updating of it gave it two subtly different meanings, one Elizabethan and one Jacobean; but in both, with several levels of irony, James was offered a lesson in English government. That lesson, as the full title of the tract put it, was that presbyterianism could be established "without any derogation to the king's royal prerogative, [or] any indignity to the three estates in Parliament."[12] Stoughton made his case in two cameo discourses well within this long and disorderly octavo. Interestingly, everything he had to say on the subject of mixed government by the estates of king, Lords, and Commons was contained in his responses to the same two passages that had provoked Martin Marprelate/Job Throckmorton into similar but more guarded reflections.

The first of these passages was Cooper's warning that the laws would be put in jeopardy if one of the estates were left out. It must be understood, said Stoughton, that Cooper could only have meant statute law. And even in regard to statute law, Stoughton maintained, presbyterianism could not place the laws in doubt, for "prelates" had never been one of the three estates. Whoever said otherwise was "guilty of high treason, to the king, and to the realm." This "treason," of course, would in 1604 have reached to Bishop Bancroft and to James himself, inasmuch as both insisted that the bishops were an estate. For the king's edification, Stoughton carefully refocused his argument in this section to adapt it to the Jacobean context: he rehearsed familiar English legal and constitutional history to prove that the assent of the "king, the nobles, and Commons of the realm" was all that was needed to make new law or repeal old law, "without prelates, bishops, or clerks."[13]

Martin Marprelate had commented on the same passage from Cooper and had drawn essentially the same conclusion, though without using the word "estate." It was when he had turned to a nearby passage in the *Admonition* —the one in which Cooper charged that the "whole drift" of presbyterianism was to turn the government of the church into an aristocracy or democracy and that the "sense and feeling" of the one would lead to a similar transformation in the state—that Martin had resorted to the language of the three estates of king, Lords, and Commons to make his reply. Stoughton did not get to that second passage of Cooper's until he had written another 160 pages of his own octavo, but when he did, he roared where Martin had whispered. In so doing, Stoughton developed quite the fullest and most penetrating version of the mixed constitution that had yet appeared in England.

Playing fondly upon Cooper's own well-chosen words, Stoughton readily conceded that the "whole drift" of presbyterianism was indeed to bring church government to what the "learned call aristocracy"—but, he added, that was all to the good. Aristocracy "and the discipline of the primitive church" differed "but in name, and not in nature," so it could "not but be beneficial unto the common weal." Moreover, there was no cause for concern about a transfer of the benefits of aristocracy or democracy to the state. That, Stoughton said in a glittering passage, already had long been done.[14]

Rather, the real danger was the spread of prelacy—prelacy, as Stoughton conceived it with considerable reason, being in no sense a monarchical regimen but an oligarchical one, a *pessimatum potestas* to be set against the *optimatum potestas* of presbyterianism. Prelacy was an innovation, a threat to the ancient order of mixed government. "Ever since the time they first began to be a people," the English "have had their wits long exercised, with the sense and feeling, of the reasons and principles, as well of democracy, as also of aristocracy." As to their ancient democracy, did not the English have "some hand and dealing . . . by one means or other" in "almost all cases of civil and criminal justice by common law"? And "which is more, have they not the sense and feeling of the making, and unmaking their own laws in Parliament? And is not their consultation in Parliament, a mere democratical consultation?" So, too, the aristocracy had long had their role in council and Parliament.[15]

Cooper's argument about a transfer from the ecclesiastical to the civil realm crashed to the ground. Stoughton asked another of his mocking questions: "what translation then is there greatly to be feared . . . when the minds of all sorts of our commonwealthmen ["common wealthes-men"] be already seasoned, with the things which he feareth? And when the common weal is already seized of the principles and reasons, which he would not have familiarly known unto it." King, nobles, and commons no longer should be afraid of "the stratagems of these uncouth, and unknown Greek names, of democracy, and aristocracy, writ in [Cooper's] book with great and capital letters." What was desired in the church was only the same "manner of government" as the English "and their progenitors and ancestors, for many hundred years together, without interruption, have used and enjoyed in the common weal."[16]

Stoughton's triumphant performance added something to the opposition version of the mixed constitution by the three estates of king, Lords, and Commons, namely history. Arthur Hall had attacked the historicity of the Commons and had a good understanding of classical categories; Lambarde had defended that antiquity but had shown little inclination to use the classical categories. The author of *A petition* and Sutcliffe, on opposite sides, barely began an examination of English history from the perspective of the three estates. None had quite taken the historicizing leap that Stoughton took; he saw clearly that the point to be established (apart from the elimination of the bishops as an estate) was the historicity not of the admittedly hoary terms of nobles and commons but of the supposedly alien and frightening principles of aristocracy and democracy in the English past. To Stoughton these words were as applicable to the English past as they were to the governance of the primitive church, for all that they were not so used. They described the ancient constitution, they described the political nature of the English "ever since they began to be a people."

It is impossible to say how influential Stoughton's book was. William Covell's *A modest & reasonable examination* (1604) noticed the sting of *An assertion* enough to include the claim of a refutation of it in its title, and to devote a few remarks to it in a preface; these have the appearance of late additions to a book already written. Covell, who dedicated his book first to Whitgift and then to Bancroft upon the old archbishop's death, caught Stoughton's point exactly: it was an attempt to take from Parliament one "of the three states (a state not of the least wisdom and gravity)."[17] But the circumstances of publication of *An assertion* suggest that it was expected to meet official displeasure, and that apparently did not occur. Yet it was by no means a rare book; copies remain fairly numerous. One thing is certain: Stoughton was not forgotten. *An assertion* was twice reprinted in 1642; a copy in the Huntington Library of the 1604 edition contains handwritten notes indicating that it was opened, if not read, in the 1630s.[18]

Perhaps the most alarming thing about *An assertion* in its own time was that it combined an obvious radicalism with social respectability and garden variety lay opinions. This combination long had posed challenges to the enemies of presbyterianism who for more than merely eristic reasons were always prepared to judge presbyterianism more radical, more dangerous than it was. The common lay presbyterian response was to deny linkage, to deny that forms in church and state were so intimately connected. Clerical presbyterians often had jeopardized that response—Cartwright and Travers are adequate witness—but Stoughton, a layman and no social radical, indeed really a lawyerly lawyer, had turned the argument of linkage upon its head, and in the doing invented what might as well be described as the Whig theory of the mixed constitution.

*

The danger attending the expression of such views was soon made evident by the mysterious demise of the College of Antiquaries, a society of scholars that had been founded during Elizabeth's reign. The college represented a considerable range of political and religious viewpoints but generally had avoided current politics in its otherwise free-flowing and candid discussions. The members were all established men, and their leading lights, William Camden and Sir Henry Spelman, were respectability itself. Spelman, for his part, was fiercely conservative. Yet the society abruptly ceased to meet after 1607, and it is probable that the one meeting that year was a futile attempt to revive an organization that actually had been defunct for a year or more. Another attempt at revival, made by Spelman in 1614, failed due to royal displeasure: James had by then conceived "some mislike" (or "a little mislike") for the antiquaries. Though Spelman's explanation of the society's previous inactivity attributed it to the age and indisposition of the members, his account broadly hints that the king's mislike of the college was political and that it had set in long before 1614.[19]

Upon the arrival of the new king, the society had abruptly shifted its discussions toward affairs of state, and to do that was certain to risk James's displeasure. To be sure, some of the opinions expressed in the antiquaries' discourses were sympathetic and useful to James's designs. Sir Robert Cotton's opinion that by "first institution and continued practice" the Scottish nations were "under the see of Canterbury" is a notable example.[20] Nor was there anything particularly offensive about the meetings on the diversity of the names of the island, on English law, and on English religion. But the members were in the habit of speaking their minds with a goodly measure of scholarly freedom. They had felt safe in doing so because their proceedings were in camera: no one but members could attend their meetings.[21] Their customary candor was in evidence when a session was held on the antiquity of parliaments. As a result, along with conventional and acceptable discourses by Camden and others, there was talk of the English Parliament as composed of the three estates of king, Lords, and Commons.

As Stoughton had done in his book, some of the antiquaries revived an Elizabethan controversy and gave it new life and shape. In this instance the point of departure was Arthur Hall's denial of the antiquity of Parliament and William Lambarde's attack on Hall, which had joined Hooker's *Order and usage* in making heavy use of the *Modus tenendi parliamentum*.[22] One anonymous discourse, standing upon the *Modus,* made only the conventional point that bishops sat by their baronies.[23] Another, attributed to John Dodderidge, stuck close to Lambarde's *Archeion* and contended that a parliament in England was properly an assembly of three "estates" of the king, the lords spiritual and temporal, and the Commons. The author also raised the matter of the ordinance as distinct from statute but left that interesting question to rest with a qualifying "in those times." Significantly, this discourse, in offering a capitular summary of the *Modus,* translated the six *gradus* of the *Modus* not as "estates" but as "degrees or tribes," quite as if "estate" were reserved for the most constant and most fundamental taxonomy.[24]

Another pertinent discourse is attributed to Francis Tate, although perhaps no more assuredly than the one attributed to Dodderidge. The text is so close, in some parts, to the Dodderidge discourse that there may be some confusion; Tate was secretary to the College of Antiquaries and conceivably he was only serving as rapporteur. Moreover, Tate apparently had expressed somewhat different views on the estates in a speech made in the Commons in 1604.[25] In any event, the discourse represents the opinion of somebody, somebody who likewise conceived of the three "estates" of Parliament as king, Lords, and Commons, who raised again the question of the ordinance (but now in the present tense, as if it were still a possibility), and who thought he was replying to Arthur Hall's denial of the antiquity of the Commons.[26]

These discourses were profoundly unhelpful to James's conception of union. A union of the parliaments would be complicated immensely by a difference in the structure of estates. And James's entire political-religious program in Scotland continued to be focused upon the idea of the episcopal estate. James would have faced a massive and cruel irony if, after so many years of trying to bring the kirk into structural congruence with the church of England, English scholars had undone in a twinkling all that work by insisting that the bishops were not an estate in England. Scottish presbyterians scarcely could have dreamed of a finer gift.

But if the antiquaries' discourses upon the estates of the realm are postulated as what triggered a suppression of the college, the question remains, how did the king learn of them, given the confidentiality of the discussions? Still another of the discourses, an anonymous one, suggests an answer. This discourse was not antiquarian in the least; it was a short address on the institution of the Parliament as it then stood. Its method, too, was different. As befitted historical scholarship, the antiquaries usually and simply discussed evidence in chronological order. This discourse, however, took a route more familiar to the sermon. It divided the question: "1. Whereof this court is composed. 2. What matters are proper for it. 3. To what end it is ordained." It differed, too, in being openly homiletic in intent, full of judgments of others' failings; none of the antiquaries' discourses on these or other topics, no matter how relevant to current affairs, took so preacherly a way. This one differed as well in matter: for all the diversity of the antiquaries, their meetings show no sign of servile royalism. This discourse did. So also it was peculiarly insistent upon the place of bishops. It held that the Parliament was composed of a head, the king, and a body. The body had two parts. There was an upper house "divided partly of the nobility temporal, who are hereditary councilors" to the Parliament and "partly of the bishops, spiritual men, who are likewise by virtue of their dignity, and *ad vitam* of this court." The "other house" was composed of the representatives of the shires and towns. As to matters "they ought to treat of," the members were warned that they consisted not "in heaping of infinite confused numbers of laws." The end of parliaments was the glory of God and "the weal of the king and his people." Meetings of Parliament were not an occasion for "particular men to utter their private conceits for satisfaction of their curiosities, or to make show of their eloquence." Men ought to be "ashamed of such toys, and remember that they are there as sworn councilors to their kings." As if to add real injury (in terms of the supposed privilege of Parliament) to the string of insults, the speaker admonished that "you must remember that you are assembled by your lawful king, to give him your best advice in matters proposed by him unto you."[27]

Everything about this discourse sets it off from its fellows: its insistence upon the parliamentary right of the bishops as spiritual men and upon their presence as vital (*ad vitam*), its denial of the right of free speech in the Commons, its almost stock set of charges against the Parliament combined with a curious use of the second person imperative in a scholarly discourse.

It is tempting to attribute this discourse to a man who was still waiting to be admitted to the society on 30 November 1604, one day after its meeting on the antiquity of Christianity. This was Launcelot Andrewes, then dean of Westminster, who wrote Abraham Hartwell on that day to press his suit for membership. Though Andrewes's rather petulant letter to Hartwell reveals something less than eagerness on the part of the college to accept him (if this was his discourse, it is not hard to see why), keeping him at bay for a long time would have been an indelicate ploy against a man whose career was soaring and whose connections to Bancroft and James were excellent. If Andrewes were the author, the time of the meeting surely would be set in 1605 or 1606, a period thin in datable meetings, according to Linda Van Norden.[28]

And if Andrewes (a veteran examiner of Marprelate suspects) were the author of the anonymous royalist discourse, the mystery of how the king learned of the subversive doctrine expounded in the College of Antiquaries is solved.[29] Two things seem likely, that James learned of the offensive discourse, and that, directly or indirectly, his displeasure led to the society's disbanding.

✳

Stoughton and the antiquaries were shouting against the wind. In 1605 and 1606 James moved decisively toward his long-planned full reintegration of the episcopal estate into Scottish life. The implementation of that policy was tightly intertwined with a palace revolution among the king's councilors in Scotland, a transformation of leadership that was at once a result and a cause of newfound strength among the partisans of episcopacy. In 1605, vigorously proepiscopal policies had been at least partially resisted by an unholy combination (or so it must have seemed to episcopalians) of the Catholic chancellor, the earl of Dunfermline, and Scottish presbyterians. They shared an abiding hatred of Archbishop Spottiswoode, if nothing else. For their part, the bishops and the earl of Dunbar, whose ambitions conflicted with Dunfermline's, could not hope to fulfill their political and personal programs unless they could convince the absent king that his hitherto trusted servant, Dunfermline, was indeed an enemy of the "estate of bishops."[30]

Dunbar's chance came as a result of a mishandled postponement of a General Assembly that had been scheduled to be held in Aberdeen in July 1605. As it became clear that the presbyterians again would use the General Assembly to resist James's all-but-certain successes via Parliament, James postponed the meeting without specifying—as was customary—a day of resumption. This menacing, indefinite suspension provoked some presbyterian stalwarts to meet anyway, in apparent defiance of the king. Dunfermline almost certainly knew of their plans, and even while he studiously affected to adhere to the king's insistence upon a postponement he did nothing to inform the king or to prevent the event.

As it turned out, the few ministers who met in defiance of the king did no more than adjourn themselves, though to a certain day. But that was enough to discredit Dunfermline, as Spottiswoode skillfully uncovered and manipulated the news about the Catholic chancellor, and enough as well to provoke the king to severity toward the ministers and their allies. With Dunfermline now compliant, the ministers were forced to recant or suffer continued imprisonment. Their explicit refusal to recant—technically, a declinature of the council's jurisdiction over a General Assembly—led to a treason trial for six of the declinature's signatories. The remainder were not tried, but clearly the independence of the kirk's assemblies—as a principle and as a practical tool—was finished. Dunbar was now firmly in charge, and in the spring of 1606 he made elaborate preparations for a proepiscopal parliament at Perth. To ensure its success, Dunbar both cajoled and bribed the nobles to support the "estate" of bishops.[31]

The first two acts of the Parliament at Perth marked the next stage of James's program. The first, "anent the king's majesty's prerogative" was rich with the language of the "imperial power" of the three kingdoms in its acknowledgment of the king's right over "all estates." It went even to the length of rescinding in advance any diminution of the prerogative "in any time . . . to come." The second, "anent the restitution of the estate of bishops," explicitly founded its authority on the principle of the first act, namely that the king was "sovereign monarch, absolute prince, judge and governor over all persons, estates and causes both spiritual and temporal." It repealed the Act of Annexation of 1587, which had impoverished the prelates to the point of the "indirect abolishing of the estate of bishops," in violation of the "ancient and fundamental policy" of the kingdom. "The maintenance of the three estates of Parliament," the act declared, was a necessary condition for the "honor, profit and perpetual stability and quietness of the said kingdom."[32] The importance that James attached to this legislation is indicated by the fact that its implementation required a substantial outlay from the crown to compensate lay interests that otherwise would have been harmed by the wholesale restitution of so much property to the dioceses. After its passage, all that was needed to complete the subjugation of the Scottish presbyteries was the restitution of direct diocesan authority over them and the synods. This control was carried out during the next few years through the establishment of perpetual, episcopally chosen or approved moderators of the presbyteries and a Scottish high commission.[33]

Meanwhile, shortly after the meeting of the Parliament at Perth, James carried out a plan to silence the remaining clerical opponents of his design. Eight of them, including both Melvilles, had been "invited" to attend upon the king at court. Fearful of the king's ultimate intentions, the band arrived at Hampton Court in September 1606 to be subjected to a program of indoctrination, humiliation, and affront that amounted to little less than terrorization.[34] The tone of the occasion was dramatized by an elaborately staged exhibition of the current worship of James I and VI, the man who as mere James VI had described the Anglican service as "an evil mass wanting nothing but the liftings." On 29 September 1606 the Scottish divines were escorted through a secret passage to the King's Chapel to observe, amid "strange music," James and Anne "offer at the altar, which was decorated with two books, two basins with two candlesticks." A German protestant visitor remarked that nothing was missing "de solemna missa" but the adoration of the Host.[35]

A more serious program was in store for the unwilling visitors. They were subjected to forced attendance at a barrage of sermons designed to show them the error of their ways—show them, that is, in the presence of the king and a select audience of Scottish episcopalians and other Scottish notables as well as a similar group of Englishmen. There were four such sermons, all promptly printed; to follow them and their deliverers is to capture the leitmotiv of court divinity in 1606 and the years thereafter. Throughout all of it, the king's and Bancroft's version of the estates were either principal notes or first harmonics.

William Barlow preached first. According to James Melville, Barlow was "all for the estate of bishops."[36] The printed text did not use the word "estate," but Barlow, in perhaps the first of all Gunpowder Plot sermons, earlier had defined the objects of the plot as the "Lucerna Israel, so is the king called 2. Sam. 21 [17]" and three "inferior lights," the "lights politic," the "lights ecclesiastical" ("priests"), and the "lights civil" of "magistrates inferior."[37] The second sermon had John Buckeridge preaching on Romans 13, a text that drew from William Laud's future tutor the statement that "tribute" was "*penditis,* or *praestatis,* not *datis*: you pay tribute and custom, and subsidies of duty and justice: you give them not of courtesy."[38] Buckeridge, unlike Cowell in 1610, was never challenged on this remarkable view of taxation. Launcelot Andrewes, the likely betrayer of the College of Antiquaries, spoke in passing of how an assembly of the body politic was a drawing together of "all the estates" at the call of Moses.[39] This point was a little ambiguous, but Andrewes was already on his way to becoming almost a parrot of the traditional view of the estates, in this respect as in so much else the king's preacher. Finally, John King preached on the royal supremacy.[40] Estates were no part of his theme, but he too was shortly to use the figure in a Gunpowder Plot sermon.[41] Other divines were soon to echo the king's and Bancroft's definitions. Oliver Ormerod, for example, wondered whether equality in the ministry would not lead to equality in "the other estates" (a question he asked with *Basilikon doron* open before him), and John Dove, in his *Defence of church government,* attempted to show that the "state of bishops" was necessary to a monarchy.[42]

Not surprisingly, the divines who preached at this second Hampton Court conference did quite well for themselves. As Peter Heylyn later put it, with pardonable exaggeration, they "gained exceedingly on the king, and great preferments for themselves." Heylyn attributed Andrewes's and Barlow's translations to Ely and Lincoln, John King's move to Bancroft's former see at London, and Buckeridge's gaining of Rochester all to the conference. No doubt there was much more behind it—the four were closely tied to the king and to Bancroft already—but John King actually felt the need to defend himself and his fellows against the charge of flattery.[43]

As for the Scots, though they were repressed they were far from persuaded. On 29 September Andrew Melville asked Richard Montague, then dean of the King's Chapel, to intercede with the king on the Scots' behalf. Montague refused, "for you are against the estate of our kirk, that is, of bishops." Melville wanted to discuss the imperfections of bishops but Montague turned to the royal supremacy. Melville said that supremacy belonged to the "presbytery." That, said Montague, "is treason in England." "But not by our laws of Scotland," replied Melville. "But you must have it so in Scotland," was Montague's retort as he "abruptly went his way."[44]

On 30 November, the preaching long over and the ministers still detained, Andrew Melville was called to account for some verses he had made upon seeing the king at worship. "When the bishop of Canterbury, sitting highest at the council-table upon the right hand, spake unto him, [Melville] took occasion to tell him plainly in his face, before the council, all that he thought." It was a long catalog; at the end he grabbed Bancroft by his sleeves and shook him, telling him that "if he was the author of the book entitled English Scottizing [the running title of *Daungerous positions*], he esteemed him the capital enemy of all the reformed kirks in Europe."[45]

✳

Melville's defiance was not emulated by the English: in England, any version of the estates of the realm but Bancroft's and James's had become a dangerous position. Court divines went on the offensive to exalt the estate of bishops and to harden the lines separating all three estates. Earlier in 1606 Bancroft had sponsored Bishop Overall's Convocation Book, an attempt to impose, as the doctrine of the church, the view that magistracy and priesthood alike existed ab initio: Adam was not only father-king but priest, and that twin authority had never lapsed in all subsequent history.[46] Buckeridge, Andrewes, and Barlow had repeated that theme in their sermons at Hampton Court. George Downame's two sermons of 1608, on the bishops and the ministry, also echoed the Convocation Book. Ministry and magistracy were "the two principal gifts of God," but as Justinian gave precedence to ministers, so do "our laws give [preeminence] to those of the spiritualty, before them of the temporalty." Downame added that scholars and students should never refuse the ministry on the ground that they were too well-born or too rich or "of their gifts, too good to be ministers."[47] George Meriton, in a sermon on nobility preached before the king early in 1607, likewise found that the patriarchs were "priests and kings in their families." Meriton's goal in this supposed panegyric to nobility was to sharpen the distinction between nobility and commons, something made difficult by the doubts about nobility fostered by "Stoics the old brokers of parity, and their successors the English Switzers." At the same time, on the ground that the "best nobles" made the "best account of the gospel of Christ," Meriton urged young impoverished noblemen to enter the priesthood as more consonant with "noble estate" than being "mayor of a town or city, or a justice of peace in the country." "I might go higher," he added, apparently hinting that noble attendance in the House of Commons was demeaning.[48]

What little remained lacking in support of the traditional estates was supplied by Bishop Andrewes, who managed the impossible feat of finding the three estates in the Bible. Preaching on a refrain in Judges— "In those days, there was no king in Israel, but every man did that which was good in his own eyes" —Andrewes found the three "estates" of captains, judges, and priests in Israel. But the scheme was "defective" until Israel acquired a king, "one over all, . . . a common father to all, that may poise and keep them all *in equilibrio,* that so all the estates may be evenly balanced."[49]

✳

From 1606 to 1640, the ideas of the three estates as king, Lords, and Commons and of mixed government by these estates virtually disappeared from English political thought. The few exceptions are almost proof of the rule. In 1610 William Hakewill, adverting to Lambarde's *Archeion,* may have described the Parliament as composed of the three estates of king, Lords, and Commons; the passage is obscure, perhaps deliberately so.[50] A youthful John Selden referred to the three "orders" of king, Lords, and Commons, but he included the bishops amongst the Lords and later changed his mind.[51] In 1613, a former or at least acquiescent presbyterian common lawyer, Sir Henry Finch, published a thoughtful legal compilation, *Nomotechnia.* Radical versions of this law French treatise had circulated in manuscript since 1604. In 1613 Finch, a religious zealot who had drifted from overt presbyterianism into millenarian Zionism, hoped to restore a shattered legal career by the publication of a "safe" version of the earlier work.[52] In it, however, he included a description of the Parliament that suggested that he was not entirely reconciled to the new order: "L'assemblie de ceux troys Estates, cestassavoir, Roy, Nobilities, & Commons, qui font le corps del Realme, est appel un Parliament, & lour decree un Act de Parliament."[53] In 1627, when an English version of *Nomotechnia,* itself a further revision, was published, the aberrant passage had disappeared.[54]

The early seventeenth century also saw one royalist usage of the three estates and mixed government in a carry-over of Arthur Hall and an anticipation of much of the *Answer.* Lord Chancellor Ellesmere analyzed the difficulties (as he saw them) of the Parliament of 1604–1610 in terms of a breakdown in the relations between the "three states" of the king, the "nobles, prelates, and lords," and the Commons. Each had its characteristic excess; following classical usage (albeit not too closely), he defined these to be tyranny, aristocracy, and democracy. Each estate also had its rightful role or interest. The king was to have his "regality, and supreme prerogative and sovereignty," the nobles and bishops "their honor and dignity," the Commons "their ancient liberties and privileges." But in "late years" the first two estates had "declined and decayed" while the "popular state" grew "big and audacious." With every session of the Parliament it "swelled more and more." Ellesmere's reflections indicate that the language of mixed government always could have made the royalist case provided that one turned away from James's preoccupation with the bishops. But it is also significant that the Lord Chancellor, another veteran of the Marprelate investigation, kept his reflections in manuscript.[55]

By the later 1620s, the English memory of the earlier confrontations had decayed. New Arminianism made the older Jacobean and Bancroftian intransigence over episcopacy seem more muted than it was; presbyterianism itself was a minor element of the English scene.[56] James's later mellowing, his anglicization, his laziness, the succession of the "soft" George Abbot after the "hard" Bancroft[57]—all these blurred the outlines of earlier clashes and make the occasional stray usage of the revised estates hard to evaluate. Henry Burton, a future independent radical in a momentarily proepiscopal phase, hoped, in 1628, for a "solemn covenant sealed by particular sacred oath of each member of the three estates in Parliament, the king, the nobles, and the House of Commons."[58] Perhaps his remark was less than innocent, a reminder that the alternative vocabulary had not entirely died out in politically minded clerical circles. Some significance might be attached to the talk of convenant and the fact that the over-wily Burton's remarks came forth in the hinge year of 1628–1629.

Equally, Burton may have meant nothing much at all. As the Puritan mood of the later 1620s approximated that of prepresbyterian Elizabethan puritanism, so might his remarks have been as innocent. A testimony to this possibility comes from Peter Heylyn's *Augustus* (1632), an "Essay of those means . . . whereby the common-wealth of Rome was altered and reduced unto a monarchy." Classical republican theory, including mixed government, was put to use to show how Octavian gathered and assured his own power by mixing it with that of the other two "estates." Strongly royalist, *Augustus* revealed a mixed government that was more sham than real; it is remarkable, then, that Heylyn comfortably used the once-alarming term "estate," even if his ostensible topic was not England but Rome.[59] It is more remarkable when Heylyn's future role is remembered. Burton's later opponent, Laud's future chaplain became the Dumézil of his age, arguing bitterly and learnedly that the three traditional estates were the universal, ancient, and reasonable order of mankind, from the days of the Egyptians, Persians, Greeks, Romans, and Gauls to his own time.[60]

Whatever their interest, these exceptions are slight against the massive silence and against the authoritative pronouncements about the estates that emerged not merely from high churchmen and royalist ultras. In the main, opposition figures after 1606 reverted to the binary language of the *dominium politicum et regale* to make their political case; quite as royalists could use classical terminology tellingly in support of their position, opposition lawyers and writers could do all they wished with Fortescue's famous dictum, which was perhaps at its greatest ascendancy in the early seventeenth century. The pattern corresponds almost exactly with the decline of overt or aggressive presbyterianism as a force in the English church from the early seventeenth century to 1640.

In the interim, men were guided by the judgment of Sir Edward Coke, for whom the three estates were the lords spiritual, the lords temporal, and the Commons—despite Coke's almost superstitious belief in the *Modus*.[61] On the matter of estates, John Cowell, the learned John Minsheu, and Sir Walter Raleigh, for all their differences, were in agreement with Coke.[62] As has been seen, later editions of Finch's legal tract decided upon silence. Camden, an expert at mincing words, wrote of three or four estates (in a way that recalls John Hooker) but made sure the clergy was among them.[63] Sir Henry Spelman's sense of historical variation was too great to allow him to come to simplistic glosses of the estates. Spelman only understood the traditional reckoning; he considered the "prelates . . . in all ages the prime part of these great councils."[64]

In the 1640s, when Englishmen again were made familiar with mixed government by the three estates of king, Lords, and Commons, some of the wisest and most learned among them thought the idea was a novelty of their own time. They were wrong, of course. Their error, however, is abundant testimony of how dangerous the idea had become. But the idea did return; and there should be no surprise that it did so by way of Scotland.

6
The Revival, 1638–1641

Sir Thomas Hope, the King's Advocate but a man who in the royalist view was "no ways to be trusted," had a sleepless night while the Scottish Parliament was meeting in Edinburgh in autumn 1639. Up at three in the morning on 22 September, he fell to prayer for divine guidance about the Parliament's "cross proceedings." He was still at it "betwixt four and five," until he saw "God would do all in his way." Hope's insomnia was not over something new in Scottish history; once again, it was "the great difficulties" in Parliament "anent the three estate [*sic*]."[1]

It might seem that nothing much had changed in Scotland since the days of James VI, but that was not true, either in general or in particular. The great din over the "estate" of bishops had died down in James's reign. Despite the false step of the liturgical demands of the Articles of Perth, which James had pursued not quite to the breaking point, James's religious policies in Scotland had shown surprisingly good sense and considerable tact. Bishops had come back, both in Parliament and in the governance of the kirk in its own proper forums, but they had not supplanted the presbyteries, which continued to function. This accidental combination of episcopacy and presbytery worked "rather well" in Scotland. A similar system obtained in Ireland, which itself served as a kind of safety valve for such antiepiscopal discontent as persisted in Jacobean and early Caroline Scotland.[2]

Of course, there did remain an irreducible hard core of opposition to anything episcopal or English in kirk matters; for all the success of James and his Scottish bishops, presbyterianism was something more in Scotland than the "negligible" element it has been described as being in early seventeenth-century England. Old Sir Thomas Hope, fretful about the estates in 1639, had in 1605 defended the presbyterians James had put on trial for treason, and he was only one of many who could rapidly revert to or acquire the presbyterian habit. In this hypersensitive situation, perhaps the most notable difference with the earlier struggle over episcopacy was that, initially at least, the main body of the ministers (who had done well financially under James's and might have done better still under Charles's and Laud's schemes to restore the kirk its ancient patrimony) were more reluctant than many of the Covenanting laity to adopt the presbyterian program. Indeed, ministers justly may have feared the new-modeled presbyterianism of the later 1630s, for it was a presbyterianism that took far too seriously for most of them some fairly dead-letter Melvillian principles about nonclerical elders in kirk assemblies. There was a menacing laicism about the early Covenanting movement.[3]

Thus, though the troubles of Charles in Scotland in the 1630s did not start out ostensibly as an attack upon episcopacy—opposition initially was focused instead upon Laud's impositions in liturgy and upon Charles's land policy in Scotland—they were prone to shift in that direction at the slightest hardening of the lines. The hardening set in rapidly. On the one side, though even the most committed opponents of episcopacy took care at first to stress reform rather than abolition so as to avoid offending moderate opinion at home and in England, the hatred of episcopacy among many of the leading Covenanters grew increasingly hard to hide. On the other side, episcopal resistance to the Covenanters became more aggressive, and Scottish bishops, despite having their own reservations about Laud's and Charles's Scottish program, took to their friends more than they sought to appease their enemies. By the end of the Glasgow Assembly of 1638, the masks had come off. The prime issue had become the abolition and defense of episcopacy, both as a means of government in the kirk and as an estate of Parliament. Sir Thomas Hope's bad night had come after nearly a year of argument and one Bishops' War; the issues raised were to persist without clear resolution until June 1640, on the eve of the second. Along the way, particularly in the spring of 1640, they were to enter into English affairs in a stunning fashion and begin the process that led to the revival in English political thought of mixed government by the estates of the realm.

*

Renewed concern about the estates of the realm in Scotland emerged more by accident than by design. Two separate lines of dispute converged during and shortly after the Glasgow Assembly of November and December 1638 to produce an unintended but increasingly self-conscious recapitulation of all the old arguments about the estates. One dispute arose from the ambiguity of the National Covenant, which had been sworn in February 1638 and thereafter as a bond between individual Covenanters and God and among the Covenanters themselves as a mutual defense pact against popery. The vagueness of the Covenant was one of its major assets, serving to link together moderates and radicals; put otherwise, textual ambiguity allowed men of differing but quite clear views to believe what they wished about it.

Part of the Covenant's ambiguity lay in its inclusion of a Confession of 1581, signed by James VI himself, to uphold the kirk of Scotland against all popery and superstition. On the face of it, nothing could be less antimonarchical or even untoward than resubscription of a confession signed (and never abjured) by James VI. But the confession had been adopted at a moment when the Melvillians were at the height of their fortunes. Archibald Johnston of Wariston, the éminence grise of the radical Covenanters, clearly thought the Confession of 1581 could be construed—at the right moment—as an abjuration of episcopacy, on the ground that the context of 1581 would permit no other interpretation. But there was a catch, one that perhaps Wariston for all his guile and preparation did not at first perceive: the Confession of 1581 itself referred to the "three estates" in addition to the kirk and the king as being parties to the confession. It was therefore possible to argue that the Covenant was a bond to preserve episcopacy.[4]

The King's Commissioner for Scotland, the marquis of Hamilton, had seen that possibility and made the 1581 confession a part of a countercovenant—known as the King's Covenant—for which he sought signers where royal and episcopal influence was strong. Then, predictably, the tables again were turned: Hope caught Hamilton off guard at a council meeting where the equally ambiguous King's Covenant was to be signed, and he extracted from the commissioner the admission that the Confession of 1581 referred to the faith as it had then stood—an admission tantamount to an unintended endorsement of presbyterianism.[5] However close to comedy they may be, these shifts over the meaning of the two covenants of 1638 set off impassioned debate about the meaning of the phrase, the "estates of the realm"—a debate, centering as it did upon an ambiguous historical document, that necessarily entailed much polemical historical research.

The second dispute that rekindled concern with the estates arose in the

Glasgow Assembly. The assembly was convened as part of a royal tactic of apparent moderation, like the King's Covenant and a series of other concessions. Behind the scenes, however, Hamilton and Charles, like the Covenanters, were preparing themselves for the alternative inherent in the situation, a resort to force.[6] Radical Covenanters thus acquired a tactical as well as a policy motive for pushing the Glasgow Assembly as far as possible toward a complete abjuration of episcopacy.

The Glasgow Assembly differed from earlier seventeenth-century assemblies in a pair of critical respects. On the one hand, the lay component was so beefed up—lay representation in the earlier assemblies having been extremely irregular—as to make the assembly all but a parliament in disguise. On the other hand, through simple intimidation the bishops were kept from attending. Charles and Hamilton more or less permitted the Covenanters to do these things without protest to give themselves grounds for repudiating the assembly if it proceeded beyond Charles's notion of acceptable reform. The bishops, for their part, prepared a protest of their de facto exclusion, and this protest brought their claim to be an estate into the picture.

It was only after the assembly continued to sit and work, in defiance of Hamilton's proclamation of dissolution on 28 November (a mere week after it began), that the other main impetus to a revival of concern over the estates of the realm revealed itself. Hamilton ordered the dissolution of the assembly when he saw that organizational control had passed to the radicals, notably Johnston of Wariston, and thus that it could not be used to endorse the liturgical reform and the moderate reform of church government that Charles and Hamilton and the Scottish bishops, with varying degrees of enthusiasm and sincerity, were now offering to Scotland. Necessarily, the assembly's refusal to respect the dissolution raised anew the matter of the king's supremacy in ecclesiastical matters, and as before that involved the question of the status of bishops.

This time, however, more was involved: after the dissolution, the assembly proceeded to the real work before it, namely the abjuration of episcopacy. If that action were not to be a mere gesture (like the resolutions of the English House of Commons before its dissolution in 1629), it had to be backed up with a claim that the assembly (which was now in membership and structure like a bishopless parliament) was the supreme authority in the sphere of religion. According to this logic, all the Parliament of Scotland (the three estates and the king) could do was ratify the actions of the General Assembly. If the Parliament failed to do so, the reasoning went, it was a stain upon the consciences of those who did not heed the kirk, but it was of no other effect. Melville's two kingdoms had returned, and with them came all the old issues.

As luck would have it, the structural parallels of the two situations—in the disputes over the covenants and in the General Assembly—were reinforced by Johnston's brilliant, dramatic production at Glasgow of long-lost registers of the General Assembly from the late sixteenth and early seventeenth centuries. To presbyterians, the early registers revealed the whole heroic resistance to James's attempts to run the kirk through Parliament. They cast the surviving registers in an entirely new light, for the compromises of the seventeenth century now could be viewed by all as shameful backsliding. Like the two covenants, the Glasgow Assembly's work and its use of the missing registers forced a resort to the past, largely in the past's own vocabulary.[7]

The excluded bishops managed to have a "declinator and protestation" read in the Glasgow Assembly on 27 November, the day before Hamilton attempted to dissolve it. As part of their case against their exclusion, the bishops pointed to the act of 1597 declaring prelacy to be one of the three estates of the kingdom and to the act of 1584 declaring it treason to impugn the dignity or authority of any or all of the three estates. Against the claim of the spiritual sovereignty of the General Assembly ("the royal prerogative of King Jesus the Son of God above all prerogatives," as Johnston put it), the bishops asserted that the assembly was null and void and could do nothing against "the three estates of the kingdom, or any one of them."[8]

The bishops' attack was strongly reinforced by Hamilton himself in his *Explanation of the meaning of the oath and covenant* (late December 1638 or early 1639), which probably drew upon the mind and pen of his personal chaplain Walter Balcanquhall, a Scot in the English church who served as Johnston's opposite number on the episcopal side. The *Explanation* set out to resolve the ambiguities of the 1581 confession by a careful rehearsal of acts of Parliament that helped to establish what the three estates were and what they continued to be. Because Hamilton had the better side of history with him, his exposition was as powerful as it was straightforward. In the 1580s, as "is well known . . . bishops, abbots and priors made up a third estate of this realm." To urge that episcopacy had been abolished by acts of the General Assembly at that time (which was the case) was to prove nothing pertinent to a "well constituted" state, for none of the acts of Parliament establishing episcopacy was ever directly repealed (which was also true). It was a "damnable Jesuitical position" to hold that what a "monarch and his three estates" had enacted in Parliament could be repealed by an ecclesiastical synod. A long documentary appendix drove the point home by citing many acts of Parliament and quoting at considerable length the relevant acts of 1584, 1597, and 1606.[9]

The Covenanters were slow to respond to the episcopal and royal argument about the estates. Indeed, in their protestation against the proclamation of dissolution, issued on 29 November, they actually referred to the three estates (as earlier declarations of the Covenanters had done) as if the phrase posed no difficulties for them.[10] Perhaps they were caught by surprise; though, inasmuch as Johnston himself had been working through the acts of Parliament for useful material, it is hard to believe that he, Hope, and other theorists were unaware of the acts the bishops and Hamilton cited. In any event, the first glimmer of a response came in a General Assembly protestation dated 18 December 1638—and not issued until after it was "revised" (reviewed and probably rewritten) by Johnston as clerk on 8 January 1639—and that response was little more than a dodge. Because of "infallible reasons," the assembly asserted, its abrogation of episcopacy was not "destructive of any lawful third estate."[11]

Substantial replies appeared only after a further month's interval. These were in the form of Johnston's "revised" answer to the bishops' declinator on 12 February and the answer to Hamilton's *Explanation* on 14 February, the latter presumably in the name of the General Assembly by authority of its standing executive committee, the Tables. Both replies asserted that the General Assembly was independent of and superior to Parliament in spiritual matters, but both also went further and directly confronted the claim that the bishops constituted an estate in Parliament.

In these performances Johnston took a good many liberties with history as well as with logic. The expression "three estates," he averred, was a mere "*stylus curiae.*" It had been used, he maintained, when there were few or no true ecclesiastics present in Parliament. On the other hand, because bishops sat by virtue of their temporalities—Johnston must have borrowed this notion from the English—the Act of Annexation of 1587 effectively had nullified their claim to be an estate. James VI and an act of 1606 had referred to the 1587 act's "indirect" abolishing of bishops.[12]

If the 1587 act—and other much less plausible shifts of interpretation— seemed to undermine the bishops' claim to be an estate, Johnston had another estate to fling into the breach. The barons or shire commissioners, he argued, were the real third estate. It was true, of course, that there had been some moves in that direction in the late sixteenth century, which

James had dismissed in *Basilikon doron.* It was also true that the subordinate position of the lairds was increasingly anomalous in the seventeenth century. But Johnston's reading of the acts of Parliament was less an argument from the past than a program for the future: the facts would be created. Even Johnston's choice of verbs hinted at this position: "There *may be* three estates without the bastard estate of bishops, abbots, pryors erected in time of popish darkness."[13]

Even where Johnston was seemingly more positive than a "may be" about the estate of shire commissioners or barons, his chronology and logic gyrated wildly. The three estates of nobles, barons, and towns existed before popish darkness—he actually said at one point—and existed de facto even when bishops did assert a recognized claim. In his reckoning bishops did or did not exist, according to whether he wanted them to be relics of superstition or seventeenth-century innovations; and when bishops were present, it was by virtue of their temporalities, not their spiritual position.[14]

*

By February 1639, however, words by themselves were insufficient means of expression for both sides. The first of the two contests known as the Bishops' Wars was already at the level of mobilization and largely bloodless tests of strength. The creation of the facts Johnston desired had to await the calling of a parliament (along with a general assembly) in August 1639, as one of the terms of the cessation of hostilities incorporated in the Treaty of Berwick.

One of the goals pursued by the Covenanters at this parliament (which gave Sir Thomas Hope his sleepless night) was the punishment of Walter Balcanquhall. His *Large declaration* —ostensibly a declaration of the king—was a documentary review of the Covenanters' positions and the royal responses and, in effect, a justification of Charles's attempt to reduce the Covenanters to obedience. Its untitled conclusion set out the king's war aims: the first (of seven) was the supremacy of acts of Parliament, the second was the preservation of each of the "three estates of Parliament."[15] When the king's new commissioner, the earl of Traquair, tried to head off the attack on Balcanquhall by pointing out that Charles would not "disclaim" the declaration put out in his "sacred" name, two Covenanting earls, Argyle and Rothes replied that the attack could not "in reason offend his gracious majesty" because the book was untrue, "dishonorable" to the king and "whole nation," and only written "to incense neighbor nations and specially England."[16]

But the heart of the program of the Parliament at Edinburgh was to create the new order Johnston had outlined in February. This was to be done with a trio of acts. The first was to be an act of recision of all parliamentary legislation in favor of bishops. The second, "anent the constitution of parliaments in all time coming," was to be a declaration of the new trinity of estates—nobles, barons, and burgh commissioners. The third act was to have revised the scheme by which the Lords of the Articles (the managing committee of the Parliament) were chosen. James had been able to rig the selection process so that the Lords of the Articles were almost automatically compliant to the king's wishes; that scheme, along with the bishops who had played the key role in producing a tame Committee of the Articles, had to go.[17]

It was not yet to be. On 14 November 1639, amid a rapidly deteriorating situation, Traquair prorogued the Parliament until 2 June 1640. The Covenanters' shrewd response was at once to obey and disobey. Johnston—though not a member of Parliament—brought in a declaration claiming that the three estates (a phrase that now comprehended the shire commissioners or barons but not the bishops) had a historic right to refuse to consent to any prorogation (a travesty of the facts). Nevertheless, the declaration went on, the Parliament would cease to meet. The catch, however, was that, although the Parliament would not meet, it would in some sense continue to exist. A Committee of the Estates (the Tables in another guise) was established for the interim.[18]

The prorogation, like the dissolution of the Glasgow Assembly, was the prelude to war. Once again the Covenanters' attack upon the estate of bishops figured prominently in Charles's official statement of the war's rationale:

[the Covenanters] strive totally to alter the frame of the Parliament, and to confound and take away the third estate, wherein the civil power of kings is so much concerned, as our father, and all his predecessors in former Parliaments . . . have been most careful to preserve.

The familiar legislation again was rehearsed. The act of 1584 declaring it treason to impugn the authority of any or all of the estates was especially prominent. "We would willingly know, how they . . . can deny, but that they have sought the breach of this act, and so are guilty of treason." So too the act recissory sought "to take away the third estate, which is treason."[19]

Charles's brave words concealed two signal truths. One was subtle. Even in royalist polemic the bishops had suffered a tacit demotion: the first estate had become the third. The other was obvious. Charles was in no position to enforce his view of the matter. The failure of the Short Parliament in April 1640 meant that he had no prospect of resisting the Scottish juggernaut. A feeble gesture of a further prorogation of the parliament scheduled for 2 June was ignored.

In rapid order the Parliament made good on its program of the previous September and much else. The "true estates" of nobles, barons, and burgesses were established by the act "anent the constitution of Parliament." In that act the critical proepiscopal legislation of 1597 and 1606 was repealed, a tacit admission that Johnston's historical interpretations would not alone create the new order. The act recissory and the act "anent the choosing of committees out of each estate" (about the Lords of the Articles) soon followed; Balcanquhall was to be "severely punished" by the terms of an act "anent the Large Declaration." The proceedings of the General Assembly were, according to plan, routinely ratified. Lifting a page from the English book, an act was passed "appointing parliaments to be held once every three year."[20] The formal structure of the Scottish revolution was complete. It was now an open question whether Charles or the Covenanters had the more dangerous position.

✳

The answer could come only from England. Politically and religiously conscious Englishmen, of course, were watching Scotland, some with sympathy and others with alarm. At some point English notables at odds with Thorough and personal rule made contact with leading Covenanters. Whether or not the story is accepted that William Fiennes, Viscount Saye and Sele, urged the Covenanters, in the last part of 1639, to make war again with England, Saye's talented younger son, Nathaniel Fiennes, was in Edinburgh late in the year.[21] Johnston was in close touch with an Anglo-Irish gentleman of radical religious views, Sir John Clotworthy. Clotworthy even left Johnston one of his "casements," a hopelessly clumsy device for supposedly secret communication; earlier he had given another to John Winthrop, Jr.[22] Laud, of course, had his own channels and own interest in the outcome in Scotland of policies he intended for three kingdoms.

In the half-year or so before the Parliament of June 1640, the Scottish business over the estates reentered England, leading to a revival of the old, distinctively English pattern of associating the revision of the estates with the matter of mixed government. As Englishmen prepared themselves for the two parliaments of 1640, they reviewed the literature pertaining to that institution, which was of necessity unfamiliar to many Englishmen who had come to maturity in the 1630s. That alone would have led to some acquaintance with the later Elizabethan and early Jacobean terms of discourse; but as had been the case before, the catalyst was Scotland.

The linkage of Scottish and English affairs lay behind the suppression of Edward Bagshaw's Lenten reading in the Middle Temple in March 1640. Bagshaw was a puritan lawyer of moderate though determined opinions; at the time of his reading he was leaning hard toward the radicals. There was good reason for his stance: Bagshaw was the recorder of Banbury, a puritan stronghold virtually controlled by the Fiennes family.[23] Lord Saye was Banbury's high steward; Nathaniel Fiennes was to sit for Banbury (a one-seat borough) in both the Short and the Long Parliament. It was doubtless because of these connections, which Bagshaw then honored, that he was chosen later to sit for Southwark—a byword for religious radicalism—in the Long Parliament. Both of Southwark's seats went to puritan "outsiders."[24]

Bagshaw later became a strong partisan of accommodation with the king and then an outright royalist. In *A just vindication* (1660), his account of the suppression, Bagshaw used a lawyer's guile subtly to refashion his position: he was a moderate pure and simple, without the radical connections or radical leanings that were in fact his in early 1640. For example, he made himself out to be a friend of the earl of Manchester, not Saye, and to be rather more favorable to the bishops than he actually was in early 1640.[25] As a result his *A just vindication,* upon which historians have relied heavily, is at least suspect. It is also inaccurate, even in the matter of dates, which are inconsistent beyond reconstruction.

Bagshaw began his reading in the last week of February 1640. He chose the Statute of Provisors (1351) for his text, an act that he could only disingenuously describe as *pro clero.* In an exceptionally freewheeling reading that raced from fifteen-hundred-year surveys of church history to unmistakable comments upon most major ecclesiastical issues of the day, Bagshaw vigorously attacked the High Commission, the whole apparatus of and rationale for ecclesiastical punishments for heresy, and, of special interest here, the civil employments of the clergy and the bishops' role in

Parliament.[26] His denial of the right of clergy to civil employments (in particular, to commissions of the peace) was phrased without qualification, as if the bishops were included. It was so reported in a contemporary account.[27] In 1660 Bagshaw denied that he intended such an inclusion, claiming that it was unnecessary to make it because bishops were of a different "sphere" than other clerks. But his own reading, in fact, effectively denied that very distinction.[28] Another point was the conventional and sound one that statutes could pass without the assent of the bishops, on the ground that they sat by virtue of the baronies. But Bagshaw raised the ante. He cast doubt upon the legitimacy of their sitting in judgment in cases of blood—that is, when it suited his case, he raised the matter of their spiritual position.[29] This was to become standard doctrine in the first year of the Long Parliament, but in March 1640 it had all the menace of an irrational heads-I-win-tails-you-lose logic. Even the strongest proof of Bagshaw's strict moderation is suspect. In his reading he advanced a scheme for episcopo-presbytery (in the form of a description of the primitive church)—one more example of license he allowed himself—and so showed himself no root-and-brancher.[30] But he was about a year too early in advancing what later became a moderate commonplace and then a species of royalism: early in 1640, episcopo-presbytery was far more a way of insinuating presbyterianism into English church government than a way of preserving episcopacy.

Bagshaw was not quite the innocent he made himself out to be. But he had uttered nothing worth the considerable political embarrassment to the government of silencing him, if his opinions are regarded purely from an English perspective. The problem was that there was no longer any such thing as a purely English perspective. In the process of being forced to abandon the reading, Bagshaw was subjected to two interviews, one with the Lord Keeper, John Finch, and the other with Laud. Both told him that his remarks were unseasonable. Either Laud made specific reference to Scotland or so Bagshaw understood him, for the lawyer's response to the charge was that he had pitched upon his topic a year before he had "heard of any opposition made against the prelacy" and that what was "moved against them in another kingdom" was of no concern to English law. Whether Bagshaw was honest or merely plausible, neither Laud nor Charles (who set Finch upon Bagshaw) was in a mood or, indeed, in a position to see matters his way. Charles's fears came out in a question he instructed Finch to pose to Bagshaw: whether the bishops could join with king and Commons to make a valid act without the presence of the lay peers or without their assent if the lay peers were a minority.[31]

Laud and Charles were not acting hysterically. Bagshaw's reading came at an exquisitely sensitive moment in Anglo-Scottish relations. Commissioners from the Covenanters were at Whitehall explaining their side of things before the English council at the exact moment Bagshaw was lecturing the students of the Middle Temple on episcopal abuses. On 3 March the Scots explained that because the General Assembly had concluded that the "government of the kirk by bishops, and civil places and powers of kirk-men . . . were two main causes" of the kirk's "evils," it did "necessarily follow" that the bishops "who did in name of the kirk represent the third estate" had to be taken away. Abolition was to be accomplished, the commissioners went on, by the acts the Parliament had attempted to pass before its prorogation: "the act of constitution of the Parliament without them," and the act "for the repealing the former laws, whereby the kirk was declared the third estate, and the bishops did represent the kirk." Without these two acts (which we saw mooted in September 1639 and made law, by the Covenanters' lights, in June 1640), "it is impossible to have a valid Parliament."[32]

To the men about Laud and Charles, who had the approach of the Short Parliament on their minds, the question was only whether or when the Scottish logic would find its English analogue. Those who had followed Scottish affairs could not but remember the sequence of escalation there. Demands for reforms not directly concerned with the bishops gave way to demands for the reform of the bishops; these were followed by demands for a clerical disabilities bill (which, of course, destroyed the bishops' right to seats in Parliament) and to the abolition of episcopacy altogether. Whether the same pattern would occur in England was unknown to all, but it was hardly unreasonable to assume that it might and that moderate professions like Bagshaw's—that reform and not abolition of episcopacy was all that was intended—were less than sincere or more than credulous. Moreover, as the Scots continued to plead their case in Whitehall even to the end of March— and, soon enough, to make their case to the Houses of Parliament—the court had to wonder whether the Covenanters could, or would, make good on the threat of the earl of Rothes to the king himself to "rip up" episcopacy in England and Ireland if Laud attempted a three-kingdoms defense of episcopacy in Scotland.[33]

Laud was prepared to probe that situation in the Short Parliament. Remarkably, he chose as his ground what would seem to be a virtually uncontested point of English law, the integrity of the House of Lords, which Bagshaw had asserted in his reading against the bishops and upon which Finch apparently had tried to trick him when he asked him whether the bishops could alone act for the Lords. The lay response in the upper house was unambiguous and so was the rejoinder from the bishops.

(As the drama was being played out, a recent session of the Scots at the council table was doubtless upon the minds of those peers who sat both on the council and in the Lords. The Scots argued that according to what by anticipation they called the "former" constitution of Parliament no act could pass "without the consent of the three estates, of which the kirk was the third." And if the law was not changed, the Parliament could not perform the "absolutely necessary" ratification of the General Assembly's works, because the bishops would have any appropriate legislation "quarrelled and annulled" upon the grounds that the acts of "1584, 1587, 1597, and 1606" prohibited their abolition.)[34]

Laud's ploy was to try to establish a distinct and perhaps controlling role for the bishops in the House of Lords. He began on Thursday, 16 April, the first day of business after the organizational preliminaries and customary addresses by the king and the Lord Keeper. Laud attempted to get the upper house to adjourn the next day, Friday, and all subsequent Wednesdays and Fridays to allow the bishops to attend convocation without the loss of their votes in the House of Lords. This proposal was phrased in terms of ancient custom; it was indeed the case that the upper house in Henry VIII's days and occasionally thereafter had forgone sitting when the bishops were so occupied. The move met predictable opposition led by Lord Saye; one unnamed bishop tried to back off a bit by suggesting that the bishops desired the adjournments not "as of right, but of courtesy." For the time being a compromise was struck. Lord Keeper Finch, who was not well, suggested that the house adjourn on Friday because of his illness. This the house agreed to do, with Robert Greville, Lord Brooke, insisting that the reason for the adjournment be so entered in the journal.[35]

But Finch could not remain ill indefinitely. The question was referred to the grand committee on privileges, a huge committee that was all but the house by another name. The meeting of convocation on 17 April and the next sitting of the upper house on 18 April both gave attention to the question; by the following Monday (20 April) the grand committee took up the question in earnest in a session so well attended that it had to be moved into the Parliament chamber. In the midst of debate "there fell something" from Laud (or perhaps Joseph Hall, the bishop of Exeter, who was then a fiercely active episcopal publicist) that the bishops "were a third estate." There was a question "whether the bishops make a distinct state in the kingdom." The bishops affirmed it, but "the house" (presumably the grand committee) denied it; "the house say there is the king, the barons, the commons; the bishops then would make four states, or exclude the king."[36] The exchange was heated. Bishop Hall and Lord Saye squared off, Hall asserting that the majority's view "about the three estates . . . would much encourage the Scots." He singled out Saye; "the lord savoured of a Scottish Covenanter." Hall was forced to recant his words the following day.[37]

Thus it was in a parliamentary session that the revival of English argument about the estates of the realm began. It was the fruit of a Laudian initiative to establish a claim that the bishops constituted an estate in England as they did in Scotland. The position was more than tenable; it was conventional in the early seventeenth century, as has been seen. But it had become dangerous in England, precisely because Laud had pushed it into an area in which it did not apply—the structure of the House of Lords. If Laud had gotten his way, his general program for uniformity in church government would have been much enhanced. Moreover, he would have constructed a technique by which the Lords could be blocked from activity by the use of the need of bishops to attend convocation. He failed; on Wednesday, 22 April, half of the bishops attended convocation and half remained in the Lords.[38] The lay lords would not be quarrelled and annulled by their episcopal counterparts.

But Bishop Hall was only partly right. Lord Saye was not a Scottish Covenanter, nor indeed did he and his fellow peers use the Scottish language of the estates. They resorted to the specifically English idiom of including the king as one of the estates as a means of excluding the bishops from the enumeration. One phrase of the debate—"make four states, or exclude the king"—is almost surely a reference to a book with which political Englishmen were renewing their acquaintance, John Hooker's *Order and usage,* in which Hooker had excluded the bishops from the three estates of Parliament but then inconsistently had suggested that the bishops were a fourth estate by virtue of convocation, which came close to being a third house of Parliament.[39] That prospect was precisely what Laud was attempting to establish and what Pym was fighting tooth and nail. There would be no fourth estate.

As the argument about the estates of the realm was revived in the Short Parliament, the only Elizabethan element not explicit was the connection between the revised anatomy of the estates and the classical theory of mixed government. But that too is found within the fecund constitutional schemings of Lord Saye. In July 1640 Saye renewed or continued a long political correspondence with Massachusetts Bay leaders. In a letter of 1636 to Saye from John Cotton there is a rare glimpse of the survival (or renewal) of the old Elizabethan antiepiscopal constitutional sensibility. In replying to a charge of Saye's that the New England way in civil matters was too democratic, Cotton chose to remember what Thomas Hooker "often" quoted out of "Mr. Cartwright": "no man fashioneth his house to his hangings, but his hangings to his house." But inasmuch as the church was a "theocracy" exercised primarily by a few (the ministers), so too the state was essentially aristocratic, for there were only a limited number of magistrates.[40]

Cotton was Bodinian in his political vocabulary. But in 1640 Saye chose the idiom of mixed government to renew the dispute, now with John Winthrop. Replying to Winthrop's version of the hangings and the house, Saye urged the governor to "put away that error." Church and state were distinct; the church could exist with any outward form of government. As for civil government, Saye suggested that "the best form of government . . . hath in it the good of all three, . . . fitly limiting each other, and thereby preventing the evils of either, that being equally poised one by the other" the interest of all would be served. The guarantee of good behavior was an annual parliament "consisting of all estates . . . having in that union supremam potestatem."[41]

✳

The revelation was complete. It lacked only a prophet. That role was assumed by Henry Parker, the leading political pamphleteer of the parliamentary cause in 1640–1642. Parker was also Lord Saye's nephew, a fact that may have more than incidental importance.

Henry Parker was the fifth and last son of Sir Nicholas Parker of Ratton, Sussex, a substantial gentleman prominent in county and even national affairs. Sir Nicholas, like Lord Saye, married a daughter of the wealthy but overextended John Temple of Stowe. But the tie between the families was not especially close. Although the Temples and the Parkers played their parts in the politics of the later 1620s and 1630s, they were more "country" than "puritan" and proved to be at most lukewarm supporters of the parliamentary cause after the war began. And Henry Parker, as a fifth son, could in no sense be described as part of a connection by virtue of hereditary position alone. Parker would have to activate the connection. He would have to become useful.

Opportunity and necessity conspired to make Parker a useful man in the 1640s. His family provided him with a solid education but little more; he had to make his own way in the world. St. Edmund Hall, Oxford (not a notably puritan foundation) and Lincoln's Inn prepared him to face an uncertain future. Parker was admitted to the bar of Lincoln's Inn in 1637, but there is no evidence of his pleading at law.[42] Parker's friend George Thomason described him, at an early point in their friendship, as a "counselor," an ambiguous term for a private man but one that hints at a special role that Parker had created for himself. He was to be a counselor, a "privado" (to use an alien word that Parker used and that was used by Virgilio Malvezzi, upon whom Parker drew) of the opposition—or, indeed, of any who would employ his services.[43]

What is most notable about Parker's public career is its frequent, perhaps invariable, connection with his need for money. Within limits, Parker's pen was for sale. He wrote, presumably on commission, for the Vintners, the Stationers, the Merchant Adventurers, and an engineer, William Wheeler. At least one of his early political pamphlets is known to have been written on demand for the future regicide Sir John Danvers.[44] Repeated hints and the logic of Parker's situation make it appear probable that he wrote most or all of his properly political pamphlets under similar conditions—that is, for gain, most likely through commission or retainer. The meshing of the two sides of his life—the representative of private, commercial interests and the writer upon public affairs—gets to the heart of being a "counselor." Parker was a publicist and a lobbyist, his value to his private clients a function in part of his public work, his political writings (seldom conducted under his own name) reflecting his utility as a private representative.

These considerations apply to Parker's first two pamphlets, *The case of shipmony* and *A discourse concerning puritans*. *The case of shipmony*, which appeared about the time of the Long Parliament's opening, delivered both more and less than its title promised. Ostensibly a review of the judgments in the case, *The case of shipmony* actually ignored (as would most of Parker's oeuvre) fine points of law in favor of more general arguments that had little to do with the substance of English law and less to do with the matter of ship money. Parker based his indifference upon principle. Because the law was confusing or contradictory to the point that what one side took for granted was "by the other utterly denied," resort had to be made to "nature," to *salus populi* ("the supreme of all human laws"), and to necessity. By these lights, Parker found, prerogative power was limited in extent and in purpose—"ample enough for the perfection, and good of the people, and no ampler."[45]

Taking the rather high road of natural law—which anticipated much of the argument of Parker's *Observations upon some of his majesties late answers and expresses*—Parker came to a discussion of the English constitution as he found it in his day and as it differed from the other polities of Europe. It was Lord Saye's constitution:

> as the English have ever been the most devoted servants of equal, sweetly-moderate sovereignty; so in our English parliaments, where the nobility is not too prevalent, as in Denmark, nor the commonalty, as in the Netherlands, nor the king, as in France, justice and policy kiss and embrace more lovingly than elsewhere. And as all the three states have always more harmoniously borne their just proportionable parts in England than elsewhere, so now in these learned, knowing, religious times, we may expect more blessed counsel from parliaments, than ever we received heretofore.[46]

This little eulogy of English government immediately followed a discussion of the three "noted factions . . . adverse to parliaments, . . . the papists, the prelates, and court parasites" who hated parliaments "because they [knew] themselves hateful to parliaments." Prelates were thus just another of the private interests (which Parker constantly opposed to the public interest). Parker came up short of calling for the abolition of bishops but left little doubt that the prelates wanted nothing less than the destruction of parliaments.[47] For advanced rather than timid reasons, Parker hesitated before root-and-branch, but *The case of shipmony* (and *Discourse concerning puritans* soon to follow) sympathized with the radicals far more than with their opponents.

Parker's fulsome praise of English government—rightly understood, rightly constituted—was accompanied by a surprising, menacing undercurrent. Parker alluded to a more global and more determined republicanism than could have been derived from his English sources:

> All other countries almost in Christendom, differ from us in this module of policy: some, but very few, allow a greater sphere of sovereignty to their princes; but for the most part nowadays the world is given to republists, or to conditionate and restrained forms of government.

Parker also raised the specter of universal revolution: "the often and great defections and insurrections, which have happened of late, almost all over Europe, may suffice to warn all wise princes, not to overstrain the prerogatives too high." If English parliaments fought "insolent princes," they were in accord with the "custom of all Europe almost."[48]

The combination of a homegrown issue (ship money) and a largely homegrown vocabulary (part common law, part legal maxims, part English historical commonplaces) with a strangely cosmopolitan and republican perspective reinforced Parker's vision of the three harmonious estates of king, Lords, and Commons in Parliament. The familiar triad of villains—papists, prelates, projectors—was opposed to Parliament (another English commonplace), but the vocabulary of the antithesis was itself republican. The opposition was between private and public, corruption and virtue, the conspiratorial Few (and the One) and the honorable Many (and the One). A prince "not seduceable" was "a thing most rare"; there was "a fatal kind of necessity only incident to immoderate power, that it must be immoderately used." The conjunction of power and the flattery of "privados" was at the root of all history: "what a bewitching thing flattery is, when it touches upon this string of unlimitable power: if this ambition and desire of vast power were not the most natural, and forcible of all sins, angels in heaven, and man in paradise had not fallen by it."[49]

The case of shipmony concealed the springs of this remarkable conceptual revolution. Parker was a borrower, but *The case of shipmony* was loath to acknowledge any assistance. The only weak clue was the use at two points of the story of Coriolanus, itself a narrative of the breakdown of the One, the Few, and the Many. In one instance, Parker compared the failure of the English to resist the Scots to the failure of the Roman plebeians to join with Caius Martius in his assault upon Corioli. In the other, Parker invoked Menenius's fable of the belly in a way that suggested that Parker was less concerned to justify the ways of the great (the Senate, as Menenius had it) than to put the king someplace less glorious than at the head of the body politic.[50]

Parker's nearly simultaneous *Discourse concerning puritans* reveals a good deal more about the shaping of his thought in late 1640 and early 1641, even as it also hinted unmistakably at a connection with Lord Saye. Parker began his *Discourse* with an observation by Virgilio Malvezzi that calumnies destroy states even as accusations preserve them.[51] Malvezzi's *Romulus and Tarquin,* from which the passage had been cribbed at greater length than Parker acknowledged, appeared in England in 1637 in the translation of Henry Carey, Lord Leppington (by courtesy) at the time and the earl of Monmouth in 1641. There was a further twist to the borrowing: Malvezzi, a Bolognese marquis who began his public career as an aristocratic constitutionalist (at the tender age of nineteen), was in England in 1640 as one of three ambassadors of Philip IV.[52]

The point about calumnies could have come as well from Machiavelli. Parker indeed did once quote Machiavelli in a favorable context. The passage, about how Saint Francis and Saint Dominic rescued the church from the ill repute of its decline, occurs in a chapter of Machiavelli's *Discourses* devoted to the *ridurre ai principe*. It is hard to avoid connecting the passage to a remark in *The case of shipmony*: "if parliaments of late be grown into dislike, it is not because their virtue is decayed, it is because the corruption of the times cannot endure such sharp remedies."[53] Parker also went to another Italian political writer, Paolo Sarpi, virtually copying extensive passages, sometimes with indirect acknowledgment, sometimes not.[54] All these sources, it turns out, were available to Parker in recent English translations, the publishers either being in the area of the law courts, or about St. Paul's Churchyard, where Parker's own publisher, Robert Bostock, and Parker's friend George Thomason could be found. It is almost as if Parker felt the need to give himself a cram course in republican theory to sustain his analysis of the English constitution.

But the sympathies with classical republicanism were limited. The themes of corruption and virtue and private and public were valuable. But "real" republicanism—classical republicanism, European republicanism—posed too many problems to be more than an experiment in Parker's thought. If Malvezzi's aristocratic notions could serve Parker, their ethos—the *concordia discors* of the baroque—was alien to Parker, who like almost all English thinkers reduced harmony to unity. And Machiavelli's politics could have but a marginal role. Machiavelli was at once too monarchical and too popular for Parker's tastes and purposes. The class politics of Mediterranean republicanism were not so much incomprehensible as unthinkable, and tactically they played right into the king's hand. Parker's own radicalism (and it was quite real) came from different sources, from some homely deductions from natural law (of which a little can be made to go a long way) and from an almost mystical sense of the identity of people and Parliament. In the end, Parker's passage on the mixture of the estates was English in its resonances.

But what had these pamphlets to do with Lord Saye? In general terms it can be said that no other political figure could have benefited more from both of them. The proposition can be made very pointedly with respect to *A discourse concerning puritans,* but it is no less true of *The case of shipmony.* The ship money trial is now remembered as Hampden's Case, but from the beginning Saye was the prime mover in the effort to test the levy's legality. Initially the viscount was to have been the object of a test case; only later did Sir Peter Temple (Saye's nephew and Henry Parker's first cousin) arrange the shift to John Hampden. Although it did not mention Saye, *The case of shipmony* raised the standard of Saye's pet political cause.[55]

A discourse concerning puritans, by contrast, was not vague at all about its pertinence to Saye. Indeed it has every sign of having been written specifically to defend the viscount's reputation. In form, *A discourse concerning puritans* was a defense of puritans from calumny. So it began with the passage from Malvezzi; so it ended as well. To be sure, Parker could not quite keep to his design or contain his energies. He took time to attack the episcopal hierarchy by means of Sarpi and, surprisingly, to give presbyterianism an equal drubbing for the same excess of clericalism. He also paraded his distinctions of the kinds of puritans. But if these excrescences are laid aside, the *Discourse* was what it claimed to be—a defense of the puritans from calumny—in a pamphlet not of fifty-eight meandering pages but a crisp twenty-five to thirty.

If the tract is so construed, a clear pattern emerges. After quoting Malvezzi, Parker examined the extraordinary looseness in the use of "puritan" and then shifted to concrete examples of misuse. He began with the Scots, who "rise up against episcopacy." According to the abusive logic of antipuritanism, "episcopacy cannot be unpleasing to any but puritans," and "no opinion can smell sharper of puritanism, then that of a church parity." Consequently, "they must needs be enemies to monarchical government." Similarly, English parliaments "have been jealous of religion" and so declared by their enemies to be puritanical. From that follows the charge of "disobedience, and disaffection to monarchy."[56]

Parker immediately turned the general calumny to a particular case: "Some scrupulous opinions make Say, Brooke, puritans, puritanism infers them mutineers, mutiny makes all that they do or say, all that they forbear to do, or say, it makes their very thoughts wicked and perverse." This was, in other words, a defense to the charge that Saye and Brooke "savoured" of Covenanters, that they were on the brink of treason ("mutiny"). Parker would not let the point drop. After the digressions he returned to the theme, taking up the charge of hypocrisy. If, *arguendo,* it was granted that some puritans were hypocrites, it was "no proof at all, that this man is such a puritan." "This man," it seems, was Lord Saye.

> If my Lord Say be such a puritan, this denotes him an hypocrite, but this does not prove that my Lord Say or Brooke, or Dod, or Clever, etc. or any the most famous puritan living is guilty of usury, sacrilege, rebellion, pulling down of churches, setting the world on fire or of renouncing the second table.

"If these things were true of particular men, calumny were needless; accusation would better suppress them." Parker could not let go. A little later, as he moved to his closing he announced that "Say, Brooke, Dod, Clever, etc. are known to me; yet no otherwise [but] as men singularly devout."[57]

These remarks, in the place they occupy, are remarkable enough. But they are more striking in that the only other contemporary puritan noted by name (and but once) is Henry Burton. Even here there is curiosity. Burton, according to the *Discourse concerning puritans,* committed only the "crime" of condemning "altar-worship." Parker later wrote a pamphlet on the topic, even though, as he confessed, it was out of his "own particular profession, interest, and . . . learning." The tract was dedicated to Lord Saye and signed (it was rare but necessary in this instance for Parker to sign a pamphlet, if only by his initials) by Saye's "most gratefully devoted servant and allies-man." There had been "former favors."[58] If Parker did not write his first two pamphlets for Lord Saye, one as an explication of his views in a pet cause and the other as a defense of the viscount's reputation, it is hard to see why Lord Saye's nephew wrote them at all.

After the Short Parliament and *The case of shipmony,* the proposition that Parliament was a mixture of the three estates of king, Lords, and Commons became increasingly common in parliamentary rhetoric. By the time of the *Answer to the xix propositions,* it was no longer recherché. But along the way it changed sides, eventually becoming a figure of at least equal interest to royalists. Indeed, by the time the king came to use the figure, Parker and the Fiennes had fairly well abandoned it. As things often work out, the moment of the apparent triumph of the opposition's use of the revised estates of king, Lords, and Commons was also almost precisely the first moment of its absorption into what later became royalism. The triumph and the reversal were but opposite sides of the same coin, though this could not be perceived at the time.

The impetus to the reversal was the great remora of Pym and his more moderate allies: root-and-branch. The church issue could shatter the fragile common front of November 1640 a good deal more quickly than the unstable coalition had been put together. The men of 1640 shared briefly in the exhilaration of a movement of national unity, even British unity. It was not to last. Perhaps the truth is that those who had doubts about the cause of reform kept their thoughts mostly to themselves, just as those who had entertained doubts about personal rule kept their thoughts to themselves.

From November 1640 to February 1641 John Pym had been successful at holding together his motley collection of allies, largely by preventing them from seeing too much of each other. There were a few but highly visible extremists, one-issue fanatics, and sectarians; beyond them lay an amorphous semiplebeian constituency of the ever-aggrieved. There were rock-steady Elizabethan-style episcopal puritans, and "downright protestants," and sturdy but angry and perplexed leaders of county and town.[59] There were conservatives, bewildered and frightened by Pym's paranoic fantasy of an enormous popish-Laudian-absolutist conspiracy but equally capable of responding to fears of the falling dominoes of religious disorder. There were the "outs" whose desires to be the "ins" made them lend their support to a cause in which they could not have fully believed, the "courtiers of the country," so to speak. There were the timeservers and crowd pleasers and those who were running as fast as they could from their collaborationist pasts of the 1630s by forging new careers suitable for the 1640s. And amid all these leaders and movers and shakers and one-man teams, there were, as always, the sheep.

Charles and Laud, by one route, and Pym, by another, had assembled all England with the reformers in November 1640. But such a situation, a country without a court, was as unnatural, indeed as perverse, as personal rule, and it was a question of when, rather than whether, the truth would out.

Pym did his best to delay the moment. As his radicals pressed him for root-and-branch, his own instincts as well as those of his patron, the earl of Bedford, suggested delay. For a while Pym had his way. The Scottish minister Robert Baillie reported that the critical petition for root-and-branch from London was in the works barely two weeks after the Long Parliament began to sit. His informants also told him that caution was necessary, a theme that was to annoy Baillie increasingly as the months wore on.[60] The petition was received by the Commons on 11 December 1640, drawing no less than fourteen speeches on whether to proceed with it further. Many of the principal figures in the later history of root-and-branch began to reveal themselves. George Digby and Falkland were against or circumspect; William Strode, Isaac Pennington of London, and Nathaniel Fiennes were predictably for it. Pym was for delay. Perhaps Falkland caught the temper of the house as well as Pym did; Falkland thought the petition was self-damning, apparently, inasmuch as he requested simply that every member of the Commons be provided with a text of the petition to read.[61]

Pym's motion for delay was designed to buy him a week's time. Somehow, there was more. The issue returned only on 13 January, when a Kentish root-and-branch petition was joined by several others of like tenor. Once again the issue was evaded: "divers spake for a long day and divers for a shorter." The next agreed-upon day, 25 January, saw another eleven root-and-branch petitions, many claiming over a thousand signatures. Some cynics thought the petitions had their origin in London. It must be said that Sir Simonds D'Ewes, a prominent man in his own county, was strikingly ignorant of the one Sir Philip Parker delivered in for Suffolk, with "above 4400 hands or names to it." Once again, the only resolution was delay.[62]

Suddenly, on 8 February 1641, the issue burst into flame. For at least eight hours the house did nothing but argue about bishops, needing no more than a technical motion to start the debate. Something like fifty speakers were reported by D'Ewes; Samuel Rawson Gardiner saw the moment as the first step in the formation of parties, a judgment that must be allowed to stand.[63]

The day was the first on which the episcopal issue came to the fore. With it came the first signs that some men supposedly among the reformers were concerned about contagious leveling. George Digby's famous attack upon the plebeian origins of the London petitioners and Edward Kirton's fear that the London petitioners included "anabaptists" were only the most notable. Kirton's remark may itself have been motivated by a budding royalist attempt to smear the puritans with the radicals' brush.[64]

Such remarks set the tone for Sir John Strangwaies's outburst of the following day in a spillover of the previous debate: "if we made a parity in the church we must at last come to a parity in the commonwealth. And that the bishops were one of the three estates of the kingdom and had voice in Parliament."[65] They also set the stage for an impassioned reply: It was said . . . that episcopacy was a third estate in Parliament, and therefore the king and Parliament could not do without them: This I utterly deny, for there are three estates without them, as namely the king, who is the first estate: the lords temporal the second, and the Commons the third: and I know no fourth estate.

No clearer echo could there have been of the debate in the Short Parliament; perhaps the echo was clearer than the original sound, for the upper house in April 1640 was not about to deny the bishops their seats in the Lords, even if they were denied their status. But that is what this speaker did. The "lords temporal" were the second estate. The speaker was Edward Bagshaw.[66] Had Bagshaw removed his mask? If so, soon enough he wanted it back. More likely, the speaker on this day was the masked Bagshaw.[67] Oddly, though, in sixteen months it was Charles who wore Bagshaw's mask.

7

The Reversal, 1641–1642

The revival of the idiom of mixed government in terms of the three revised estates was exhilarating. It was also banal. Certainly there was the high drama of impassioned utterance in Saye's maneuverings in the Short Parliament, in Parker's needling in *The case of shipmony,* in Bagshaw's outburst of February 1641. Whether they were episodes of daring or of malicious triumph, these were direct, if verbal, challenges to the foundations of Caroline policy in three kingdoms. Much of the excitement, however, was in the gesture of defiance, in the exhibitionism of the broken taboo. Such moments have their mornings-after when, in sharper light, they appear flaccid and trite. The historian duly notes the reprintings in the early 1640s of Martin Marprelate and William Stoughton; the revival of mixed government, so far as it has been seen, was little more than a new edition of an old text.[1] The circumstances, the timing, and the personnel of the revival possess a certain interest, but not the words. Coming from the quarters they did, the words were predictable.

What was new, and what could never have been predicted in February 1641 was what would come during the next fifteen months: an astonishing reversal of positions on mixed government on the eve of civil war. The king's apologists laid claim to mixed government with the revision of the estates it had nearly always entailed. A parallel course led Henry Parker and Nathaniel Fiennes to a position in which mixed government and the revised enumeration of the estates was less an expression of their cause as it stood in spring and summer 1642 than an embarrassment to it.

The reversal was not perfect, it was not complete—many on both sides objected to it—but it did occur. It was odd in light of the past and troubling with respect to the future, yet it caught well the paradoxical moment of the eve of civil war. From the royalist perspective, the adoption of the idea of the mixed constitution summarized the bitter ironies of eighteen months of the Long Parliament. The parallel rejection by leading theoreticians of the opposition reflected the genuine revolutionary perplexities of the same moment, which earlier reticences and later tergiversations obscured. The reversal, then, arose out of quite particular circumstances of thought and action.

It could be argued, perhaps, that Arthur Hall's sarcasms and Ellesmere's private ruminations furnished adequate precedent or tradition for the version of mixed government in the king's *Answer to the xix propositions.* In a sense, this view is true: a theory of a balanced constitution could as well be rigged to serve the king's purposes as his opponents'. But Hall had not had to contend with the bishop question and Ellesmere in 1611 chose to ignore it, though at the cost of rendering his reflections unsuitable to the aims of his master, who had built the theme of one book and the policy of two kingdoms upon the defense of the estate of bishops and the royal supereminence above all the estates. Had Laud's enemies not revived the language of mixed government, such royalist experiments might have been by themselves adequate grounding, either as precedents or as analogous responses, for the employment of the language in the *Answer*. But the revival of the language of mixed government by the opposition—set against the royal defense of the estate of bishops—had destroyed the opportunity for innocent adaptation.

The stunning transformation arose partly out of the struggle for control of the means of war and partly out of the struggle over the bishops. Both were part of the ongoing commentary in deeds as well as thoughts on James's maxim of no bishop, no king. As the episcopal side of the transformation was played out in the Long Parliament, the issue at stake was by turns the question of bishops' votes in the upper house and their spiritual function altogether. There was no straightforward progression from the supposedly lesser step of excluding them from the Lords to the greater one of excising them entirely from the church. From the beginning the two were intertwined, even—or perhaps especially—when moderates or those who would lead them on claimed there was no such connection. So also the fate of the bishops was linked in tactics and long-established habits of thought with the fate of the king. Predictably this connection too was denied. Inevitably the denials did as much to establish the language and logic of debate as the assertions. The denials spoke, sometimes accurately, as to motivation. But they did not and could not speak to the question of structure, of what was the next step the moderates professed not to want to take. On that there was substantial if uncomfortable agreement. As always there were two sides. The friends of the king and bishops were proven right, but their own activities did much to validate their worst fears by forcing their opponents into those successive steps that most opposition leaders denied—with varying measures of sincerity, duplicity, and self-delusion—that they wanted or intended.

The struggles over the fate of the bishops took place and set up the reversal in three separate but related and overlapping phases. The first was an effort to reform the church in a way that would have avoided altogether the need to discuss the issue of whether the bishops were an estate. This effort was a proposed combination of episcopacy with presbyterianism—a scheme, rich with overtones of mixed government, that had a history dating back to the Reformation. In early 1640 it was a daring reform proposal; in 1641 it was rejected by the parliamentary leadership; by 1642 it had become a royalist staple.

The second phase, which took place amid the debates over the bill to remove the clergy from civil employments including seats in the House of Lords, was a direct confrontation with the question of the status of the bishops. Supporters of the bill were surprised to find that the bishops' defenders in the two houses reached for the traditional notion of the estates. These defenders were dangerous because of their eminence and their position in the center-right of the reform coalition. It was one thing for court divines and Laudian agents like Balcanquhall to argue for the traditional enumeration of the estates. It was another for so renowned a defender of liberty and property as John Selden to do so.

The third phase was a paradoxical outgrowth of the second. The claim that the bishops did not constitute an estate characteristically had been coupled with the proposition, rarely gainsaid, that they sat in the upper house by virtue of their baronies. Selden, notably, challenged that orthodoxy, and even he could not upset it. But the proposition was designed to explain a fact, the lack of an episcopal veto in the proceedings in Parliament. In a context in which the removal of the bishops was not at issue, it was harmless; when the root-and-branch or the clerical disabilities bill was at stake, it was explosive. In those circumstances, the peerage of the bishops, hitherto a subject with which the temporal peers were not especially concerned, acquired a new and personally menacing significance for them, a significance that was amplified several times over by the nasty politics of crowds, by ugly threats made through petitions from "all

England," and by purge. The result was to compress the fate of the bishops within the fate of the Lords: the assault upon the bishops came to be viewed as part of a more generalized assault upon the Few.

✳

On 9 February 1641, the same day that Strangewaies and Bagshaw tussled over root-and-branch and the three estates, James Ussher, archbishop of Armagh, complained of a false pamphlet put out in his name.[2] This was the first public signal of the movement to defuse both Laudianism and root-and-branch by combining features of episcopacy and presbytery. Charles (or John Gauden) later wrote of "presbytery . . . in a conjuncture with episcopacy"; episcopo-presbytery is an accurate if awkward term for what was desired.[3] The usual name was "primitive" or "moderate" episcopacy. "Primitive" episcopacy embodied the humanist and reformation ideal of a return to purer times. Those earlier days were inescapably associated with an ideal of simple bishops sharing responsibility for the governance of the church with their own clergy.

Schemes of that sort had been part of English protestantism from its beginnings. Proposals with some or all of the key elements survive from the time of Henry VIII and Edward VI.[4] They were particularly well advanced in the heady days of Archbishop Grindal, though they faded with Grindal's fall.[5] By the early seventeenth century they may have been revived as a fallback position after the failure of presbyterianism to maintain public acceptability.[6] From the purely English perspective, then, such ideas were part of the reforming heritage, and Bagshaw's hinting of his favor for the scheme in his Lenten reading doubtless reflected a revival of reformist aspiration during the last days of the Laudian church.

A purely English perspective, however, was not possible in 1640–1642. What in England was an almost entirely unimplemented ideal had attained a measure of institutional realization in Scotland and Ireland. Ussher drew upon his Irish experience in formulating his scheme for England; doubtless few Englishmen were aware of how much Scottish presbyterianism was actually embodied in it.[7] To most Englishmen, Ussher's plan must have seemed like a test model of the English future. The situation was different in Scotland, where there had been four decades of experience with episcopo-presbytery, for that is what had resulted from James's reimposition of episcopacy in Scotland. As has been remarked, the system worked reasonably well. But this success was not known or understood in England in

1640, for the Covenanters were in revolt over precisely that mixture and were urging their English counterparts to have none of it.

The pamphlet of which Ussher complained was not his but well might have been mistaken as his. *Directions propounded and humbly submitted to the high court of Parliament, concerning the Book of Common Prayer and episcopall government* was the work of Ephraim Udall, the son of the great Elizabethan presbyterian leader John Udall.[8] It had little to say about the details of the proposed combination, but its general drift was clear enough: preaching bishops (preaching being at once "primitive" and puritan) were to be joined to "assistants" and "presbyters." By itself, Udall's scheme was little more than a straw in the wind. It is possible, however, that it reflected at an early date the ideas of a much more important man, John Williams, bishop of Lincoln, who along with Ussher was the prime undertaker of the great attempt at compromise.

Ussher's own simple and elegant scheme had begun to circulate as early as December 1640, though all surviving versions mention the Triennial Act and so cannot be earlier than 15 February 1641. But Richard Baxter knew it was circulating in 1640, and Sir Simonds D'Ewes, who acknowledged a "most intimate and dear familiarity" with Ussher in December 1640, held to a distinctly Ussherian line on root-and-branch before the Triennial Act.[9] Ussher's plan took the whole of the presbyterian system and superimposed upon it bishops or superintendents, "call them whether you will." Shrewdly, Ussher translated the presbyterian terminology into a more comfortable English idiom, the better to show how little really needed be done; the local minister and deacons became the rector and sidesmen or churchwardens, the classes were revived rural deaneries. Diocesan, provincial, and national synods capped the system.[10]

Williams, for his part, was actively engaged in the high politics of church reform, in the "aristocratic constitutionalism" of an inner group trying to bring under its sway the most eloquent and committed of its opponents. Like the earl of Bedford, Williams mingled the prospect of reform with unveiled blandishments.[11] He met with Alexander Henderson, promising royal favor if the Scots would quit encouraging root-and-branch in England. These meetings failed and served only to send the Scots back to their desks to resist the new dangerous tendency.[12] With English divines Williams had more success, perhaps because he had more to offer. At his bidding, the upper house ordered him in March 1641 to set up an advisory group of ministers to work under his Committee on Religious Innovations. Williams managed to fill it with all shades of orthodox protestant opinion.[13]

The two Smectymnuans (Smectymnuus was an acronym formed of the initials of the authors of *An answer to a booke* (1641), a root-and-branch response to Joseph Hall's *Episcopacie by divine right*: Stephen Marshall, Edmund Calamy, Thomas Young, Matthew Newcomen, William Spurstow), Edmund Calamy and Stephen Marshall, shared the puritan fold with Cornelius Burgess, who had close ties to Bedford; the first two quickly, the last more slowly became root-and-branchers, if that was not what they had been all along.[14] Ussher, John Prideaux, and John Hacket (Williams's chaplain) represented a moderate stream of puritanism and wished to maintain episcopacy. Robert Sanderson was an acceptable Laudian who had been engaged by Laud to prepare a few concessions in liturgy and ceremony, though not in church government.[15] Williams sat these men down at his table, and perhaps with the benignity of a little lordly hospitality he told them that "the king, was ready to lance every sore, and let out the corruption, only keeping up the places of bishops and dignitaries, among which themselves, being men of great godliness, and learned, did deserve a share, and should be remembered."[16]

This also happened to be the ideologically predominant opinion in the Commons—so the Scots presbyterian Robert Baillie was told and what he had to report home with no enthusiasm. The Committee on the Minister's Remonstrance were, apart from Selden (whom Baillie called "the avowed proctor for the bishops"), "all . . . for the erecting of a kind of presbyteries, and for bringing down the bishops in all things, spiritual and temporal, so low as can be with any subsistence: but their utter abolition, which is the only aim of the most godly, is the knot of the question."[17] Baillie was probably wrong about Selden. Remarks in the *Table talk,* likely from about this time, show him too to be one of the flock. Bishops and presbyters, he said, were like deputy lieutenants and justices of the peace or like the president of the College of Physicians and his colleagues.[18]

Equally worrisome to Baillie and others of his persuasion was the possibility that Williams might succeed with his churchmen. They must have been tempted. Cornelius Burgess, about whom Baillie had doubts, explained the aim of ministers to the Commons as the restoration of the "primitive times" when "many things" were not done "by the bishops alone, but by the bishops and clergy, *concensiente plebe.*"[19] And if Burgess, an associate of Bedford, could so express himself, friendly rivalry demanded that the former and future firebrand preacher, Calybute Downing, a clerical protégé of the earl of Warwick, express himself on the topic too. It was Downing who set Charles's teeth on edge with his famous incendiary sermon to the Artillery Company of London and became Baillie's "familiar friend." But Downing also could soothe; in *Considerations toward a peaceable reformation in matters ecclesiastical* (1641) he wrote that "middle counsels are seldom safe in affairs of state, yet seldom hurtful in business of the church" and warned "not to blast all . . . with an anti-Christian brand."[20]

The breadth of support for the compromise can be seen in the efforts in its behalf made by close associates of Hyde and Falkland—John Hales and George Morley—and by the renegade Scotsman, friend of Pym and Williams, John Dury.[21] All three produced pamphlets that favored episcopo-presbytery and were as well overtly rational and irenic in the spirit of Richard Hooker. Dury set out to show that episcopo-presbytery was the common denominator of most protestant countries: the Lutherans used bishops, superintendents, and clerical consistories, and the "seniors" of Transylvania, Poland, and Bohemia were the "very same" as bishops. Even the Calvinist Dutch and Germans made some distinctions among the clergy.[22] Morley also argued that episcopacy was the "universal tradition of the whole Catholic church," neglected only by a few churches "in the west of Europe" that were at odds with "all the Christians upon the face of the earth." But he was careful to show his support for an episcopacy that shared ordination and jurisdiction with a body of presbyters.[23] Hales offered a vision of supervisory episcopacy of some practical power, yet one in which the bishops were elected either by the presbytery or, in another formulation, "the church . . . either representative or collective."[24]

Despite having such broad support, the movement failed because the extremes would not stand for it. Within the puritan camp there were strong notes of tension. There is no evidence that Calamy and Marshall succumbed to irenic pressures as did, perhaps, Burgess and Downing. As Smectymnuus was afoot even as Williams held his meetings, *An answer to a booke* was all seeming sweetness; but there was at least one pamphlet, from an anonymous insider, that revealed a grasp of the situation faced by leading English puritans.[25] Whoever wrote *Certaine reasons tending to prove the vnlawfulnesse and inexpediencie of all diocesan episcopacie (even the most moderate)* had a sound notion of what he called "petite episcopacy." It consisted of small dioceses with a constant moderatorship over church assemblies and "a negative or double, or at least a casting voice, when things come to be voted." And as much as he did not like it, the author knew that in the Commons the "fast (though perhaps secret) friends of petite episcopacy" held the balance of power. The author of *Certaine reasons* was preparing for the bitter-end struggle of a man who thinks he has lost and knows only one reason to continue the fight. Consider, he wrote, the "desperate condition" of those who have fought "this holy war against the bishops' office," consider what "ireful and revengeful minds hereafter" will do when they get the victory. "If we will not, or cannot attempt any thing with hope, yet we may do it at least through fear."[26]

Meanwhile the Scots switched from blandly confident affirmations of root-and-branch to nervous attacks on compromise. They had had previous experience with "limited prelacy" and "limited episcopacy," they said, and had discovered that a single mold would spoil the loaf. Baillie argued that "limited episcopacy" always led to "episcopacy as it now stands." Henderson said that all the restrictions in the world, all the mixture with presbytery that could be devised, would not change the essential nature of episcopacy and its ungodliness.[27]

There were also problems on the other side, brought about by Williams's eccentric behavior. The same anti-Laudian Williams who rushed about accepting the plaudits of the people and affecting popularity after his release from the Tower also preached to the king at Whitehall that the "Geneva discipline" was "fit only for tradesmen and beggars."[28] The negotiations hardly could afford such doings any more than they could afford Williams's being caught out trying to bribe one of John Pym's servants in the early part of May, supposedly to assist the entry of opposition leaders into the government by passing on to the king the intelligence gained.[29] But perhaps Williams was only responding to an earlier serious breakdown in confidence between him and leaders of the Parliament. Sir John Lambe, dean of the Arches and a man in severe trouble with both Houses of Parliament for his long and compliant career as an ecclesiastical administrator, made an abject submission to Lord Saye, part of which may well have involved his turning upon Williams, notionally his superior.[30]

Finally, there was no guarantee that Charles would go along with these proposals. Williams was letting it be known that Charles "told him Canterbury had drawn him to the canons' making against his judgment," but Charles also made it clear at some point in 1641 that Ussher's scheme would never get his assent, a decision he regretted in 1648 and ought to have regretted in 1642.[31]

The date of the failure of episcopo-presbytery cannot be established firmly. As late as 9 April, Williams's committee was still working the vein of anti-Laudian reform of ceremony and doctrine.[32] By 12 May, almost certainly, the church government compromise had fallen apart. On that day two members of Williams's subcommittee of divines, Burgess and Hacket, argued different sides of the question of retention of deans and chapters before the Commons.[33] Inasmuch as the revenues from the abolition of deans and chapters, to the extent that they were not absorbed by the laity, were to help pay for the reformation of the church, Hacket's defense of deans and chapters indicates that his master or the king had decided to keep things much as they were.

Williams finally introduced his own bill for church reform into the Lords on 1 July 1641. The bill was long and complex and would have provided for the mitigation of a good many abuses. A body of "assistants" from each county—not diocese—was to share with the bishop responsibility for ordination and jurisdiction. Sir John Lambe was to be thrown out of a job; deans and chapters were to be reformed, their excess revenues devoted to buying in impropriations. Clergymen were not to hold secular employment, with certain exceptions; of course, the exclusion from civil function was not to extend to the bishops' place in the Lords. The bill received its second reading on 3 July and was committed to the whole house, a mimic of the Commons' procedure with the root-and-branch bill.[34]

It was only after the effort at compromise had failed that the last and best-known proposal to combine episcopacy and presbytery was coming into circulation. Sir Edward Dering's plan was of the same stamp as Ussher's, save that it had a pronounced laic bias that was alien to the archbishop's scheme and to most of the others. Dering called for the abolition of archepiscopacy (no mean thing in Kent), a new-modeled episcopacy based on the shire, and humbled bishops who shared responsibility with organized presbyteries. Dering later claimed to have first expounded this proposal on 21 June 1641, in a moment of public apology and reversal on root-and-branch; on that day there was some discussion of a choice between "a constant president in the presbytery" (episcopo-presbytery) or a "temporary and elective" one "at the will of the presbytery" (presbyterianism).[35] Dering may well have had reason, as will be seen, to blow out of proportion some casual remarks made on 21 June. But it is interesting to note that two days before his supposed introduction of his scheme in the Commons, Dering announced by another route that he suddenly had taken the king's cause to heart. On 19 June he proposed a wholly gratuitous "royal subsidy" that would have increased Charles's bargaining power with the Scots while decreasing the English Parliament's hold on both.[36]

Dering, who had acquired substantial knowledge of the printing trade as a result of committee work in the Commons and who was a publicity seeker usually embarrassingly quick to get his speeches into print, never published an acknowledged version of his plan or his supposed speech on it until his celebrated *Collection of speeches* of January 1642.[37] Bad as his troubles were when the *Collection* appeared, they would have been worse still if he openly and fully acknowledged that his proposal had been published in three anonymous editions in the third or fourth week of July 1641.[38]

When Dering did print his proposal on the eve of his defection to the king, his original sixteen points became twenty-six. More significantly, the proposal had become more conservative and more refined in traveling around Kent in autumn 1641.[39] Its contents were absorbed in the famous Kentish royalist petition of January 1642. Even after the appearance of the *Collection* (an instant success after it was banned), the earlier version continued to be reprinted. Under different titles, the proposal reappeared in June 1642 and again in January 1643.[40] All in all, Dering's proposal may have been the most frequently reprinted pamphlet of the period. As the incorporation of the scheme into the mainstream of Kentish royalism may indicate, it was important to just those men who sought to tame Charles in 1640 and to defend him in 1642. It also played its part in the making of the *Answer to the xix propositions.*

*

The second phase of the struggle that led to the reversal of positions unfolded in Parliament simultaneously with the abortive effort to establish an episcopo-presbyterian system. What happened was that, when the issue was addressed in terms of whether the bishops were an estate, the bishops found surprising support among men who had been highly critical of them. Earlier, few people had expressed strong feelings about the subject. It often had been said that the bishops sat in the upper house by virtue of their baronies, not by virtue of their spiritual position. When that proposition was advanced to argue that the bishops had no veto in the House of Lords, as it had been from the days of Elizabeth to the Short Parliament, the right-from-barony argument had received a kind of general, nodding assent. The argument only served to prove a fact that needed neither proving nor changing: if an episcopal claim to be an estate meant the bishops ought to have their own negative voice, then the bishops were not an estate in most people's eyes. But when that same proposition was used to assert that the bishops had no claim at all to sit in Parliament, except by virtue of what was granted to them by the king or by the king and the other constituents of Parliament, the stakes became different, the facts became different. Then the question came down to the right of bishops or the church to be a part of the unchanging order of things—to be an estate. When that became the issue, the bishops found defenders among men otherwise not their closest friends.

That came as a shock to the archenemies of the bishops: the "estate" of the bishops proved to have strong defenders outside the Laudian circle. For the later career of the *Answer,* the most notable of these was Edward Hyde. Hyde had been perturbed by what his friends Falkland and Culpeper allowed into the *Answer,* but his response was not sudden. From the beginning Hyde believed the survival of episcopacy and the bishops' claim to be an estate were inseparable. When the bill to disable the clergy from civil employment was introduced into the Commons on 30 March 1641, many (even Falkland) thought that the removal of the bishops from the Lords would be a barrier of reform that would hold off further attack: "if this bill were once passed, a greater number in both houses would be so well satisfied that the violenter party would never be able to prosecute their desires." The future chancellor would have none of it. The change would affect the king's interest, in the very real sense that it reduced the number of his certain supporters in the Lords. And it was, simply, revolutionary:

> It was changing the whole frame and constitution of the kingdom, and of the Parliament itself: that if they were taken out of the house, there would be but two estates left; for that they as the clergy were the third estate, and being taken away, there was nobody left to represent the clergy: which would introduce another piece of injustice, which no other part of the kingdom could complain of, who were all represented in Parliament, and were therefore bound to submit to all that was enacted because it was upon the matter with their own consent.[41]

But this was one argument Hyde was bound to lose: he spoke for the future, not the present. Even Falkland did not stand with him, professing that he had never heard that the bishops were an estate of the realm, but if they were, the upper house would defend their right.[42]

Hyde's position nevertheless communicated clearly to his still-friends among the parliamentary leadership that efforts to abolish bishops would be met by this almost atavistic reply. Although Hyde's moderation was perhaps not as great as has been argued, he was no royalist or episcopalian ultra, and his rejoinder meant that a continuing expression of the reform cause in terms of the abolition of the estate of bishops would meet determined resistance from within the fragile common front.[43]

Hyde might be dismissed as an early defector, but John Selden could never be dismissed, and Selden did an about-face on the place of the bishops when he perceived the call for their reform (which he supported) shaping into an assault upon their very being. His earlier views are clear from *The privileges of the baronage in England, when they sit in Parliament.* In this work he took a conventional line. He argued that bishops in the upper house could not prevent an act from passage even by their unanimous disapproval. Moreover, there could be a parliament without the presence of the spiritual lords. Precisely this sort of argument had been used to make the case that bishops were no estate of the realm. Selden could not have been unaware of the drift of his remarks.[44]

But when the fate of the bishops was on the block in 1641, Selden rose to an entirely unexpected defense of their right. In the debate of 8 February 1641 and later in a similar one on 10 March, Selden argued vigorously that the bishops sat in Parliament as the representatives of the clergy. He emphatically rejected the view that the episcopal franchise was inherently rooted in a royal grant of a barony. In the February debate he is reported to have said that root-and-branch would "abolish ecclesiam . . . the clergy are the church." When Selden was challenged for this statement, a Mr. Vaughan defended him by interpreting his remarks to mean that the episcopal writ of summons referred specifically to the spiritual role of bishops.[45] So indeed Selden himself argued in the debate on the secular employments of the clergy on 10 March, a debate in which Selden "puzzled all the house." He entered the fray only after the opponents of the bishops had managed to utter their usual positions. One was the frequent, almost automatic attempt to trivialize the episcopal presence by making it hang entirely upon baronies. The other position was a twin to the first, in the view of the root-and-branchers; Selden spoke after William Strode contemptuously referred to the bishops' claim to be "one of three estates in Parliament." If fear of an episcopal veto lay behind Strode's remark, Selden said, the fear could be dismissed: the bishops had no such veto. Yet they did represent the clergy. Rather tauntingly, knowing full well the anticlericalism of those around him, Selden suggested that if the clergy were not represented by bishops then they had to be represented some other way.[46]

It was a dazzling performance and for John Pym an alarming one. Pym felt the need to patch things up by means of some desperate ad hoc recollections of John Hooker's *Order and usage.* He argued that the bishops sat in the Lords only by virtue of their civil position but in convocation by virtue of their spiritual position. Given Pym's hostility to convocation, that was no solution, only an acknowledgment that it would be difficult to convince men that bishops had no spiritual function whatever.[47]

Selden elaborated his position in unusually systematic sections on bishops in his *Table talk* and in remarks on the king. As always, he took an idiosyncratic line. He conceded that it was possible—legally possible—for the bishops to be removed from the upper house or to be abolished from the church: "All is as the state likes."[48] Nonetheless it would be wrong, not because of a supposed episcopal divine right, but because the bishops and clergy for no good reason would be divested of their rights, because presbyterianism would solve nothing, and because the king would be harmed. In his inimitable way, Selden reduced the complexities of the case to a few pithy propositions, of which three may serve to highlight the rest:

To take away bishops' votes is but the beginning to take them away.

The three estates are, the lords temporal, the bishops are the clergy, and the Commons, the king is not one of the three estates as some would have it (take heed of that) for then if two agree, the third is involved, but he is king of the three estates.

The bishops being put out of the house, whom will they lay the fault upon now: when the dog is beat out of the room where will they lay the stink?[49]

The defense of the right of bishops and the clergy to be present in the great council, to be a part of the state (rather than to be a kind of internal colony of men ruled but, unlike other subjects, not having any share in rule) was too much to respond to directly. Few men were prepared to take up Selden's suggestion that the clergy be represented in Parliament in some other way than by bishops, and few were prepared to grant any real importance to convocation. After the religious debates of February and March 1641, leaders of the opposition seldom resorted to the language of estates. Opposition leaders made no more grand gestures such as had occurred in the Short Parliament, or as Bagshaw and Strode had attempted in the Commons.

Not surprisingly, however, the bishops and their friends did continue to insist upon their claim to be an estate. John Williams would make the point in May 1641, and it was the more telling because Williams was a Calvinist, an enemy of Laud, and an old ally of Lord Saye (until he and the viscount fell out over the bishops in the spring of 1641).[50] John Warner, bishop of Rochester, confided similar remarks in his diary.[51] Orlando Bridgeman, a common lawyer and the son of a bishop, brought the matter up in a debate on Strafford. With apparent contempt, this Straffordian noted the incongruity and hypocrisy of charging the earl with treason for supposedly attempting "to take the legislative power out of the three estates" but not calling it treason "if you take it out of one of them [the bishops] and put it into the other two." Bridgeman was later one of those most distressed by the king's *Answer.*[52]

These first encounters with the defense of the bishops as an estate were additional preparatives to the reversal. Those who would hold together the common reform front were put on notice that the attack on the bishops— if phrased as an attack upon their right to be an estate—would be met by men equally determined to assert it. Had the friends of the bishops been universally discredited as Laudians or courtiers or as part of the great amorphous plot against protestantism and property, had the claim of the bishops to be an estate continued to be part of a Laudian strategy of aggrandizement (as it appeared to be in the Short Parliament), then the denial of bishops' right to be an estate would have made continuing sense for opposition thinkers. Instead, it proved to be a too-sensitive indicator of the strains the religious issues were placing on the common front. Talented and ambitious men like Hyde were put off by it; and if he and his friends and allies (who included the Digbys) were at the fringes of the reform coalition, they were also valuable for that very reason. The dissent of a man like Selden was at least symbolically more damaging. Like Archbishop Williams, he was generally viewed as a victim of the plot, a sufferer in the name of liberty as Williams was for the true reformed religion.

If the reformers found this aspect of their argument more trouble than it was worth, their opponents had every motive for embracing the claim of bishops to be an estate. But it also became possible for partisans of the bishops and the king to disengage themselves from that claim, through the alternative justification of the bishops' votes in the Lords, namely that the bishops were peers. Along with the pressure of events, this alternative provided an attractive way to couple the defense of the bishops with a more general cause, the rights of the temporal peers of the House of Lords.

*

Neither the opponents nor the partisans of the bishops were immune to inconsistency. Those who claimed that bishops were not an estate also claimed that their spiritual function made it impossible to sit in cases of blood. Consistency is not to be expected in matters so important as the trial of Strafford, where the solid block of episcopal votes made the prospects of a conviction appear slim. Likewise, while defenders of the bishops relied upon the counterclaim that bishops were or represented an estate, many also claimed that bishops sat by right of peerage. Both Archbishop Laud and his chaplain, Peter Heylyn, were assembling materials to make this case in 1641.[53] By May 1641 political pressure and crowd politics gave a brutally practical, experiential meaning to this proposition, which might otherwise have merely gathered dust in Lambeth or the archbishop's lodgings in the Tower. The new meaning, derived from circumstances in which deeds changed the sense of words, conflated the attack upon the bishops with an attack upon the independence of the upper house. Nothing was further from the minds of most of those who led the reform coalition—nothing more abhorrent to some, nothing more dangerous to the cause in the eyes of others. But it occurred, and it paved the way for the reversal.

On a strict accountancy, the two claims made on behalf of the bishops were incompatible. One asserted, the other led away from the traditional anatomy of the three estates. The bishops' claim to be an estate was couched in the logic of representation, certainly by Hyde and Selden. Finer points of the notion of representation could be left vague; the bishops simply stood for the clergy. The claim of bishops to peerage, on the contrary, entailed the conventional wisdom about peerage, which was for two reasons irreconcilable with their claim to be a distinct estate. First, it was held that temporal peers (who had to be the norm) were not representatives; they sat only for themselves. Second, the received view (though some men knew it was inadequate) was that the personal writ of summons was rooted in tenure—a point held to be as true of the spiritual peers as of the temporal. Given these assumptions, it was therefore a practical as well as a theoretical impossibility that bishops could sit and vote both as representatives of the clergy and as barons.

A few participants in the debate perceived the difficulty. This fact apparently underlay Pym's line of thought when he separated the episcopal presence in the upper house from the episcopal presence in the convocation. And apart from Pym's obvious hostility to convocation and the scanting, therefore, of the representative episcopal role, Pym's reasoning foundered upon the same rock that earlier had snagged his guide, John Hooker, who could not make up his mind whether there were three or four estates of Parliament.

Selden's perception of the problem was more incisive, for it brought into play his enormous learning. Indeed, it is possible to follow the development of the underlying questions from one end to the other through Selden's scholarly career. His first work, *Jani Anglorum facies altera* (1610), which he had brought upon the world in his twenty-sixth year, contained a passing remark that Parliament was composed of three "ordines" of king, magnates, and people.[54] In 1610, Selden was no revolutionary nor even much of a reformer, and the usage seems innocent enough. For all his anticlericalism, he had no designs against the bishops or the episcopal presence in Parliament. But Selden was quite clear on the connection of the bishops' seats with baronial tenure. In the first edition (1614) of *Titles of honor,* Selden dropped any mention of the estates or orders, though the episcopal presence was still understood in terms of baronial tenure.[55] The radically different second edition (1631) of the work revealed, in general, how far Selden's learning had advanced and, in particular, how he had rejected his youthful, conventional views. As he now saw it, post-Conquest bishops usually were barons by tenure, but their presence in Parliament had nothing to do with that. Bishops had sat in the witenagemot and similar councils before there were baronies. Their presence at these meetings, which Selden regarded as true precursors of Parliament, was by an aboriginal and never abrogated spiritual right.[56]

At the same time, Selden's philological-historical investigations into the nature of barony led him to find a decisive break in English history about the time of King John, after which baronial tenure itself no longer sufficed to cause a personal writ of summons to be issued. Only some of the tenants-in-chief (or barons) received them. Moreover, in time some men who were not barons by tenure received writs of summons anyway. "Honorary" or "parliamentary" barons (who had a right to a writ of summons) thus were made distinct from tenurial barons by a process of historical development. Richard II's use of letters patent to create barons simply sealed a long move away from feudalism. In this analysis Selden came to conclusions not unlike those that Sir Henry Spelman had reached a few years earlier.[57] But whereas Spelman tended to stress the original, feudal character of the summons to Parliament, regarding the later developments as a kind of defection, Selden was perfectly content to see the later, honorary barons by writ of summons as the proper, the criterial outgrowth of a long process of change.

Therefore nobody really sat in what came to be the House of Lords by right of baronial tenure. All sat, essentially, by a writ of summons, the bishops receiving theirs by one route that led back to Anglo-Saxon times and reflected their spirituality, the temporal peers by another route, which had to do with the separation of the personal right and obligation to give counsel from its tenurial origins.

There was not any mention of estates in the 1631 edition of *Titles of honor*. The matter was essentially irrelevant to the purposes of that work, and it involved a kind of polemical reductionism antithetical to the scholarly delicacy of Selden's enormous compilation. Selden continued to believe the conventional proposition that the presence of the lords spiritual was not necessary to the passing of a bill in the House of Lords. Yet the Selden of *The privileges of the baronage* (1642) was also the Selden of the *Table talk* and the bête noire of the religious debates. And for these latest, highly charged expressions of support for the right of the bishops, Selden teased out the polemical and somewhat crude conclusions that were to be had for the looking in the 1631 edition of *Titles of honor*: that the bishops were an estate, and that barony by tenure was irrelevant to the Parliament as it now stood. Two remarks in the *Table talk* can only be understood as the politicization of a lifetime of learning: one that the right of bishops to sit in the Lords was the same as that of the other peers, and another that the temporal peers were representatives of the commonwealth quite as much as were the knights and burgesses of the lower house.[58] Both remarks put Selden in an enviable position. He could assert that the bishops were one of the estates and could assert their equivalency of status with the temporal peers, but only because he had digested (and, arguably, simplified) his own learning in such a way that the logical incompatibility of the bishops being both peers and the representatives of the clergy had disappeared. He accomplished this feat by destroying the axioms upon which that incompatibility had been based. The temporal peers also sat by writ of summons—divorced from barony—and they had a public, rather than a wholly personal role, as did the bishops. Focusing upon the writ of summons allowed for a distinctly royalist interpretation—grace and favor—to explain the House of Lords (perhaps this underlay some of the implications of *Titles of honor* in the 1631 edition, which appeared when Selden was seeking to recover from the debacle of 1628–1629). But the same focus permitted Selden to divorce the public function of members of the upper house from something so private, so personal, so exclusive as feudal tenure had become. Individuals had a right to be called personally to the upper house, but if that right was personal to them or similarly individuated to a diocese, that only explained who was called, not why they were called.

Edward Hyde also perceived the incompatibility of the episcopal claim to be an estate and the claim that the bishops were "merely" peers, though Selden's subtleties eluded him. But he was unable to convince Falkland and Culpeper, who persisted in holding that the bishops were peers. Their position was in fact more convenient than Hyde's, and it had the practical effect of Selden's subtleties though lacking them. Their stance bespoke an indifference, if not quite a hostility, to the claims of Laudian high church-manship. For the time being, it corresponded to the dispositions of perhaps most of the royalist common lawyers, although that would come to change.[59] Above all, their position was exquisitely tactful about the relation of royalist politics to the disturbing datum that the king agreed in the parliamentary way to the exclusion of bishops from the House of Lords when he signed the clerical disabilities bill finally submitted to him in February 1642. To renege openly upon their position by calling the bishops an estate would be to jeopardize the painfully won appearance (and to an extent, the reality) of constitutional moderation and even cooperativeness that the king's friends had sedulously cultivated.

But there was never a general abandonment of either position by either side. For most royalists and parliamentarians, fastidiousness of argument tended to give way to redundant capacity and overkill. The most that can be said—it is enough, for it describes the reversal—is that the claim by the opposition that the bishops were not an estate because they were barons proved to be more and more embarrassing; conversely, the indifference of some royalists to the bishops' claim to be an estate or simply the advancing of the alternative but strictly incompatible peerage argument became increasingly attractive. The circumstances leading to both tendencies were the same.

*

There were two crucial moments for the forging of these positions, corresponding to the two moments of greatest stress in the Long Parliament. One was the period bracketing Strafford's trial, the introduction of the bishops' exclusion bill in both houses, and the introduction of the root-and-branch bill in the Commons (April–May 1641). The other was the period extending roughly from late November to early February 1642, when great pressure was put on the bishops and on the temporal lords to conform to the wishes of opposition leaders in the matters of the exclusion of the bishops and control of the militia. In both instances the business of the bishops was linked with an obviously secular, and indeed, military matter; and in both instances the abnormal politics of crowds, petitions, and overmanagement played a part.

By April and May 1641, crowd politics and pseudo-mass politics were an established feature of the Westminster scene, but up until that point their focus had been narrowly ecclesiological or religious. In a world like that of Caroline England, religion and politics were inextricably linked, yet religious agitation, even in its more extreme forms, had been as much dissociated from politics as it could have been. In 1640, the traditional May Day riot, slightly postponed, was turned into a tumult against the archbishop of Canterbury. Another tumult about the persons of the high commissioners meeting in St. Paul's occurred in October 1640; the privy council, which ordered the Lord Mayor to make inquiry, was distinctly annoyed at the jury's lack of zeal in seeking the offenders.[60] Still closer to the first meeting of the Long Parliament, on 1 November, a group of about sixty persons made its way into the convocation house in St. Paul's and went about "breaking open boxes and taking away and tearing of divers records and papers and beating, and evil handling the proctors and other officers who did endeavor to withdraw the said seditious persons from their outrages."[61] Then, too, there were the peaceful demonstrations: the triumphal processions for the freed Burton, Prynne, and John Bastwick, and the conduct of Williams when he had been freed (Williams had amused himself and the crowd by swatting Peter Heylyn's pulpit with his episcopal staff during Heylyn's service).[62] This was the local setting of the London petition for root-and-branch; George Digby's doubts about the significance of its 15,000 signatures hardly was generated by the petition itself but rather by an already full context of popular religious activity.[63]

So far, all those who saw or pretended to see a political base to these religious tumults were wrong. To be sure, the menace of linkage was to be inferred. But it had not occurred, and those who, like George Digby, were quick to make the inference could be accused of bad faith. Indeed, because the predicted outcome did not result, the religious agitation, even at its most aggressive and disorderly, seemed the more remarkable, the more genuine, the more holy.

By the time of Strafford's trial and attainder, however, the situation had changed: the religious and political causes now had become intertwined. The bishops' votes in the upper house seemed crucial to the outcome of the case, so they were excluded from participation in this matter of blood. But then the temporal peers showed themselves surprisingly resistant to conviction. The subsequent shift to a bill of attainder changed only the outcome, not the sentiments of the majority who had held out against conviction. Passage of the attainder was assisted, if that is the word, by the popular politics that previously had been witnessed only with respect to the bishops. And, disturbingly, whereas the earlier anti-Laudian tumults came from one-knew-not-where, the later anti-Strafford mob activities had at least a measure of sympathy, and more than likely complicity, from opposition figures in the lower house.[64]

The facts speak for themselves. Except for the complicity of a member of the Commons, the names of the Straffordians (those in the Commons who voted against the attainder) would never have been posted in Palace Yard. Moreover, a curiosity of timing, to put the most neutral construction on it, in an acutely date-conscious era saw the matter of Strafford and the bishops' exclusion bill coming before the Lords at virtually the same time, and both coincided with the traditional but now politicized May Day riot. The bishops' exclusion bill was sent to the Lords on 1 May, a time when the privy council clearly expected trouble, which it anticipated by requiring the Lord Mayor to have in readiness an additional 800 members of the trained bands to cope with the disorders and "insolencies" that were so well known "that it needs not to be repeated."[65] The presence of John Lilburne, then simply a darling of the sectaries, in the anti-Strafford crowds made the connection clearer. Sir Simonds D'Ewes saw 7,000 "citizens," "many of them captains of the city and men of eminent rank," exerting pressure on the Lords on 3 May. What royalists saw was Lilburne at the head of them, threatening that the crowd without weapons would swell to "40 or 50,000 in arms who if they cannot have the Lord Strafford . . . will have the king's person." Lilburne, brought before the upper house for these words, claimed that he was merely reciting what he had heard others say.[66] He was set free, but it cannot be accidental that on the same day (4 May) Lilburne was being investigated by the Lords, the lower house, at the instigation of John Pym's half-brother Francis Rous, was declaring that the Star Chamber judgments against Lilburne were illegal and warranted reparation from the public coffers.[67]

Against this turn of events, the earl of Essex and Lords Mandeville and Saye led an attempt to exclude from voting on the attainder any peers who would not take the Protestation, the test oath that Pym devised after his revelation of the Army Plot. This was to be the first of many disputes over the Protestation and the first exploration by key opposition figures of the purge of the upper house that was to preoccupy them in the winter months of 1641 and 1642.[68] George Digby's father, the earl of Bristol, began to show his own increasing impatience with the reform cause with which at least initially he had been identified; his name was first on a list of peers who announced that they were intimidated by the crowds.[69]

May was far from over, however, and the upheavals continued, with the political and religious issues locked together beyond separation. Large crowds assembled outside St. James, where the Queen Mother resided. Two people were killed in a riot of about 1,000 seamen around the Tower on 11 May. There were further tumults in St. James on 18 May; the same day saw a hysterical millenarian libel placed near the Parliament, which the Lords interpreted as a threat of antiepiscopal rioting. They decided in advance that if the predicted violence were not suppressed they would adjourn. An appeal from the upper house to the Commons for assistance in controlling the disorder was met by a studiously ambiguous and unhelpful response. The Commons appointed two of its most radical members, Henry Martin and Arthur Goodwin, to manage the conference with the Lords. Their message to their parliamentary colleagues was that the lower house was uncertain whether it could suppress the tumults in the vicinity of the Queen Mother, that it would be best if she departed the realm (as the crowds wished), and that the good subjects' "jealousies" about her entourage were well founded.[70]

This was the atmosphere surrounding the upper house's consideration of the bill to exclude the bishops (and all other clergymen) from civil employments, the bill that was presented to weak sisters among the reformers as the bill that would end the terrors of root-and-branch. In fact, though the bill was sent to the Lords on 1 May, they could not consider it until 6 May because of preoccupation with the attainder. Then they were not given much time; the root-and-branch bill was introduced in the Commons on 28 May. Again, the shaky were encouraged to believe that root-and-branch was only a ploy to get the bishops out of the Lords, but because the Lords remained adamant in their refusal to countenance episcopal exclusion, the ploy increasingly became the goal itself. If the Lords would not be intimidated by a threat, then the threat itself had to be executed as a punishment or at least as a show of force. At the introduction of the root-and-branch bill in the Commons Pym all but acknowledged that the attempt to exclude the bishops by bill was dead and that he would pursue the other strategy. The bishops, he thought, ought to remove themselves voluntarily from the upper house; if they did not, he would pursue them with criminal charges.[71]

*

Clearly it was never easier for temporal peers to share the perspective of their embattled spiritual colleagues. A man who was not one of them, but whose learning and connections brought him to a better understanding of the peerage than any other man in England—Selden—caught precisely the temper of the reconciliation between temporal and spiritual lords:

> Bishops have the same right to sit in Parliament as the best of the earls and barons—that is those, which were made by writ. If you ask one of them (Arundel, Oxford, Northumberland) why they sit in the house, they can only say their fathers sat there before him and their grand-father before him, etc. And so says the bishop: he that was a bishop of this place before me sat in this house, and he that was a bishop before him, etc.[72]

John Williams reprised the theme in a rambling defense on 24 May of the bishops' right to their places, basing his argument on the double logic that the bishops were an estate and that they were also a part of the Few. "The prelates of this kingdom, as a looking-glass and representation of the clergy, a third estate, if we may speak either with Sir Edward Coke, or ancient acts of Parliament, have been in possession [here] of, these thousand years and upwards." This purely clerical representative role remained intact through all time, from its Saxon foundations (Williams cited Lambarde and Spelman) to the present, Williams claimed. So Williams had not let fall the baton passed to him unwillingly by his languishing and discredited opponent Laud. Williams was careful to disavow Laud's claim that the bishops had a veto, but Williams's position was no less striking for that. However, it was the other part of the bishops' "double capacities" that interested Williams in May 1641 and that gave him the rhetorical resources for his altogether extraordinary defense. The other side was barony, conventionally understood. "The princes of the Norman race indeed, for their own ends, and to strengthen themselves with men and money, erected the bishoprics soon after into baronies." And that, implied Williams, was a matter of equal concern to the temporal peers, a "matter of freehold" that carried with it "the legislative power."[73]

At every turn in his examination of the several clauses of the exclusion bill, Williams attempted to equate the attack upon the bishops with an attack upon the lay peers, or to involve them in it one way or another. Referring to Bagshaw's argument in the Middle Temple, which he thought underlay the drafting of the bill—this was probably a veiled allusion to Lord Saye—Williams pointed out that the same logic that would exclude the clergy from intermeddling in civil affairs could be used to exclude the temporal peers because it was based on a statute of Richard II that mentioned only the gentry as candidates for service as justices of the peace. Even a salvo in the bill that was designed to protect noble clergymen from its penalties was turned by Williams to his own account. Clearly this provision was intended to assuage the feelings of a few noble clergymen and their near relations, yet Williams suggested that it actually showed a contempt for the nobility.[74] In his conclusion Williams threw logic and clear argument the rest of the way overboard, in favor of the appeal to the emotions that had increasingly determined his subject matter. Williams somehow managed to construe the bill to throw out the bishops as an act of parliamentary suicide and thus ipso facto void, like an act "to take away the votes of all the commons, or all the lords." Which of these prospects he wished to suggest was the serious one was well indicated by a series of quotations from 1 Corinthians, chapter 12, Paul's famous homily on the body politic, one source of conservative theories of order.[75]

Wary of his enemies, Williams cast his speech in deviousness and innuendos. No such wiliness was necessary to Henry Pierrepont, Lord Newark. More clearly than Williams did, Newark pursued the theme that Selden had outlined, though he said nothing about the bishops being an estate. His emphasis was upon the indefeasible diocesan right of peerage, which he saw as no different from that of the temporal peers: "I think he is a great stranger in antiquity, that is not well acquainted with the bishops sitting here: They have done thus, and in this manner, ever since the Conquest; and by the same right, the other peers did, and your lordships now do." The pasts of the two peerages were the same, and so would be their futures. "What bench is secure . . . ? And which of your lordships can say then, he shall continue a member of this house, when, at one blow, twenty-six are cut off?"[76]

The ambiguities of the bishops' position remained. Their "double capacities" were never quite capable of resolution. While a strongly proepiscopal petition from Oxford University (Selden's constituency) in May 1641 feared that the attack on the bishops was essentially anticlerical and would issue in "a universal cheapness and contempt upon the clergy," a pamphlet, *A short treatise of archbishops and bishops,* went the contrary route, anatomizing the whole kingdom, lay and clerical, as "nobility and commonalty," with lords spiritual shorn completely from the "clerks," who were joined with the mere "laymen."[77]

But the reversal had begun, and it cropped up in surprising ways. Sir William Elyott wrote D'Ewes in July 1641 that his "wretched vicar," seeing "nothing as yet to concern" him from the upper house, continued to pray for his bishop, Matthew Wren, "till the upper house and the king hath declared" otherwise. He would, that is, insist upon the concurrence of the three estates of the *Answer,* the king, the Lords, and the Commons.[78] Equally pertinently, Sir Thomas Aston was casting the bishops in a role more naturally allotted to the lay nobility, the role of counterpoise—in the *Answer*'s remarkably passive formulation, the role of "screen and bank." The bishops, Aston claimed, have been the "ballast which have poised the barks of monarchy, to sail safely in the sea of the vulgar, . . . the medium 'twixt tyranny and anarchy."[79]

But if episcopal partisans had gained an idiom, perforce the bishops' opponents were losing theirs, for the two were the same. Lord Saye had made a commitment to the revised anatomy of the estates that was now turning into an embarrassment, and he was not ready to abandon it on 27 May—a day on which, it would seem, the upper house was given its last chance to pass the bill to exclude the bishops, for the next day saw the introduction of the root-and-branch bill in the Commons. Instead Saye put so fine a construction on the truth that it might as well have been a lie. The question of the moment, he said, was not "root and branch" but only whether "superfluous branches" would be removed, whether bishops would be "reduced to what they were in their first advancement over the presbyters." That was true—it was the question "before us"—but "Old Subtlety" was doing his cause no good with the next day's activity surely known to him. Nor was Saye any longer in resonance with the majority of his own side of the house in defending the Commons from the charge of infringing upon the privileges of the Lords in seeking to remove some of its members. There was, he said, no breach of privilege in either "estate's" proposing by way of bill to the other what the other house had power to accept or reject. That too was true, but it was no longer a winning strategy to call the houses by the names of "estates."[80] Too many peers had come to agree with Saye for him to get his way.

Similarly, when the bishops' exclusion bill was renewed after the recess, Oliver St. John's attempt at persuasion in a conference with the Lords (27 October 1641) was seriously marred by his insistence that the bishops were not a "third estate and degree." His argument led him to concede that bishops were nobles and indeed routine members of the upper house. As he searched for a few precedents in which acts or petitions had passed without the bishops, he was forced to acknowledge the usual pattern: "the degree of nobility in all ancient records, is prelates, earls, and barons."[81] Root-and-branch or bishops' exclusion could not survive such arguments in their favor.

The identification of the cause of the bishops with the fate of the lay peers soon became a determined royal policy. Over the summer men were translated to the episcopate to increase the king's certain votes in the upper house. George Digby was raised to the peerage primarily to protect him from a Commons intent on punishing him for publishing his rousing defense of Strafford, but he also had a vote. The threat of further ennoblements was clear; Saye tried to persuade the upper house to close its doors to "usurers."[82] Charles encouraged Bristol to fan dissension between the houses over religion, and by the fall the king, through Secretary Nicholas, was regularly in touch with Bristol regarding the management of an obstructionist strategy in the Lords.[83] Because Charles was now bedecked in the moderate habit of a man who had signed virtually every bill presented to him by the two houses, it was now in his interest to preserve that image and yet preserve his power by using the House of Lords as a barrier against further "reform."[84]

✳

The ingathering of the Few posed challenges to those who wished to pursue the cause of reform. Indeed, one problem was that there was little left to reform, apart from the place of bishops in the state and the church. There was little left to do but be afraid and to act on fears, which led, as early as Pym's Ten Propositions of 24 June 1641, to proposals for parliamentary control of virtually all significant court appointments and to vaguer claims of a parliamentary interest in the management of the military establishment. But neither these proposals nor any others could go forward as bills, without the assent of the upper house, and as Charles tried to build the barrier higher, his opponents, including leading opposition peers, were actively trying to pull it down.

The new opposition theme, which emerged in summer 1641 and shaped the politics of winter 1641–1642, was the "good correspondency" of the two houses—that is to say, the agreement of the Lords with the Commons. The events of May had proven there was only one way to accomplish "good correspondency," a campaign using elements of the purge and of intimidation to reduce the upper house to a suitably purified or terrified remainder. To those who supported "good correspondency," the scheme had something of the air of preserving aristocracy by going right to the point of destroying it. To those opposed and to a few emergent civil radicals (and perhaps inchoately to a much larger constituency in the streets), it was little less than the destruction of the independence of the Few.

The campaign began to be intensified on 30 July 1641. Sir Philip Stapleton moved, John Pym seconded, and Nathaniel Fiennes spoke immediately in favor of a proposal to exlude from office in church and commonwealth anyone "either lord or other" who refused to take the Protestation. The Commons quickly had the vote published, an irregular proceedure designed solely to apply pressure to the upper house. For several days the Lords did little but fume. They sent down messengers to request a conference with the Commons to see "whether the House of Commons will own said paper," a lordly phrasing indeed. Pym sent his own messengers back with no reply to the question but rather a lecture on the "parliamentary way" of giving a reason for the conference. The members from the Commons then told their lordships how important "good correspondency" was: "whosoever is the cause of the contrary, . . . the sin may lie at his door." The quarrel was patched over, but not before Pym tried unsuccessfully to put nine bishops in a *praemunire* for being on the wrong side of a division in the upper house.[85] Almost immediately before the September recess, a dispute between the two houses over contradictory direction to the country concerning religious observance drove home the meaning of sin. On the same day (8 September) that a majority in the upper house sent out an order for "the suppression and search of scandalous libels against nobles," six high opposition peers publicly protested against the order of their own house concerning religious observance. The sin was not to lie at their door. Charles, in his own words, was "not much sorry" to hear the news of the dispute; meanwhile Secretary Nicholas had begun to call the lords who protested the "party of the Protestors."[86]

After the September recess, the assault upon the Lords began in earnest.

Casting precedent to the winds, the Commons renewed the failed bill to exclude the bishops and other clergy from civil employment, rushed it through their own house, and sent it to the Lords on 27 October 1641. Once again the upper house refused to abandon the bishops. As with the events of May 1641, the struggle over the bishops was connected with the politics of the control of force. In May it had been Strafford and the Army Plot; in autumn and winter 1641 it was the need to raise an army to fight the rebellion that had broken out in Ireland and to put the English kingdom in a "posture of defense."

The Grand Remonstrance, passed in the Commons by a narrow margin on 23 November and presented to the king on 1 December, was a part of an appeal not so much to the king as to the country against the evil and malignant party of papists, bishops, and courtiers. In particular, the malignants had prevented further reformation in the parliamentary way:

> They have had such a party of bishops and popish lords in the House of Peers, as hath caused much opposition and delay in the prosecution of delinquents, hindered the proceedings of divers good bills passed in the Commons' house. . . . what can we the Commons [do], without the conjunction of the House of Lords, and what conjunction can we expect there, when the bishops and recusant lords are so numerous and prevalent that they are able to cross and interrupt our best endeavors for reformation . . . ?[87]

There could be no good answer because the problem was misstated. Only with the agreement or indifference of most of the protestant lords did the "popish" lords and bishops get their way. And the "divers good bills" were really then but one, the bill to disable the bishops. That one bill indeed was a victim of the lack of "conjunction," as was the failure to prosecute "delinquents," who again were the bishops. In effect, the Grand Remonstrance charged the upper house with having bishops and popish lords who would not act against bishops and popish lords. Charles's own reply to this part of the remonstrance (written by Hyde) was to stand upon the ancient constitution and parliamentary way that up to that moment had failed to present him with a problem. The bishops' votes, he said, were "grounded upon the fundamental law of the kingdom and constitution of Parliament," but inasmuch as he was presented with no bill—Charles must have enjoyed this—"we will give you no answer at this time."[88]

But as early as 3 December, well before Charles's reply, Pym answered the great question of the remonstrance. He threatened to remove the screen and bank, personally informing the upper house in a conference that if it did not "join with us" in passing "good bills," the Commons and the minority of "good lords," as he called them, would take their grievances directly to the king. What that meant on 3 December no one, not even Pym himself, could really know.[89]

Fortunately for Pym he did not quite have to find out: the crowds, the petitions, and a foolish maneuver of the bishops, now led by Williams, did his hard work for him. A return to crowd politics in November and December marked a growing hysteria in London that was compounded by the appearance of royalist gangs to face the crowds and by Charles's appointment of a ruffian, Thomas Lunsford, to control of the Tower. Some particularly nasty demonstrations after Christmas, designed to cause the Lords to accept the exclusion of the bishops, led on 27 December to a formal withdrawal of Williams and eleven other bishops. Two days later, Williams and the others declared that all proceedings in the upper house were void until the bishops could come and go in safety. Reasonable as the claim was, from the point of view of men who were being removed from the upper house not by votes but by the mob, it was a disaster. Williams's declaration raised the shade of Laud's claim in the Short Parliament—that the house could not function in the bishops' absence.[90] Williams had denied this point in his defense of the episcopal franchise in May; he was a notorious conniver and, for those who chose to believe in such things, the beast had just revealed its true form. But there was more: if the bishops would not attend, the lay lords hardly could be expected to stand by them forever. The twelve signatory bishops were impeached, sent to the Tower, and—rather to prove the validity of the Commons' case against the impeached bishops—a number of nonsignatory bishops were allowed (and perhaps pressed) to attend the upper house in January.[91] Underlying the episode was the unstated but well-understood supposition, amply borne out by events of the next two weeks, that neither Charles nor the armed cavalier enthusiasts were able to protect them.

Still, after the debacle of the Five Members and Charles's abandonment of the city on 11 January 1642, the House of Lords managed to hold on for another month against mounting and ultimately intolerable pressure. Throughout December and January, the "good lords" entered formal protestations upon losing key votes, as they had done on 9 September, to "discharge" themselves by name of responsibility for the evils of the kingdom.[92] These were the correlative of the suggestions made by Pym and later by Denzil Holles that the good lords and the Commons go directly to the king without the malignant lords. Both Hyde and the Venetian ambassador interpreted these protestations as denunciations of the bad lords to the people.[93] In desperation, Charles tried to strengthen his friends in the upper house with some ennoblements from the Commons, but the Commons, meeting in Grocer's Hall, passed resolutions to prevent him from doing so without their consent. These votes revived in substance the object of a bill read only one time the previous June, a good measure of the deterioration of the situation.[94]

"God forbid that the House of Commons should proceed in any way to dishearten people to obtain their just desires": so John Pym said when the Lords pleaded with the Commons on 28 December to join them in setting a guard about the Parliament.[95] Whether or not Pym and his friends orchestrated the events of December and January, they did not let the opportunity pass. On the day Charles left London, armed petitioners from Buckinghamshire (encouraged or abetted by John Hampden) informed the Lords of their hope that they would "co-operate with the House of Commons."[96] Petitioners to the Lords from Essex on 20 January associated the removal of the bishops and popish lords with the relief of the economic crisis, a note reiterated in many petitions and one—whatever the real extent of economic distress—that could not have been taken as anything other than a threat. Even at this date, the upper house remained behind the bishops. The Lords, choosing their words with care, thanked the petitioners for their good will "in relation to the privileges of Parliament and the safety of Ireland" but refused to make further undertakings: "for the rest of their petition, this house will take it into consideration in due time."[97]

The key day in the campaign was 25 January. A petition from Hertfordshire set the tone. All the nation's problems, it asserted, stemmed from "the want of compliance" of the Lords with the Commons; the "total decay of trade" could be remedied only by the removal of the bishops and popish lords. Obviously taking a cue from Pym and the good lords, the petitioners made a note of their special affection for "those noble lords and gentlemen in both houses whose endeavors are for the public good" and claimed a "liberty to protest" against the "enemies to this kingdom, who refuse to join with those honorable lords, and the House of Commons." The Lords' response was "to conceive" that the petitioners had "good intentions," but that was as far as they were prepared to go; two courageous peers, Thomas Wriothesley, earl of Southampton and Francis Leigh, Lord Dunsmore, dissented to even this qualified response. Soon petitions from Devon and Exeter were introduced by the young earl of Bedford to much the same effect. Behind these petitions lay others that might as well have been personal missives from Pym and St. John, for one came from Tavistock and another from Totnes, the small boroughs for which the two leaders sat.[98]

The Lords spent the rest of the day—it was a long one—at a conference requested by the Commons and managed by Pym, in which Pym harangued the Lords on the significance of four additional petitions ("they had received more"). These petitions were "the cry of all England," he said, and as the petitions linked the "agony, terror, and perplexity" of the kingdom to the bishops and popish lords, so did Pym. The Commons were "in no part guilty," and the Lords knew "what is to be done." If they failed, the Commons would be "sorry" that it would be "enforced to save the kingdom alone, and that the House of Peers should have no part" in England's preservation.[99]

At the next day's debate on the conference, the king's cousin, the duke of Richmond, moved that the Lords adjourn for six months. A flurry of outrage from the good lords led to the last of their protestations. They wished to be on the record that the young duke was inadequately punished.[100] Later the earl of Warwick, a very good lord, brought in some seamen and young men who wanted the persons responsible for their miseries to be "declared." They prophesied that, if relief was not forthcoming, "multitudes" would take to "that remedy . . . next at hand." On 29 January the seamen returned for an answer. The Lords promised one as "speedily as may stand with the great affairs of the kingdom."[101]

Two days later the screw was tightened again. Another petition threatened to move to the "next remedy." This "horrible petition," as Hyde called it, this petition of the "rabble threatening a mutiny" as it was styled in a royalist compilation, illustrates more clearly than any other petition the purposeful or accidental coordination of crowd and leadership that marked these "daily assaults upon the Lords."[102] The petition was printed by William Larnar, known later as a close associate of John Lilburne, and contained directions for assembly in More Fields. From there the petitioners, the spokesmen for "many thousand poor artificers in and about the city of London," were accompanied to the Commons by John Venn, a London militia captain with close ties to the city members. A delegation was admitted and the petition was read. The problems of the kingdom, including the petitioners' own hunger, were "chiefly and originally" trace-able to the bishops and the popish lords. The step short of that "next remedy" they warned of was that the names of the opposers of reform "be publicly declared." They had one further thought: the abolition of the House of Lords. The good lords ("those noble-worthies . . . who concur with you") ought to "join with this honorable house, and to sit and vote as one entire body."[103]

According to D'Ewes, the petitioners wanted "instant remedies."[104] They restated their demand for the list of names as they stood at the bar. Pym's response was all but a repetition of his ploy of 3 December: "This is of great importance. We must go to the lords and if they will not join with us we must join with them and show His Majesty these things."[105] Denzil Holles, the son of the earl of Clare, managed the conference with the upper house in a way that left no doubt what use was to be made of the petition. It was an extreme statement, he said, but so were the times; the Lords alone "should be guilty of all the miseries that may happen."[106]

The next day saw a crowd of angry women outside the houses with a petition of their own in their hands and vengeance on their minds. Several peers were jostled by them and by some porters. By now the resolution was at hand.[107] One stumbling block was removed on 1 and 2 February, when the Lords agreed to petition the king to put the forts of the kingdom into acceptable hands; by 4 February petitioners to the Lords from Surrey were thanking them for their partial "concurrence" with the Commons but reminding the peers that the bishops had not yet been removed and urging them on to a "constant union." On 5 February, the Lords finally caved in on the votes of bishops; Kentish petitioners thanked them three days later for their "good correspondence." They promised to defend the House of Lords "so far as your lordships shall continue to hold correspondence and concurrence with the said House of Commons." When the impressment bill passed on the same day, the peers were immediately rewarded, as it were, by a decision of Suffolk petitioners to leave most of their company at home "in obedience to a late order of the House of Commons."[108] Indeed, the Commons, after two months of ignoring the tumults, took the appropriate measures to ensure there were no more: like the petitioners from Suffolk, the opposition leadership no longer had any doubts about the "continued concurrence" of the Lords with the Commons.[109] There was only one problem. The House of Lords was nearly empty.[110]

*

"God had placed us (my lords) betwixt the king and his people; let us play our parts. . ."; thus did Henry Carey, earl of Monmouth, try to rally his colleagues shortly after the king left London.[111] But the screen and bank had only three weeks left and, in a sense, Charles himself had removed it when he went looking for his birds in the Commons on 4 January 1642. As winter gave way to spring, a majority of the peers went home, many to await his call. The ultimate issue having been joined—the contest between king and "people"—most of the peers decided that their fortunes, all things considered, were best subordinated to the king's. Charles became their screen and bank.

For a while the opposition could enjoy its triumph. The radicals and the hotheads had a field day. On 31 January, the day of the "horrible petition," Sir Arthur Haselrigg wanted the Commons to go covered to the Lords. Early in February Strode amused himself by suggesting an ultimatum to the Lords on the impressment bill: "If they refuse us, to go to them no more."[112] Dering, on his way out at the same time as the malignants in the upper house, reported at the beginning of February that a "gentleman of the house" told him that he wanted to "bring the lords down into our house among us."[113] Such sentiments were hardly characteristic of the political instincts of most of the Commons, but they emerged at a moment when the House of Commons was arguably the "democracy," the third classically defined "estate," as it had never been before.

The triumph was real: the king had lost the one contest he had chosen to fight. But it was also hollow. The deepest political difficulties emerged with "democracy," and they were not much mitigated by such shoddy victories. The breaking of the House of Lords had chased away the bishops and popish lords, but it had also chased away the greater part of the protestant peerage, and there was nothing to show for it except hypocritical assents to two bills passed under the most irregular circumstances, circumstances that Charles had thought treason: "they [the Five Members and Lord Kimbolton] have endeavored . . . by force and terror to compel the Parliament to join them in their traitorous designs, and to that end have actually raised and countenanced tumults against the king and Parliament."[114]

For a true believer like the London turner Nehemiah Wallington, the crowds of walking petitioners were the result of God's stirring up of "all sorts, high and low, rich and poor, of both sexes, men and women, old and young, bond and free, both in the cities and the countries."[115] But there were other ways of looking at it. "The insurrections of the apprentices (as all ungoverned multitudes) are of very dangerous consequence, but God, who works miracles, can out of such violent actions bring comfortable effects."[116] The real "miracle," however, was not the "comfortable effects" but the nervous suspension of the gentry's fear of Hydra; in more settled times few of the Commons would have taken issue with the sneer underlying Sir Thomas Aston's description of the radical petitions:

> So rare a gift have the illuminated fancies of this all knowing age, that old women without spectacles can discover popish plots, young men and apprentices assume to regulate the rebellion in Ireland, seamen and mariners reform the House of Peers, poor men, porters and laborers spy out a malignant party, and discipline them.[117]

8
The Answer

One more matter needs to be considered before we return to the focal point of this study, the king's *Answer to the xix propositions*. The preceding account suggests rather a higher degree of political polarization by May 1641 than usually has been acknowledged in recent studies of political history of that period and in broader studies of the political culture of the early seventeenth century. The full range of issues is complex and beyond the scope of this study, but it can be argued that the political culture of early Stuart England was more confrontational than these studies recognize, even though older views of a formed, structural political opposition party are clearly unsatisfactory.[1] To be precise, it will be suggested that the political culture of the seventeenth century had no steady or reliable means of differentiating between confrontational and nonconfrontational ("consensual" or "organic") politics.[2] If recent scholarship shrewdly has perceived the factionalism and back-door accommodation inherent in what used to be called unthinkingly "the opposition," it is allowable, indeed necessary to insist upon the confrontational aspects of accommodation, consensus (when enforced by test oaths and purges), and the pursuit of office.

The terrain of later Tudor and Stuart politics and political thought was astonishingly constricted. So, at least, it appears to the modern political mind, attached as it is to assumptions based upon the ideas of pluralism and a political continuum and removed as it is from the qualitative and frequently rhetorical schemes by which political thought and action were then modified. Conversely, the modern scholar sees gradations that seventeenth-century Englishmen could not see and therefore could not act upon. Tudor and Stuart political culture had but the most rudimentary idea of a political spectrum, of an extended series of subtly discrete gradations from servility to sedition. There was no clear idea, such as underlies modern political activity, that the acceptable and unacceptable in policy or idea were linked to similar boundaries of means; indeed there was no clear notion of the permissible and the impermissible or of the constructive and the unconstructive. In short, there was no loyal opposition, no automatically disloyal opposition, no political failure that did not contain within it the prospect of treason, and not much treason apart from obedience to Rome that could not also be regarded as a constructive political act. Characteristically, political failure was associated with the commission of a crime, political success with preferment and power. To lose was to be impeached and convicted, attainted, put in contempt, imprisoned; to win was to do these things to one's opponents, to escape their fate, and to enjoy the spoils so obtained, for the fruits of victory were seldom otherwise to be had. A stalemate, a draw, was effected or recognized less by some intermediate level of reward or punishment than by some combination of both, not a *via media* but a clash of contraries.

Tudor and Stuart observers caught this lability of politics, and it is a measure of the limitations of the system that they were puzzled and distressed by it. The problem, simply, was that an unpredictable, often irrational switching mechanism derived jockeying for preferment, opposition, crime, and treason out of substantially identical conduct. That mechanism was royal grace and favor, which came in several varieties—genuine, forced, and feigned.

As Arthur Hall had it, for opposition in the Commons

> you may be frowned on by princes and others, yet they will know you well enough, commend you in secret, glad to win you to employ in service, judge you wise, honest, and worthy to be trusted, not a butterfly, a six weeks' bird: whereas if you follow their humors, if their turns be served, if you play the hireling, they perhaps will smile upon you for the time, never trust you, but in the end shake you off.[3]

The duchess of Newcastle, nearly a century later,

> heard my lord say, that it is a great error and weak policy in a state to advance their enemies, and endeavor to make them friends, by bribing them with honors and offices, saying "they are shrewd men, and may do the state much hurt": and on the other side, to neglect their friends, and those that

have done them great service, saying "they are honest men, and mean the state no harm."[4]

In a similar vein, Clarendon described the paradox of John Pym, who was in November 1640 "and for some months after, the most popular man, and the most able to do hurt, that hath lived at any time." Precisely for this reason he and his patron Bedford were the targets of "the first design" of the court "of softening and obliging the powerful persons in both houses." But the prospect of the chancellorship of the Exchequer led Pym to abate his "sharpness in the house" and led—so says Clarendon, who, even if he were wrong, is interesting in his analysis—to Pym's loss of reputation in the Commons, a circumstance that made him less useful to the court than he was when in high dudgeon against it. "He found that he was much better able to do hurt than good; which wrought very much upon him to melancholic."[5] But two days before Pym was charged with treason, rumor still had it that he would be given office. The political mind even then could not easily make a distinction we make by reflex.[6]

Sir John Bramston, a man with a long memory, spoke of the commingling of opposition and preferment as a deep-rooted phenomenon. Some members of the Long Parliament made speeches "to show they had parts, and might do good or hurt; intending that the king, finding them able to do mischief might take them off by preferring them, as he had done Wentworth, Digges, and others formerly." It was "a most pernicious course," but "his son Charles Prince" had kept to it, even though "for one he gained he lost two or three or more; for all, seeing the way to preferment was by opposing, were sure to pursue the beaten track."[7] It was, surely, an aged path. Martin Marprelate, it may be remembered, thought John Aylmer's radical reformism was a "snare" to catch a bishopric; one wonders about Throckmorton's own motives.[8]

The incalculability of politics understandably led men to muse upon the fickle goddess Fortune. Sir Thomas Wentworth, in his opening remarks to the Council of the North upon assuming its Lord Presidency, attributed his sudden reversal to "the rich dispensation of a sovereign goddess" who had guided him "within the space of one year" from imprisonment to his viscountcy and new office.[9] But if it is hard not to sympathize with those dizzied by the vertiginous politics of faction and favor, it is also true that Wentworth's story was at once extraordinary and routine, like the winning ticket in a lottery. Who would win or lose, why one would win or lose, these were foreseeable to none; that there would be such winners and losers, however, was obvious to all.

The difficulties of such a system, or lack of system, were perceived, certainly by 1641. The Grand Remonstrance of November 1641 rose, for once, beyond mere partisanship in its analysis of the problems caused by politics conducted by means of criminal charges. Although it was pleading its own case in seeking to have a veto over ministerial appointments, the Commons leadership summarized a problem that was as much a habitual one for the king (*mutatis mutandis*) as it was a novel one for a House of Commons:

> It may often fall out that the Commons may have just cause to take exceptions at some men for being councilors, and yet not charge those men with crimes, for there be grounds of diffidence which lie not in proof.

> There are others, which though they may be proved, yet are not legally criminal.

> . . . we may have great reason to be earnest with His Majesty, not to put his great affairs into such hands, though we may be unwilling to proceed against them in any legal way of charge or impeachment.[10]

The problem, of course, was not to be solved in the seventeenth century.

There were other dimensions. Political judgment hung on qualitative distinctions devoid of clear, substantive, and, especially, commensurable content. Whether or not an opposition was a crime depended, in the final analysis, on whether it was given that name; and this determination too often depended on motivational, even rhetorical characteristics. What was done or what was said was no more important, perhaps even less important, than the presumed intention behind it. The altogether hysterical denials that the Scots of 1640 were rebels were English and Scottish attempts not to argue conduct—the facts spoke for themselves—but intention. The carry-over into the casuistry of the English civil conflict of 1642 was the parliamentary claim, at once absurd and necessary, that a subject was not in rebellion against his king if he did not intend to make war against him; the clanging of swords and the smell of powder were not testimonies of the intention.[11] But this reasoning was only more dangerous, not more strained, than the recitation of the causes that had led to James Whitelocke's imprisonment in 1613. Whitelocke's rhetoric, not his law, did him in:

> in all the course of his writing [he] never used so much as a modest phrase of tenderness or loathness to deal in so high a cause, or of referring or submitting himself to better judgment, or making the case difficult or doubtful. . . . Whereas it might have become him either to have declined to deal in a cause of that greatness, or at least to have handled it in reverend and respective manner. . . .[12]

Rhetoric mattered, gesture mattered. It was not simply an analysis of political psychology that led Charles in 1629 and afterward to describe his opponents in the Commons as "distempered" and as "ill-affected men." It was also a way of stating the problem caused by men whose political ideals were actually the same as those of "wise and moderate men" and "religious, grave, and well-minded men." The stock in trade of the "evil spirits" was not so much ideology as innuendo, the "casting out" of "some glances and doubtful speeches." This kind of analysis was a necessary requirement of a system in which similar, even identical words and actions were often to be found in friend and foe.[13] Compounding the problem, nevertheless, were the sometimes arbitrary constructions placed upon particular formulations or usages. Here words themselves were used to gauge intentions, frequently with the slimmest justification. "Sovereignty" was not a word that the lawyers liked much to hear.[14] Everyone knew that "priest" and "presbyter" were mere variants of the same etymon, but to use one or the other was to toss in one's lot with a religious faction. As we have seen, the latent meanings supposed to be entailed in one version or another of the estates of the realm had much to do with who used the doctrine and whether it was used at all. In these cases, doctrine tended to dissolve itself into rhetoric; rhetoric itself was a matter of word gestures, a code of intentions or presumed intentions not clearly spelled out in the doctrine itself.

To the extent that this view is correct, it places certain aspects of politics of the first six months of the Long Parliament in a somewhat different light than recently has been cast upon them. At the heart of the matter is the perception—doubtless correct—that the leading opponents of Charles's policies in late 1640 and 1641 were moderate men—given a notion of a spectrum of possible positions—who sought a settlement for the nation and preferment for themselves. They were not a formed opposition, a quasi-institutional "party," but men bidding for place at court and for a solution to the problems—not highly ideological—that had prevented the court from acquiring the financial stability it so desperately needed and local governors from exercising their own blend of local and national authority to the satisfaction of their communities, their masters at the center, and themselves.[15] Because the schemes for office were partly and imperfectly but intermittently realized across the first six months of the Long Parliament, because the wishful rumors of further accommodation continued, because large parts of the strategy of leading members of both houses continued to place great stock on the control of the men about the king (the evil or good councilors as the case might be), and because more radical designs were not evident, the harsher and more confrontational aspects of the politics of the period have been minimized.

But a difficulty arises when one asks what expectation was held by the seekers of office, the accommodators, in the event of failure. The answer must be "the plot"; the only guarantee that parliamentary leaders had that force or the legal process would not be turned on them was that they would control the apparatus of state before it could be utilized against them. In a revealing oxymoron, Clarendon wrote that after Bedford's death those who sought office were "desperate in their hopes."[16] Conrad Russell has pointed out that the parliamentary leaders lost "their escape route" when the Spanish captured Providence Island in the autumn of 1641; they had needed one for some time, probably since Pym revealed the Army Plot early in May, and certainly when Charles, late in May, threatened to go to Edinburgh to settle with the Scots.[17]

Under the circumstances, then, the pursuit of place was itself an aggressive act, a confrontational mode, just as overt opposition sometimes was taken for a bid to serve the king. Neither the royalists who fled in late 1640, nor Sir Thomas Aston, who seems to have secured an escape route of his own before he began his campaign to save the church, would have disagreed.[18] Such was the result of a political system that could not distinguish the pursuit of office, political opposition, and criminal activity. Each of the three was a manifestation of the same root cause: ambition.

✳

These principles were fully operative during the position shifting regarding the estates. If they help explain how aggressive politics could be shielded by the pursuit of place, they also suggest that the reversal of terminology and arguments was one of those rhetorical or gesticular devices by means of which the "ins" and the "outs," the aggressors and the aggrieved, could be perceived, when it appeared to many constitutional royalists that the roles of king and Parliament had shifted.

To be sure, not everyone changed his language. When the bishops were ousted from the House of Lords, some of the opponents of the bishops and the king revived their earlier description of the kingdom as composed of the three estates of king, Lords, and Commons. They had fought for it, and they were not to be denied their revenge. Sir Thomas Wroth, a radical gentleman from Somerset, introducing an adulatory petition to the House of Commons from his county on 25 February 1642, spoke of the wonders done and to be expected from the "high and glorious assembly of the three estates in Parliament."[19] Early in March Sir Robert Harley attempted to lecture royalist justices of the peace in similar terms, justifying the activity of the houses as a responsibility incumbent upon each of the "three estates."[20] Victory tried to call a halt to the process of reversal; the bishops were out and at last the question should have been settled.

But it was not to be. There was already a new motive for the opposition to regret ever having brought up the estates of the realm, and a new motive for royalists to adopt it. This new motive lay in the king's refusal to sign the militia bill, the passage of the militia ordinance (5 March), and the issuance by the king of commissions of array to counter the parliamentary levies under the militia ordinance. Sir Thomas Wroth, of course, did not know it, but his remark of 25 February came shortly after the last piece of legislation enacted by the three estates of king, Lords, and Commons in England for eighteen years.

The ordinance, as an alternative to the bill or petition, had been gingerly explored in August 1641, when fears about the king's intentions in going to Scotland were at a height and when the usual fears of armed recusants were also in the air. No one except Henry Martin seems to have believed that ordinances could do much more than bind the members of the two houses or (more significantly) make some emergency provisions during the absence of the king from the realm. The latter contained within it the possibility of limitless extension, and the obvious constitutional dangers left most men reluctant to proceed. But Martin was prepared, on 27 August, to "wish" that the house "might account . . . an ordinance to be of equal force and power with an act of Parliament."[21] By 8 February 1642 Martin, the only genuine republican in the house, was ready to go a good deal further. Replying to a suggestion that the bill to exclude the bishops ought to be presented to the king with reasons for its passage, he blandly suggested that the assent of both houses was "sufficient." The king was "not to have a third house of Parliament to counsel him otherwise." Martin went on to argue that as the "whole commons" chose the House of Commons, the king chose the Lords, so his "vote was included in the Lords' votes." The "custom," as he called it, of "le roy s'avisera might be left aside."[22]

In late February and early March the opposition officially adopted Martin's position as it stood in August 1641. Martin's unambiguous embrace of bicameral sovereignty in early February 1642 suggests that the playboy revolutionary had a good idea where the leadership then stood and recalibrated his own position accordingly. If so, then the leadership did not lose a step in applying the tactic used against the upper house to the king: to invite assent and then go ahead without it, invoking emergency as justification.

On 28 February, Charles refused to assent to what would have been the militia bill. The Commons' official response was to declare the denial "dangerous" and to refer with knowing vagueness to "some speedy remedy" by "both Houses of Parliament."[23] The nature of the remedy discussed that day is revealed by a ciphered passage in Sir Ralph Verney's diary: "If a king offer to kill himself we must no[t] only advise but wrest the weapon."[24] This is what the militia ordinance came to be: the signal for an arms race to secure the weapons necessary to secure Parliament *and* the king's person by preventing one of them from having any.

To most of those who accepted it the militia ordinance was an emergency measure, justified only by the threat of the great popish plot, a new version of which was conveniently revealed in a letter addressed to Pym and found in the street by a watchman on 15 March. To these nervous moderates the militia ordinance was not to be a precedent.[25] There were other views, however. Some were prepared to make the emergency permanent. Unnamed "others" in a debate on obedience to the militia ordinance on this day argued, according to D'Ewes, that the ordinance had to be obeyed because it was "warranted by law of God by the law of nature and of necessity."[26] On 2 April, Nathaniel Fiennes revealed himself to be one of these "others." Fiennes did "most ignorantly and untruly affirm that the king had no negative voice in passing those acts of Parliament which both houses had agreed unto but was to assent to them."[27] Fiennes pursued the point from a different angle on 15 April by producing a tale of a Worcestershire shoemaker who was "glad to hear that no ordinances of the houses could bind or ought to be obeyed without the king's consent given to it."[28] So Fiennes came to hold the theory of bicameral parliamentary sovereignty more or less as Martin had presented it on 8 February; the only difference, trivial in the context, was that Fiennes thought the king was bound to assent and Martin thought his assent unnecessary.

As Fiennes and Martin were pushing the new politics along in the Commons, an anonymous broadside appeared in the streets and shops, "Published for the good of the commonweal." This was *A question answered: how laws are to be understood, and obedience yeelded? necessary for the present state of things, touching the militia,* doubtless the most influential broadside of the civil war.[29] In it, Henry Parker (see Appendix 2) began to construct the political theory that stood Parliament through the early years of war and later became (ironically but not illogically) a proof text for the levelers.[30] As matters stood in April 1642, *A question answered* was the public elucidation of the line of thought that Parker's cousin Nathaniel Fiennes was advocating in the Commons. Charles thought it extremely dangerous. He sent a copy to the Lords with a recommendation that its author be discovered and punished for his "seditious and treasonable distinctions."[31]

A question answered blithely, almost gaily, conceded the brutal fact that more scrupulous men like D'Ewes could not bring themselves to face: by the letter of the law the militia ordinance was illegal. "Let it be granted," Parker said. And then Parker revealed the political theory of the permanent emergency. There was, he argued, an equitable as well as a literal sense of every law, and if the letter and the equity (or "spirit" or "reason") were at odds, equity controlled. Equity did not have to be expressed; if a general turned his artillery upon his own soldiers, he "did *ipso facto* estate the army, in a right of disobedience." If the distinction were not admitted, Parker went on, then any monarchy, even "a legal and mixed monarchy" was the "greatest tyranny." That would be "an absurdity." So did Parker explicate necessity and the law of reason, the catch phrases of the proponents of naked bicameral sovereignty in 1642.

The positions taken by Fiennes and by *A question answered* were incompatible with the doctrine that the three estates were the king, the Lords, and the Commons. There was no room for a balance or a royal negative voice. Martin's contemptuous dismissal of a third house of Parliament expressed what Fiennes and Parker preferred to leave unsaid: there were two estates and a royal employee, no doubt with tenure. For the opposition, the reversal was complete. Parker and the Fienneses, the great propagandists of the revised anatomy of the estates in 1640 and 1641, had no use for it in mid-1642.

✳

    The opposition had been twice burned by its version of the mixed, balanced constitution of king, Lords, Commons—first when the tumults and political pressure had put the bishops more firmly among the Few than could have been imagined in the days of Thorough and the canons of 1640, and second when it became embarrassingly clear that a coherent logic for the ordinance required an abandonment of the assumption that the king was on an equal footing with the two houses. Strangely but clearly, the opposition had discovered for itself several ironic meanings of James's now hoary "no bishop, no king."

    In April 1642 the king's friends asserted the rights of both and adopted the very language their opponents had discarded. The earliest instance of the line of thought embodied in the *Answer* appeared in an anonymous pamphlet of April 1642, *A plea for moderation.* [32] The pamphlet was part of the great surge of Kentish royalism of spring 1642, a royalism that brought into an exhilarating, courageous alliance such men as Sir Edward Dering, Sir John Culpeper, and the earl of Bristol. Either of the latter two could have written *A plea,* but exact attribution is not important; the merger of the royalist-based political accommodation pursued by Bristol, the religious compromise sought by Dering, and the language memorialized by Culpeper and Falkland in the *Answer* makes an attribution as irrelevant as a survey of the pamphlet's contents is important.

    The Pleader was all for the middle ground between vicious extremes. He was a "Magna Charta man" and yet would "give Caesar his due." He despised the "hierarchical power of bishops" but would not admit he must "have no bishops at all." Echoing the line taken by Selden, Newark, and Williams, he noted that bishops of old had had a "deciding power both in temporal and spiritual matters . . . all which before popery was thought of"; put another way, the Pleader was quietly countenancing the right of the bishops to vote in the upper house. In a republic, he continued, presbyterian polity was perhaps allowable: no king, no bishops. But the Pleader had another design for his country—the plan of "that English Seneca, Sir Edward Dering in a treatise of his." [33]

    The Pleader's language was initially of the tribe of Fortescue. "Prerogative" and "liberty of the subject . . . *meum* and *tuum*" must "go hand in hand." King and people must come to a right understanding, he said, quoting from "a good speech though from a bad man," Strafford. But uncontrollably the Pleader shifted into a different idiom, that of Ellesmere and Arthur Hall. The king had been the one wronged: "I hope with us he may be esteemed a third estate in Parliament."[34]

A plea and the *Answer* shared a great deal: the constitutional royalism of disheartened reformers, a language prepared to consider the king as an estate of the realm, the political perception that made the leap natural, even if it was contrary to the king's position as of 1640. The two statements even shared defects. As the *Answer* could not maintain the logic of the classical balance without reverting to the Fortescuean language of *dominium politicum et regale,* so too *A plea* muddled classical and binary or Fortescuean terminology. As the *Answer* drifted unsteadily from calling the Commons the "democracy" to warning the gentry-dominated Commons of the frightful example they set for "the common people," so *A plea* wandered off into similar warnings about "the anti-governists" who would heap up "a load of higher and greater crimes" than those yet perpetrated.[35]

A plea was heard, or perhaps its insights were being reproduced spontaneously. In March, as has been seen, Sir Robert Harley was laying down the law to his royalist neighbors on the Herefordshire bench about the "three estates." Late in April they gave it right back in a letter that circulated among royalists in several counties beyond Herefordshire: "You tell us truly that the constitution of this kingdom is comprised of three estates. . . . it is a triple cord and it would be dangerous to untwist it: if you leave out either it will not be so strong." Each estate had a negative voice. If anyone had "power of binding" it was the king rather than the Commons; laws, lands, and parliaments flowed from him. The writs of summons caused men to be elected to the Commons not "to govern" but to join with the king and Lords in legislation.[36]

Thus the components of the royalist reversal were also complete by April 1642. The principles of the *Answer* entered into the official correspondence so late as mid-June only because when Hyde joined the king at York he had a propaganda backlog to overcome.[37] A strange symmetry revealed itself on the parliamentary end; the opposition also was having trouble keeping up with the war of words. That is a partial explanation of why there was no direct answer from the Parliament to the *Answer to the xix propositions* when it first appeared and why a reply to the king's answer to the declaration of 26 May was issued six months later.[38]

Yet there was an answer to the *Answer,* one that may have had its origins in the parliamentary paper jam. At least this is how many took Parker's *Observations upon his majesties late answers and expresses,* as an unofficial but authentic representation of opposition thinking upon both the *Answer* and the declaration of 26 May. On 22 July Francis Rous wanted one of the first replies to Parker's *Observations* investigated as a scandalous pamphlet. The next day, D'Ewes rose to his great moment of open defiance, his own public confession that he had been duped. The official declaration in response to the *Answer,* composed by a committee headed by Nathaniel Fiennes, was finally about to be voted when D'Ewes exclaimed that a "great part of this declaration was already printed in a pamphlet of observations, and that part of it also is confuted in print by him that hath answered that observator." The house would be dishonored to "put out for their declaration" what was already to be found "in a budget or a pocket."[39]

Parker's *Observations* skirted the passages on mixed government in the *Answer.* Just once it used the word "estate"; it briefly bandied about the vocabulary of classical constitutionalism—monarchy, aristocracy and nobility, ochlocracy, and democracy. But Parker's heart was not in it.[40] He hardly could entertain the claim of the king to be an estate, *at least* an estate, in a pamphlet the major goal of which was to establish the inferiority of the king to the houses. But the greatest irritant was "democracy." Tendentiously quoting the *Answer* on the screen and bank, Parker made it appear that the nobility *and* the gentry were the screen and bank. Indeed it was almost always the nobility and gentry *conjunctim*; Parker did all he could to minimize the imputation of democracy to the House of Commons. The *Answer* had pointed to the menace of Wat Tyler and the "dark, equal chaos of confusion." Parker took no notice; he made it appear as if the king were accusing his enemies of an "aristocratical usurpation."[41] We are left with a monumental irony: Parker was as terrified of the *Answer* as Hyde was. There was one difference: in effect, Parker had written it, in *The case of shipmony.*

But that was not the only irony surrounding the *Answer.* The *Answer* turned out to have predicted the future in the reverse order in which it already had occurred. The *Answer* was the product of a two-year struggle in which an attack upon the bishops led to an attack upon the Lords, which led at last to an attack upon the king. The *Answer* put it the other way around: "the second estate would in all probability follow the fate of the first." Order collapses, order is restored. In this contradiction we may take comfort: things are never as bad as they seem.

But why? A seventeenth-century Saxonist may provide a clue. Like his father Henry, Sir John Spelman was a royalist, an episcopalian, and an antiquary. Surely this biographer of Alfred had at some time encountered the words of the Wessex king or those of Aelfric and Wulfstan about those who pray, fight, and work. If he had, he chose not to remember them but rather their image, their imagination—the three-legged stool.

> The high court of Parliament therefore resembling a chair of three feet, the two houses make but two of the three, which without the third is lame and useless (as to making of law) but with the third become a firm and useful seat, and makes that sacred *tripos* from whence the civil oracles of our law are delivered.[42]

Of course, Spelman was wrong. The two houses proved themselves anything but lame and useless, with the king or without. And Spelman's tripos was not a king-stool—Spelman used other means to assert the supremacy of the king. Nevertheless, if Charles's and Spelman's definition of the estates was of no use to them in its decade, by the progressive exercise of imagination it came to be the received version of the ancient constitution for the next two hundred years. We all must sit on something.

Appendix 1
Hyde's Religious
Position in 1641

In his remarkable study, Brian Wormald argued that Hyde's religious position in 1641 was considerably more flexible than the accounts in the *History* and the *Life* would lead one to believe.[1] In one respect, the argument can be carried a good deal further than Wormald saw fit to make it: there is no reason to suppose that Hyde was opposed to the episcopo-presbyterian schemes afoot in 1641. Friends from the Tew circle, George Morley and John Hales, supported it, and there is little reason to think that they were at odds with their political friend.[2] Indeed, Hyde may well have continued his toleration, at least, for the schemes through the Uxbridge negotiations and even into the Restoration, when they were vigorously promoted by John Gauden.[3]

But as Wormald discovered a high churchman in the *History* and the *Life* and found him at odds with the ecclesiastical moderate he detected in 1641, he tended to dismiss the significance of the facts of Hyde's conduct in 1641 and 1642, the outlines of which Wormald did not contest.[4] At root, Wormald caricatured both Hydes—the man of 1640 and the man of the exile—and as a result created two straw men, each terrified of the other. No doubt Wormald is correct in identifying high church influence upon Hyde the writer, a haze of affection for Charles and his churchmanship that led Hyde to emphasize his own importance in the church debates of 1641.[5] On the other hand, as Wormald also carefully indicates, his later development did not preclude later acknowledgment of his difference with Laud, a major part of which, it would seem, was Laud's view that the bishops constituted a part of the peerage.[6] Wormald does not challenge the nature of Hyde's disagreement with Falkland; instead he states that the underlying dispute was the more political adiaphorism of Hyde and the more spiritual adiaphorism of Falkland.[7]

Precisely: Hyde was *always* the political churchman Wormald so brilliantly describes, and the *History* and *Life* do not contradict it. Hyde's support for the bishops never came from *jure divino* principles but from a deep and unshakable faith of their value in the whole community. Hyde was unbending but not for doctrinal reasons. Nevertheless, there was a religious component; in community life God had instituted order and the bishops, if they behaved themselves along with everyone else, were an important part of the structure. For this reason Hyde could not follow a true *politique* like Culpeper. Hyde's attitudes during and after 1641 were kindred to those of Elizabethan and early Jacobean churchmen: his position did not differ significantly in texture or in substance from Richard Hooker, even to participating in the great ambiguity of Hooker's views. Did Hooker's reasonable religion include or exclude those who disagreed? Was adiaphorism a position that opened or shut doors? Hyde, having Scottish presbyterian and English root-and-branch before his eyes, naturally was attracted to the latter prospect and its leading Jacobean exponent, Bancroft; he seems to have seen Bancroft as a staunch defender of bishops and good order but little more—a Laud without the absurdities and the sharp edges. It may have been a myth, but it served Hyde well.[8]

Moreover, it appears that Hyde was perceived as a somewhat more committed defender of the church by his friends than Wormald has allowed. Hyde was inundated with letters from and in support of Thomas Triplet, a member of the Tew circle not mentioned by Wormald. Triplet had entered a business arrangement with George Lilburne, the uncle of the future Leveller and a strong puritan in his own right. These dealings went astray and, according to Triplet and other friends of Hyde, Lilburne turned the dispute into something resembling a puritan crusade, a matter made easier by the presence of the Scots in the north. Triplet's house was plundered, and Lilburne tried to interest John White's committee in the Commons in Triplet. Hyde, not Falkland, primarily was urged to sort the matter out, and this friendly prodding was done in language that suggests that Hyde would share a substantial antipuritan animus.[9] Similarly, other associates of Hyde took it quite for granted that Hyde was receptive to highly skeptical comments about the great doings: one correspondent, for example, commented cynically in January 1641 on the "new great statesman of Hackney," Calybute Downing, and confided that "all the clergy" expected trouble along with Laud.[10] If Hyde was cooperative with those in the puritan fold whose idiom was so different, it probably was not because he shared their cultural assumptions.

Moreover, whatever may have been Hyde's disagreements with Laud, in February 1642 Hyde was enough in the archbishop's trust that Laud chose to confide in him a very troublesome matter. Having been visited by a certain "Mr. Hunt," either an extortionist or an agent provocateur, Laud took immediate counsel with his trusted servant Richard Cobb and with Hyde, who were both at that moment in Laud's "inner chamber" at the Tower. This indicates strongly that Hyde's memory in the *History* and the *Life* of a personal friendship with Laud at this time was neither a mirage of hindsight nor a misdated recollection of the days before 1640.[11]

In summary, a careful reading of Wormald contains, in its qualifications, the view advanced in this study: that with no more than the usual exaggeration Hyde's position in 1641 was substantially as it was presented in the *Life* and the *History,* the position of a man with a deep attachment to the structure of the church as it stood.

Appendix 2
Henry Parker and
A question answered

A question answered is anonymous. Peter Heylyn offered a prima facie absurd remark that it was "affirmed" to be Selden's.[1] More plausibly, Ernest Sirluck suggested that John Marsh was its author, because Marsh's *An argument or, debate in law* . . . (30 September 1642) likewise was conconcerned to show that the king's legal command could be disobeyed on the grounds of equity. Sirluck simply suggested that *A question answered* was a "prior abstract" of *An argument, or, debate in law*.[2]

Because Sirluck did not provide any detailed evidence for his view, an elaborate rebuttal is unnecessary. Admittedly there are resemblances, but Marsh himself described his tract as partly derivative: "I have borrowed some of the Parliament's grounds to expatiate myself upon."[3] This statement should not be taken lightly, especially because it casts doubt whether *An argument or, debate in law* was a "prior abstract" of anything by Marsh. Second, the resemblances, though close, are not complete. Marsh's notion of equity is somewhat different from that of *A question answered*; it is much more closely bound to common law maxims and statutes.[4] Indeed the originality of Marsh's position is that he sought to provide a respectable legal underpinning to an argument that in *A question answered* treated law with casual disregard. Indifference to the nuts and bolts of the law was a Parker trait and one that Marsh, an official of Lincoln's Inn, hardly could have shared with him. If *A question answered* was a "prior abstract" of *An argument or, debate in law*, Marsh must have had a decidedly malleable personality. There are formal similarities, too. "The king says X, the parliament says Y" is a style common to both pieces. But it is also to be found in Parker and several militia tracts about the time of Marsh's.[5] One slightly later, *Touching the fundamentall lawes,* in fact, is much closer to *A question answered* than Marsh's piece.[6]

The single strong argument against an attribution to Parker is George Thomason's failure to attribute it to his friend. It is idle to speculate upon Thomason's silence if indeed Parker was the author. The strongest argument for Parker's authorship is the following parallel from *A question answered* and Parker's *Observations,* which antedated Marsh's book by three months:

A question answered

. . . when the militia of an army is committed to the general, it is not with any express condition, that he shall not turn the mouths of his cannons against his own soldiers, for that is so naturally and necessarily implied, that it's needless to be expressed, insomuch as if he did attempt or command such a thing against the nature of his trust and place, it did *ipso facto* estate the army, in a right of disobedience, except we think that obedience binds men to cut their own throats.

Observations (p. 4)

And we cannot imagine . . . that any generalissimo can be so uncircumscribed in power, but that if he should turn his cannons upon his own soldiers, they were *ipso facto* absolved of all obedience, and of all oaths and ties of allegiance whatsoever for that time . . . : wherefore if there be such tacit trusts and reservations in all public commands [etc.].

Further textual parallels could be made. A nontextual argument is intriguing. Several students, including Sirluck himself, have by a process of mental association turned to Parker immediately upon discussing *A question answered* (Sirluck even stresses the place of "equity" in Parker's work).[7] William Haller and Lois Schwoerer did it; so did a royalist declaration shortly after Parker's *Observations* appeared.[8] The intuition, I suggest, is sound.

Notes

The place of publication is London unless otherwise stated.

Chapter 1

1. Charles I, *His majesties answer to the xix propositions of both houses of parliament* (1642) [British Library (hereafter cited as BL), E. 151 (25)], 18. For a convenient edition of the celebrated passage see Corinne Comstock Weston, *English Constitutional Theory and the House of Lords, 1556–1832* (1965), 263–65.

2. Edward Hyde, earl of Clarendon, *The History of the Rebellion . . . , Also, His Life* (hereafter cited as *Life*), 2 vols. (Oxford, 1843), 2:938, 944.

3. Ibid., 2:950.

4. Ibid., 2:950, 953. Cf. the shrewd intuition of Harold Hulme in "Charles I and the Constitution," in *Conflict in Stuart England . . . ,* ed. William Appleton Aiken and Basil Duke Henning (1960), 123 and n. 22.

5. Clarendon, *Life,* 2:953.

6. Ibid., 2:941, 953. Edward Hyde, earl of Clarendon, *The History of the Rebellion . . . ,* ed. W. Dunn Macray (hereafter cited as *History*), 6 vols. (Oxford, 1888), 1:357, 406, 568.

7. The next three paragraphs assume that Hyde's position on the church in 1640–1642 was rather closer to the tenor of his remarks in *History* and the *Life* than Brian Wormald's account (see n. 38) suggests. For a discussion of this important point, see Appendix 1.

8. Clarendon, *History,* 1:406–07; idem, *Life,* 2:941.

9. Clarendon, *Life,* 2:940–41.

10. See p. 148.

11. See pp. 179, 181–82.

12. The standard accounts of the *Answer's* later influence are Weston, *English*

Constitutional Theory; Corinne Comstock Weston and Janelle Renfrow Green-berg, *Subjects and Sovereigns; The Grand Controversy over Legal Sovereignty in Stuart England* (Cambridge, 1981); Julian H. Franklin, *John Locke and the Theory of Sovereignty: Mixed Monarchy and the Right of Resistance in the Political Thought of the English Revolution* (New York, 1978).

13. Samuel Rawson Gardiner, ed., *Constitutional Documents of the Puritan Revolution, 1625–1660,* 3rd ed. (Oxford, 1906), 250. Some of the propositions were less extreme though no less hostile than those involving parliamentary control of executive power; they made Charles appear less conciliatory than was actually the case.

14. *Answer,* 5.

15. Ibid., 10–11.

16. BL Harley (hereafter cited as Harl.) 163, f. 207b.

17. See Chapters 3 and 4; see also pp. 98–102.

18. *Answer,* 13.

19. Ibid., 12–13. "Proper" is used nine times on pp. 11–14; the second proposition had given the rhetorical opening by using the word.

20. Ibid., 17.

21. This paragraph summarizes Chapters 3–8.

22. *Answer,* 17–18.

23. Ibid., 18; cf. 11.

24. Ibid., 24. For some treatment of the association of arms and the commons in early Stuart England, see J. G. A. Pocock, *The Machiavellian Moment: Florentine Political Thought and the Atlantic Republican Tradition* (Princeton, 1975), 357. See also Thomas Hedley's important 1610 speech in Elizabeth Read Foster, ed., *Proceedings in Parliament, 1610,* 2 vols. (New Haven, 1966), 2:170–97, especially 194–97; Sir Thomas Smith, *De republica Anglorum,* ed. L. Alston (Cambridge, 1906), bk. 1, chap. 23; William Shakespeare, *Henry V,* act 4, sc. 8. It is well to note that the military virtues of the English commons almost always are worked out with reference to France.

25. James Harrington, *The Political Works,* ed. J. G. A. Pocock (Cambridge, 1975), 198.

26. *Answer,* 18.

27. For the distinction see Charles Howard McIlwain, *Constitutionalism Ancient and Modern* (Ithaca, 1958). For recent reevaluation see Donald W. Hanson, *From Kingdom to Commonwealth: The Development of Civic Consciousness in English Political Thought* (Cambridge, Mass., 1970), vii and 24–26, 134. Cf. Pocock, *Machiavellian Moment,* 27, n. 30. Weston and Greenberg give considerable attention to *gubernaculum* in *Subjects and Sovereigns*; see their index s.v. "*gubernaculum.*" But the point, especially of the dual usage of "government" in the *Answer,* was earlier handled in Michael J. Mendle, "Mixed Government, the

Estates, and the Bishops: A Motif of English Political Thought" (Ph.D. diss., Washington University, 1977), 100–103.

28. *Answer,* 18.

29. Ibid., 19–20. The claim of the Commons to be a council is a much underrated claim. For another example, see the declaration of 19 May 1642, in Edward Husbands, ed., *An exact collection* (1643), 197: "the two Houses of Parliament being the supreme court and highest council of the kingdom, were enabled by their own authority" to defend the kingdom.

30. *Answer,* 20–21.

31. Ibid., 21–22.

32. BL Cotton Ms. Nero C. x., f. 115 recto; Smith, *De republica,* bk. 1, chap. 18; Sir Thomas Aston, *A remonstrance against presbitery* (1641), B4 recto. See also Thomas Wilson, cited in Lawrence Stone, ed., *Social Change and Revolution in England, 1540–1640* (1966), 117. An anonymous speaker on the Resiant Bill of 1571 resolutely distinguished the commons of the "manual or mechanical arts" from the "nobility, knights, and soldiers"; BL Cotton Ms. Appendix 47 (formerly Add. Mss. 5009–5010), ff. 78–79. This distinction is similar to the text in T. E. Hartley, ed., *Proceedings in the Parliaments of Elizabeth I,* 2 vols. (Wilmington, Del., 1981), 1:226.

33. See pp. 180–82.

34. Husbands, *Exact collection,* 363.

35. Weston and Greenberg, *Subjects and Sovereigns.*

36. Sir Roger Twysden, *Certaine Considerations Upon the Government of England,* ed. J. M. Kemble (1849), 14, 127–32. But cf. Monmouth's translation, "a well constituted aristodemocratical government," in Giovanni Francesco Biondi, *An history of the civill warres of England,* trans. Henry Carey, earl of Monmouth, 2 vols, in 1 (1641), "Introduction," C2 verso.

37. *Answer,* 22.

38. B. H. G. Wormald, *Clarendon: Politics, History, and Religion* (Cambridge, 1952), is the classic study of Clarendon's and Falkland's religion, but see Appendix 1.

39. Clarendon, *Life,* 953; Clarendon, *History,* 1:311–12, 357.

40. Ibid., 1:118.

Chapter 2

1. Georges Duby, *The Three Orders: Feudal Society Imagined,* trans. Arthur Goldhammer (Chicago, 1980). Jacques Le Goff, *Time, Work, and Culture in the Middle Ages,* trans. Arthur Goldhammer (Chicago, 1980), 53–57, 110–16, and passim; Jacques Le Goff, "Les trois fonctions indo-européennes, l'historien et l'Europe féodale," *Annales* 34 (1979): 1187–215.

Because English usage did not usually discriminate between "order" and "estate"—certainly "estate" was not a gentler term—the distinction drawn by Duby and Le Goff between these words is ignored here.

2. Jean Batany, "Des 'trois fonctions' aux 'trois états'?" *Annales* 18 (1963): 933–38.

A useful survey of the work of Dumézil and his students is C. Scott Littleton, *The New Comparative Mythology* (Berkeley, 1966).

3. Georges Dumézil, *Archaic Roman Religion*, trans. Philip Krapp, 2 vols. (Chicago, 1970); Bernard Sergent, "Les trois fonctions des Indo-Européens dans la Grèce ancienne: bilan critique," *Annales* 34 (1979): 1155–87.

4. Julius Caesar, *The Gallic War*, with a translation by H. J. Edwards (Cambridge, Mass., 1958), bk. 6, 13–15.

5. Batany, "Des 'trois fonctions.'"

6. Daniel Dubuisson. "L'Irlande et la théorie mediévale des 'trois ordres,'" *Revue de l'Histoire des Religions* 188 (1975): 35–63.

7. Duby, *Three Orders*, 99–110.

8. See Duby, n. 1; Ottavia Niccoli, *I sacerdoti, i guerrieri, i contadini. Storia di un' immagine della società* (Turin, 1979).

9. Duby, *Three Orders*, 6.

10. Boethius, *King Alfred's Anglo-Saxon Version of Boethius De Consolatione Philosophiae*, ed. and trans. J. S. Cardale (1829), 90–91; a better translation is in Dorothy Whitelock, ed., *English Historical Documents, 500–1042*, 2nd ed. (New York, 1979), 919.

11. S. J. Crawford, ed., *The Old English Version of the Heptateuch, Aelfric's Treatise on the Old and New Testament and his Preface to Genesis* (1922), 71–72. The translation by William L'Isle of Wilburgham was first published in 1623 as *A saxon treatise. . . .* See also Aelfric, *Aelfric's Lives of Saints*, ed. Walter W. Skeat (1890), pt. 3, 120–25, and Wulfstan II, archbishop of York, *Die "Institutes of Polity, Civil and Ecclesiastical,"* ed. Karl Jost (Berne, 1959), 33, for the other usages of Aelfric.

12. Attributed mistakenly to Aelfric in Thomas Wright, ed. and trans., *The Political Songs of England, from the Reign of John to that of Edward II* (1839), 365. A modern facsmile text is Wulfstan II, *A Wulfstan Manuscript*, ed. Henry Royston Loyn (Copenhagen, 1971), f. 71; cf. Wulfstan, *Die "Institutes,"* 55–58.

13. Aelfric, *Lives*, 120–25.

14. See pp. 182–83.

15. Eric Mercer, *Furniture, 700–1700* (New York, 1969), 31–37.

16. Le Goff, "Les trois fonctions," 1206.

17. Duby, *Three Orders*, 21–43, especially 31, 37–38, 41. See Huguette Taviani, "Le mariage dans l'hérésie de l'An Mil," *Annales* 32 (1977): 1074–89.

18. Duby, *Three Orders*, 5.

19. Claude Carozzi, "Les fondements de la tripartition sociale chez Adalbéron de Laon," *Annales* 33 (1978): 683–702.

20. Duby, *Three Orders*, 54, 139–46, also 192–205.

21. Taviani, "Le mariage"; Malcolm Lambert, *Medieval Heresy: Popular Movements from Bogomil to Hus* (New York, 1977), 26–29.

22. Le Goff, *Time, Work, and Culture*, 53–58; idem, "Les trois fonctions," 1193.

23. Duby, *Three Orders*, 171–74, 285, 287.

24. Jacques Paul Migne, ed., *Patrologia cursus completus . . . series latina*, 221 vols. (Paris, 1844–1864), 159:679.

25. John of Worcester, *The Chronicle of John of Worcester, 1118–1140*, ed. J. R. H. Weaver (Oxford, 1908), 32–33. The manuscript illustration in the Durham Cathedral Library is reproduced in Jacques Le Goff, *La civilisation de l'Occident médiéval* (Paris, 1972), plates 117–18.

26. Gerald Robert Owst, *Literature and Pulpit in Medieval England* (Cambridge, 1933), 548–93; Stanley Bertram Chrimes, *English Constitutional Ideas of the Fifteenth Century* (Cambridge, 1936), 96; Alfred William Pollard, ed., *Fifteenth-Century Prose and Verse* (1903; reprint ed., New York, 1964), 176–77.

27. Reginald Pecock, *The Repressor of Over Much Blaming of the Clergy*, ed. Churchill Babington, 2 vols. (1860).

28. Owst, *Literature and Pulpit*, 554. Duby and Le Goff view the anomaly of the merchant as being partly responsible for the decline of the scheme; Duby, *Three Orders*, 325, and Le Goff, *La civilisation*, 325–26. Cf. Niccoli, *I sacerdoti*, "Epilogo: Le quattro verità," 125–37.

29. David Hume, *History of England*, 8 vols. (1822), 6:19, n. 1.

30. William Stubbs, *The Constitutional History of England in Its Origin and Development*, 3rd ed., 3 vols. (Oxford, 1884), 2:163, 171–73, 176.

31. For a recent restatement see George Osborne Sayles, *The King's Parliament of England* (New York, 1974); the earliest doubts were raised by Frederic William Maitland in his introduction to the *Memoranda de Parliamento* (1893), reprinted in Maitland, *Selected Essays*, ed. Harold Dexter Hazeltine, Gaillard Lapsley, and Percy Henry Winfield (Cambridge, 1936), 1–72, and in part in Maitland, *Selected Historical Essays*, ed. Helen Cam (Cambridge, 1957), 52–96.

32. Albert Frederick Pollard, *The Evolution of Parliament*, 2nd ed. (1934).

33. Ibid., 78–80.

34. Helen Cam, "The Theory and Practice of Representation in Medieval England," *History* 38 (1953), reprinted in *Historical Studies of the English Parliament*, ed. E. S. Fryde and Edward Miller, 2 vols. (Cambridge, 1970), 1:275. Cam also alluded to the work of Dumézil (264–265), a very early recognition indeed of his work's relevance to historians.

35. A. F. Pollard, *Evolution*, 62–64.

36. Ibid., chap. 4. Thirning's speech is available in Stanley Bertram Chrimes

and Alfred L. Brown, eds., *Select Documents of English Constitutional History, 1307–1485* (New York, 1961), 192–93.

37. Text in Chrimes, *English Constitutional Ideas*, 97, attributed to Henry Beaufort; reattribution by John Roskell, "The Social Composition of the Commons in a Fifteenth-Century Parliament," *Bulletin of the Institute of Historical Research* 24 (1951): 171–72.

Stafford's scheme anticipated by about eighty years the similar formulation for France of Claude de Seyssel in *La monarchie de France . . .* , ed. Jacques Poujol (Paris, 1961), 121–26.

38. Chrimes, *English Constitutional Ideas*, 120–24, 167–91.

39. A. F. Pollard, *Evolution*, 70.

40. *Times* (London) *Literary Supplement*, 3 July, 10 July, and 17 July 1924.

41. Chrimes, *English Constitutional Ideas*, 1–65 passim, 81, n. 2, 85–98. Ruth Mohl, *The Three Estates in Medieval and Renaissance Literature* (1933; reprint ed., New York, 1962).

42. Chrimes, *English Constitutional Ideas*, 101–06. But see Albert Frederick Pollard's review in *History* 22 (1937): 164–65, and see Geoffrey Elton, *"The Body of the Whole Realm": Parliament and Representation in Medieval and Tudor England* (Charlottesville, 1969), 15.

43. Chrimes, *English Constitutional Ideas*, 99–126 passim.

44. As translated in Bertie Wilkinson, *Constitutional History of England in the Fifteenth Century (1399–1485)* (1964), 303. Original text in Chrimes, *English Constitutional Ideas*, 116.

45. Chrimes and Brown, *Select Documents*, 260–61.

46. Ibid.; Wilkinson, *Constitutional History.*

47. Chrimes, *English Constitutional Ideas*, 106–15; Bertie Wilkinson, "The Deposition of Richard II and the Accession of Henry IV," *English Historical Review* 54 (1939): 215–39. Chrimes and Brown, *Select Documents*, 350–53. Wilkinson, *Constitutional History*, 398–439; cf. Bertie Wilkinson, ed., *The Creation of Medieval Parliaments* (New York, 1972), 91–102, 109–13.

48. See pp. 87–88, 101–04.

49. Elton, *"Body of the Whole Realm,"* 7 and n. 7, 19, 26–31.

50. Ibid.; 22.

51. James Dyer, *Cy ensuont ascuns nouel cases collectes per le iades tresreuerend iudge, mounsieur Jasques Dyer* (1585), ff. 59v–60r, no. 7388 in A. W. Pollard and G. R. Redgrave, *A Short-Title Catalogue . . . , 1475–1640* (hereafter cited as STC) (1946).

52. Elton, *"Body of the Whole Realm,"* 22.

53. Caroline Skeel, "The Influence of the Writings of Sir John Fortescue," *Transactions of the Royal Historical Society*, 3rd ser. 10 (1916): 77–114. Skeel's article remains a stern warning to any attempt to downplay Fortescue.

Chapter 3

1. Weston, *English Constitutional Theory*. Her relevant underlying articles are "Beginnings of the Classical Theory of the English Constitution," *Proceedings of the American Philosophical Society* 100 (April 1966): 133–44, and "The Theory of Mixed Monarchy Under Charles I and After," *English Historical Review* 75 (1960): 426–43.

2. R. W. K. Hinton, "The Decline of Parliamentary Government under Elizabeth I and the Early Stuarts," *Cambridge Historical Journal* 13 (1957): 122, and idem, "English Constitutional Theories from Sir John Fortescue to Sir John Eliot," *English Historical Review* 75 (1960): 410–17; Pocock, *Machiavellian Moment*, 354–55. See also Hanson, *From Kingdom to Commonwealth*, 249 and n. 109. Cf. Hume's judgment on the three estates of king, Lords, Commons, quoted in Chapter 2.

3. Weston, "Beginnings," 137.

4. Weston, *English Constitutional Theory*, 22.

5. New evidence notably on and about John Hooker (see n. 72) and Thomas Egerton, Lord Ellesmere, in Louis A. Knafla, *Law and Politics in Jacobean England: the Tracts of Lord Chancellor Ellesmere* (Cambridge, 1977), 80–81, 254, 307, for the sixteenth and early seventeenth centuries; for 1640–1642 see Michael J. Mendle, "Politics and Political Thought, 1640–42," in *The Origins of the English Civil War*, ed. Conrad Russell (1973), 219–45.

6. Weston and Greenberg, *Subjects and Sovereigns*, 40–41, 284.

7. Weston, *English Constitutional Theory*, 27 and n. 34. Since then the matter has received greater attention, albeit without greater perceptiveness: Weston and Greenberg, *Subjects and Sovereigns*, and Weston, "Concepts of Estates in Stuart Political Thought," in *Representative Institutions in Theory and Practice, Studies Presented to the International Commission for the History of Representative and Parliamentary Institutions, no. 39* (Brussels, 1970), 87–130.

8. In the *Discourses*, Machiavelli wrote of "tre stati" of "Principato, Ottimati, e Popolare." Elsewhere he glossed the latter two as "qualità." Of course, he meant by "stato"—in this instance—a kind or form of government, as elsewhere he wrote of "lo stato regio" and "lo stato populare." He did not intend "estate" in the northern European sense. Machiavelli's first English translator, Edward Dacres, was careful on this point, more notable inasmuch as Dacres often reached for the nearest cognate in his able if literal translation of the *Discourses*: "three kinds of state." See Niccolò Machiavelli, *Opere*, ed. Mario Bonfantini (Milan, 1963), 96, 99 (bk. 1, chap. 2); 142 (bk. 1, chap. 18). Cf. idem, *Machiavels discourses upon the first decade of T. Livius*, trans. Edward Dacres (1636), 10, 16.

9. Charles I, *His maiesties declaration concerning his subiectes in Scotland* (1640), 22–23; this reiteration is only a part of a longer story. See Chapter 6.

10. For Hall, see pp. 61–62; for Ellesmere, Chapter 5.

11. For this side of Fortescue see Stanley Bertram Chrimes, "Sir John Fortescue and His Theory of Dominion," *Transactions of the Royal Historical Society,* 4th ser. 17 (1934): 117–47, and idem, *English Constitutional Ideas,* conclusion: The "Spirit" of the Constitution; Felix Gilbert, "Fortescue's 'Dominium Regale et Politicum,'" *Medievalia et Humanistica,* fasc. 2 (1944): 88–97. For his influence see Sir John Fortescue, *De Laudibus Legum Angliae,* ed. and trans. Stanley Bertram Chrimes (Cambridge, 1942), civ–cvii, and the still commanding article of Skeel, "Influence of Fortescue."

12. Thomas Elyot, *The boke named the governour* (1531; facsimile reprint, Menston, Yorks., 1970).

13. The early, very limited English dictionaries of the seventeenth century, from Robert Cawdrey's *Table alphabetical . . . of hard vsvall English wordes* (1604) on, gave due attention to these words.

14. Elyot, *Boke,* ff. 1, 2, 6, 7.

15. Thomas Starkey, *England in the Reign of King Henry the Eighth. A Dialogue between Cardinal Pole and Thomas Lupset,* ed. J. M. Cowper (1872), 181.

16. Ibid., 169–70, 181–83.

17. Weston, "Beginnings," 137.

18. Weston, *English Constitutional Theory,* 15.

19. The Fleet, ca. 20 November. Stephen Gardiner, *Letters of Stephen Gardiner,* ed. James Arthur Muller (Cambridge, 1933), 420–21. See Franklin LeVan Baumer, *The Early Tudor Theory of Kingship* (1940; reprint ed., New York, 1966), 150. The letter had considerable currency through publication by John Foxe in *Actes and monuments* (1563), 746.

20. Stephen Gardiner, *A Machiavellian Treatise,* ed. and trans. Peter Samuel Donaldson (Cambridge, 1974), 144–45.

21. Henry Ellis, ed., *Original Letters Illustrative of English History,* 2nd ser., 4 vols. (1827), 2:187–95.

22. Stephen Gardiner, *De vera obedientia* (1553; reprint ed., Leeds, 1966).

23. Winthrop S. Hudson's *John Ponet (1516?–1556), Advocate of Limited Monarchy* (Chicago, 1942) contains a photographic facsimile. To facilitate reference to any text, I have used the original signatures.

24. Gen. 9:6.

25. John Ponet, *A shorte treatise of politike power* ([Strasburg?] 1556), A4 recto. Here and in later citations printers' abbreviations are silently expanded.

26. Ibid., A4 verso, A 5.

27. Weston, "Beginnings," 139.

28. Ponet argues that resistance to oppressors is the justifying function of nobility; in the extreme case true nobility is founded in tyrannicide. Only if the nobility fails does a private man have the right and duty to kill a governor. But that is the present case. After a reminder in the manner of John Ball that all men "came of one man and woman," Ponet describes the attributes, in his view, of the

contemporary nobility: "their lusty hawking and hunting, nimble dicing and conning, carding, their fine singing and dancing, their open bragging and swearing, their false fleering and flattering, their subtle piking and stealing, their cruel poling and piling, their merciless man murdering, their unnatural destroying of their natural country men, and traitorous betraying of their country" (*Shorte treatise,* G7 recto). I have repunctuated, substituting commas for a series of rhetorical question marks; I have read the original "fliering" as a variant of fleering.

29. Geoffrey Elton, ed., *The Tudor Constitution* (Cambridge, 1968), 16.

30. John Aylmer, *An harborowe for faithfull and trewe subiectes* (Strasbourg [*sic*: London], 1559), H4 recto.

31. Ibid., H3 recto.

32. Ibid., but omitted in Elton's excerpt.

33. Ibid.

34. Ibid., omitted by Elton.

35. See Aristotle, *Politics,* ed. and trans. Sir Ernest Baker (New York, 1962), bk. 2, chap. 1, 5–11. According to Weston, Aylmer was "familiar" with the *Politics*; see Weston, *English Constitutional Theory,* 17, n. 16.

36. Aylmer, *An harborowe,* H3 recto, emphasis added; Elton omits the first three words.

37. Ibid.

38. Elton, *Tudor Constitution,* 11, n. 1. The phrases "in my judgment" and the vague "those that" make little sense if one supposes that they refer to a group of speakers whose views were accepted by Henry; surely these words are an *apologia* for a once-lost cause. My view accords with that of Joel Hurstfield, *Freedom, Corruption and Government in Elizabethan England* (Cambridge, Mass., 1973), 39–40. But cf. Rudolph W. Heinze, *The Proclamations of the Tudor Kings* (Cambridge, 1976), 153–77.

39. Ibid., 28. The act was repealed *in toto* in 1 Edw. VI.

40. Aylmer, *An harborowe,* omitted by Elton.

41. Ibid., H4 recto, emphasis added; "But the state," etc. omitted by Elton.

42. Martin Marprelate, *O read ouer D. John Bridges* [the Epitome] (1588), E1 verso. This and other Marprelate tracts have been consulted in the Scolar Press facsimile edition, *The Marprelate Tracts [1588–1589]* (Menston, Yorks., 1970).

43. Weston and Greenberg, *Subjects and Sovereigns,* 273, n. 24.

44. John Strype, *Works,* 21 vols. in 25 (Oxford, 1812–1840), 8:16; Felicity Heal, *Of Prelates and Princes: A Study of the Economic and Social Position of the Tudor Episcopate* (Cambridge, 1980), 216.

45. Smith, *De republica,* xxvii–xxix.

46. Hinton, "English Constitutional Theories," 420, with useful historiographic summary, 418–19.

47. J. W. Allen, *A History of Political Thought in the Sixteenth Century* (1961), 263.

48. Weston, *English Constitutional Theory,* 16 and n. 15; Weston and Greenberg, *Subjects and Sovereigns,* 10, 12.

49. In a letter of 1565, Smith gave some account of his purposes consonant with the account given here. Although no man will admit to inconsistency, Smith came close, admitting he lacked scholarly resources to fill "gaps." For the letter, see Smith, *De republica,* xiii–xiv, or Mary Dewar, *Sir Thomas Smith: A Tudor Intellectual in Office* (1964), 111–12. Alston's treatment remains the most sensitive.

50. Smith, *De republica,* bk. 3, chap. 9.

51. Chrimes, *English Constitutional Ideas,* 323.

52. In *De republica Anglorum* Smith admits to no such purpose. But Smith is a notable figure in the history of linguistics. For this side, see Dewar, *Thomas Smith,* 16–20 and 214 for bibliography; Bror Danielsson, *Sir Thomas Smith, 1513–1577. Literary and Linguistic Works (1542, 1549, 1568)* (Stockholm, 1963). Interestingly, Smith and Gardiner had a controversy over Greek pronunciation in the 1540s.

53. Smith, *De republica,* bk. 1, chaps. 1, 2.

54. Ibid., chaps. 3–5.

55. Ibid., chap. 6.

56. Ibid., chaps. 7, 8.

57. Ibid., chap. 9 (history), chap. 15 (nature); bk. 2, chaps. 3, 4 (current practice); the quotation is from bk. 1, chap. 9.

58. Hinton, "English Constitutional Theories," 420; Weston, *English Constitutional Ideas,* 16.

59. Smith, *De republica,* bk. 1, chaps. 10, 16.

60. Ibid., chap. 16.

61. Ibid. ("four sorts"); cf. xvi and app. B. On the complicated matter of the borrowings, the most recent statement is in William Harrison, *The Description of England,* ed. Georges Edelen (Ithaca, 1968); see his index s.v. "Smith."

62. Smith, *De republica,* bk. 1, chap. 18.

63. Ibid., bk. 2, chap. 1.

64. Ibid.

65. Ibid., bk. 1, chap. 7.

66. Harrison, *Description,* 149, 152.

67. Cf. Smith, *De republica,* bk. 2, chap. 1: "For as in war where the king himself in person, the nobility, the rest of the gentility, and the yeomanry are is the force and power of England: so in peace and consultation where the prince is to give life and the highest commandment, the barony for the nobility and higher, the knights, esquires, gentlemen and commons for the lower part of the commonwealth, the bishops for the clergy." And see Lambarde: "Like as in war, where the

king is present in person; and with him, the nobility, gentry, and yeomanry; there is the force and puissance of the realm: Even so in peace, wheresoever the prince is as the head, to give life, (that is to say) to yield the highest and last assent; and where the barony, consisting of the lords spiritual, and temporal; and the commonalty, made up of the knights, and burgesses." The three estates are found repeatedly after this passage. William Lambarde, *Archeion, or A Discourse upon the High Courts of Justice in England,* ed. Charles Howard McIlwain and Paul L. Ward (Cambridge, Mass., 1957), 126, 128–30. The borrowing was not noticed by Lambarde's editors.

68. Smith, *De republica,* bk. 2, chaps. 1, 4.

69. Ibid. The point is not certain but can be seen in Smith's puzzlement about the extension of martial law to situations short of "open war" (bk. 2, chap. 3) and in the passage in bk. 1, chap. 9, touching King John's liege homage to Innocent III, noted and emphasized by Hinton, "English Constitutional Theories," 420. But Hinton's contention that this is the most "extreme statement in the book" is incorrect. Smith's point is merely that John's action was not binding on him or his successors because it was not an act of Parliament. Without an act of Parliament, how else could a king in war and diplomacy be bound? If he could not bind himself, how could he bind his successor? The point is not a general one about the power of the king-in-Parliament to do what the king alone cannot, but about how the king alone can maneuver himself, if he wants to, out of his own free will. And Smith at least implies that such a deed is possible, and in that limited sense law controls prerogative. However, Smith's remark comes in the context of an argument that England is a monarchy because its kings, with this one exception, never received investiture from pope, emperor, or foreign prince. The passage calls to mind the preamble of the Act in Restraint of Appeals and raises the question whether even an act of Parliament could undo the imperial dignity of the crown. It is hard to believe that Smith would have believed that such a deed was legally possible; it is the political equivalent of a right to self-mutilation.

70. Smith, *De republica,* bk. 2, chap. 3. The dispensing power as a factor in political thought is usefully discussed in Weston and Greenberg, *Subjects and Sovereigns,* 22–34.

71. In this analysis I adhere to the general tenor of the argument of McIlwain, *Constitutionalism.*

72. See the very fine edition of Vernon F. Snow, *Parliament in Elizabethan England: John Hooker's Order and Usage* (New Haven, 1977).

73. Ibid., 3–28.

74. Ibid., 45, 122 and nn. 1, 2.

75. Ibid., 50–57; Maud V. Clarke, *Medieval Representation and Consent, A Study of Early Parliaments in England and Ireland, with Special Reference to the* Modus Tenendi Parliamentum (1936; reprint ed., New York, 1964). See also

J. G. A. Pocock, *The Ancient Constitution and the Feudal Law* (New York, 1967), 43, for seventeenth-century estimations of the *Modus*.

76. Snow, *Parliament in Elizabethan England*, 145.

77. Ibid., 133; Clarke, *Medieval Representation*, 388.

78. William Prynne, *The fourth part of a brief register . . . of parliamentary writs* (1664), 593, 604−05. Even though Prynne was a great proponent of the rendition of the estates as king, Lords, and Commons—even to the refashioning of the evidence—his hatred of the *Modus* knew no bounds.

79. Clarke, *Medieval Representation*, 382−83; Snow, *Parliament in Elizabethan England*, 141−42.

80. Snow, *Parliament in Elizabethan England*, 78.

81. Ibid., 181. Hooker regarded "degree" and "estates" as synonymous in this context (ibid., 152).

82. Ibid., 152−53.

83. Lambarde, *Archeion*, 132; Snow, *Parliament in Elizabethan England*, 95−96.

84. Lambarde, who believed parliaments of king, Lords, and Commons were immemorial, would not humor the doubts of "any man" who should "suspect, that any of the two lower estates of the assembly" derived authority from later, post-Conquest laws (Lambarde, *Archeion*, 138, cf. 129). Arthur Hall did just that, at least with respect to the lower house and perhaps—by virtue of the argument from conquest—to both houses. Lambarde had to be reticent ("any man"): Hall was Burghley's ward; *Archeion* was dedicated to Robert Cecil and perhaps was originally intended for his father. See Wilbur Dunkel, *William Lambarde, Elizabethan Jurist, 1536−1601* (New Brunswick, 1965), 130. A somewhat better study of Lambarde is Retha Warnicke, *William Lambarde, Elizabethan Antiquary, 1536−1601* [1973], but see Snow, *Parliament in Elizabethan England*, 89 n., for bibliographical caveats.

85. Sir Simonds D'Ewes, *Journals of all the parliaments . . . of Queen Elizabeth*, rev. Paul Bowes (1682), 350.

86. See Chapter 4.

87. On Hall, the basic but unsatisfactory work remains Herbert Gladstone Wright, *Life and Works of Arthur Hall of Grantham* (Manchester, 1919); see also J. E. Neale, *Elizabeth I and her Parliaments*, 2 vols. (1969), 1:247−48, 253−57, 260−61, 333−45, 407−10; and Snow, *Parliament in Elizabethan England*, 98−101.

88. Arthur Hall, *An Admonition by the Father of F. A.*, was an appendix to the account of his privilege case, *An Account of a Quarrel between A. H., Esq., and Melchisedech Mallorie, Gent.*, reprinted in *Miscellanea antiqua Anglicana*, ed. Robert Triphook (1816).

89. Hall, *Miscellanea*, 78−81.

90. The retraction is in H. G. Wright, *Arthur Hall*, 181; reprinted and

miscited as "Herbert" by Snow, *Parliament in Elizabethan England*, 107–08. This admittedly obscure passage, probably difficult by design, was received with varying interpretations. My reading concurs with Weston and Greenberg, *Subjects and Sovereigns*, 283–84, n. 15, that Hall changed his enumeration of the estates; Snow, *Parliament in Elizabethan England*, 106–08, argues the contrary. It does not matter, however, to the present argument which view is correct, for if Hall did not exchange his system of estates, he smirked at the kings, Lords, Commons plan: the three estates "as they are called." The clerk was not taken with Hall's sincerity; see Neale, *Elizabeth and her Parliaments*, 1:407.

91. Neale, *Elizabeth and her Parliaments*, 1:407.

Chapter 4

1. Elton, *"Body of the Whole Realm."*

2. Richard Bancroft, *A sermon preached at Paules Crosse the 9 Februarie, . . . 1588* (1588/1589). Notably, the claim of a divine right is what caught the eye of many puritans; see Stuart Barton Babbage, *Puritanism and Richard Bancroft* (1962), 27–29, and W. D. J. Cargill Thompson, "Sir Francis Knollys' Campaign against the *Jure Divino* Theory of Episcopacy," in *The Dissenting Tradition: Essays for Leland H. Carlson*, ed. C. Robert Cole and Michael E. Moody (Athens, Ohio, 1975), 39–77.

3. Walter Travers, *A full and plaine declaration of ecclesiasticall discipline* (1574), 55, 158–61, 177–79. Travers's scheme of presbyterian discipline limited the eldership to pastors and doctors; the laity entered only as "the people."

4. Claire Cross, *The Royal Supremacy in the Elizabethan Church* (New York, 1969), 24–25; Elton, *Tudor Constitution*, 330–35.

5. Cartwright in John Whitgift, *The Works of John Whitgift*, ed. John Ayre, 3 vols. (Cambridge, 1851–1853), 1:390.

6. Ibid., 1:393, 2:554.

7. For the very different texture of the presbyterian movement *in toto*, see Patrick Collinson, *The Elizabethan Puritan Movement* (1967) and idem, "Episcopacy and Reform in England in the Later Sixteenth Century," in *Studies in Church History*, vol. 3, ed. G. J. Cuming (Leiden, 1966), 91–125.

8. Whitgift wrote of the "whole state of the clergy of greatest account," in apposition to "a few persons" who supported presbyterianism, but he never seems to have thought that presbyterian ministers were not a part of or were in principle against the idea "of the whole state of the clergy"; Babbage, *Puritanism and Bancroft*, 19.

9. James Kirk, "'The Polities of the Best Reformed Kirks': Scottish Achievements and English Aspirations in Church Government after the Reformation," *Scottish Historical Review* 59 (1980): 22–53.

10. Melville's position was clearly indicated in the *Second book of discipline,* especially in chap. 1, nos. 4 and 5. For a text see David Calderwood, *The History of the Kirk of Scotland,* ed. Thomas Thomson, 8 vols. (Edinburgh, 1842–1849), 3:530–55. It is characteristic of the hold of the figure of the three estates that the *Second book* concluded by showing the "utility that shall flow from the reformation to all estates" (Calderwood, *History,* 554).

For recent doubts about the hold of the two-kingdom theory on Scottish thought see Arthur Williamson, *Scottish National Consciousness in the Age of James VI* (Edinburgh, 1979).

11. *Acts and Proceedings of the General Assemblies of the Kirk of Scotland from the Year M.D.L.X.,* ed. Thomas Thomson, 3 vols. (Edinburgh, 1839, 1840, 1845), 2:474.

12. Gordon Donaldson, "Lord Chancellor Glamis and Theodore Beza," *Scottish Historical Society Miscellany* 9 (1951): 97, 99 n. 1.

13. Ibid., 103.

14. Julian H. Franklin, ed. and trans., *Constitutionalism and Resistance in the Sixteenth Century: Three Treatises by Hotman, Beza, and Mornay* (New York, 1969), 113, 118–29. Beza did not define the components of the estates, but he did separate them from the king; the estates were subjects. And Beza approvingly noted later medieval assemblies of estates in which the clergy participated. Additionally, he surveyed the estates of other countries; these included the clergy.

15. François Hotman, *Francogallia,* Latin text by Ralph E. Giesey; trans. J. H. M. Salmon; ed. Giesey and Salmon (Cambridge, 1972), 292–95. But see 444–47, where the clergy are recognized as having been one of the estates after their wealth had grown excessive.

16. Cited ibid., 75.

17. See Chapter 2, n. 37.

18. Franklin, *Constitutionalism and Resistance,* 164.

19. James Melville, *Autobiography and Diary of Mr. James Melvill with a Continuation of the Diary,* ed. Robert Pitcairn (Edinburgh, 1842), 118–19. See the account in Calderwood, *History,* 3:578, for the seeming sweetness and moderation of the proposal.

20. Calderwood, *History,* 3:578.

21. Melville, *Autobiography,* 119.

22. John Bruce, ed., *Letters of Queen Elizabeth and King James VI of Scotland* (1849), 63–64. Gordon Donaldson, "Foundations of Anglo-Scottish Union," in *Elizabethan Government and Society,* ed. Stanley Thomas Bindoff, Joel Hurstfield, and C. H. Williams (1961), 304–05.

23. Gordon Donaldson, "The Polity of the Scottish Church, 1560–1600," *Records of the Scottish Church Historical Society* 1 (1953): 212–26. For *stylus curiae,* see Chapter 6, p. 119.

24. *Acts of the Parliaments of Scotland,* ed. Thomas Thomson and Cosmo Innes, 11 vols. (Edinburgh, 1814–1844), 3:293. Hereafter cited as APS.

25. APS, 3:292–93 (the first of Black Acts); see Gordon Donaldson, *The Scottish Reformation* (Cambridge, 1960), 212–13. Although intended to apply to a later moment, 1596, Maurice Lee's remark that episcopacy for James was "a means to . . . the exaltation of the power of the king" is exactly right; see Lee's "James VI and the Revival of Episcopacy in Scotland: 1596–1600," *Church History* 43 (1974): 51.

26. Calderwood, *History,* 4:451.

27. Ibid., 4:460.

28. Gordon Donaldson, "Scottish Presbyterian Exiles in England, 1584–8," *Records of the Scottish Church Historical Society* 14 (1963): 67–80.

29. Gordon Donaldson, "The Attitude of Whitgift and Bancroft to the Scottish Church," *Transactions of the Royal Historical Society,* 4th ser. 24 (1942): 95–115 passim.

30. Pierpont Morgan Library (New York), Ms. MA 276 (hereafter cited as PML), 9. Neale identified these speeches of Throckmorton's in *Elizabeth and her Parliaments,* 2:9, 110–11, 150–52, 169–73.

31. PML, 23, abbreviations expanded.

32. Leland Carlson, *Martin Marprelate, Gentleman: Master Job Throckmorton Laid Open in His Colors* (San Marino, Calif., 1981), 6, 106 and n. 31, 107, correcting Neale, *Elizabeth and her Parliaments,* 2:164 and 174.

33. Martin Marprelate, *Hay any worke for cooper* (1588/[1589]), 27. Carlson, *Martin Marprelate.* A preliminary report on Carlson's research appeared as "Martin Marprelate: His Identity and His Satire," in Carlson and Ronald Paulson, *English Satire* (Los Angeles, 1972), 3–53. In both works Carlson used Throckmorton's speeches as important texts in his efforts to identify Martin.

34. [Richard Bancroft, supposed author,] *Tracts ascribed to Richard Bancroft,* ed. Albert Peel (Cambridge, 1952), 42. Bancroft, citing Foxe in support of episcopacy, wrote of the four "degrees" (here, archbishops, bishops, ministers, deacons) of the "ecclesiastical estate" (ibid., 137).

35. Text in Calderwood, *History,* 4:254–69; see especially 256, 259–61, 264–65.

36. Bancroft, *Sermon,* 72–73; see also 82, 84.

37. Richard Bancroft, *Daungerous positions . . .* (1593), 128; see also 20–21, 44–45, 137.

38. [Richard Bancroft,] *A survey of the pretended holy discipline* (1593), 300–306.

39. Ibid., 7–38; quoted phrases from 7, 9, 12, 14.

40. Richard Hooker, *Of the Laws of Ecclesiastical Polity,* ed. Ronald Bayne, 2 vols. (1907), 1:356 (bk. 3, xi, 20).

41. Thomas Cooper, *An admonition to the people of England* (1589), 87, see 82.

42. Bilson, for all his hostility to presbyterianism, had the gravest doubts about the civil position of the clergy. See his *True difference* . . . (1586), bk. 3, 302, where the Parliament is called the "temporal states of this realm," and 308, where the clergy are said to have no negative voice, by English law, and no right whatsoever to make civil laws, by the law of God. However, Bilson was unremittingly firm on the royal supremacy (bk. 3, 293–312 ff.) and in bk. 3, 308, seemed to doubt the historical right of the commons to make laws. For the prosecutions under 23 Eliz. c. 2, see Carlson, *Martin Marprelate*, 78, 80–81.

43. Cooper, *Admonition*, 92–93.

44. Ibid., 160.

45. Marprelate, *Hay any worke*, 25–26; cf. Cooper, *Admonition*, 87.

46. Marprelate, *Hay any worke*, 26.

47. Ibid., cf. Cooper, *Admonition*, 92.

48. See pp. 98–102.

49. Marprelate, [the Epitome], D3 verso, cf. E2 recto.

50. Aylmer's true position was evident even in Martin's quotation: every city should have its "superintendent." That word was used widely among the English, as among the German reformers, to denote the godly bishop (episcopus=supervisor); ibid., D4 verso.

51. Ibid., E1, recto and verso.

52. Ibid., E1 verso–E2 recto; cf. John Aylmer, *An harborowe for faithfull and trewe subiectes* (1559), H3 recto.

53. John Penry, *Th' appelation of John Penri* ([La Rochelle], 1589), 32–33.

54. Paul L. Hughes and James F. Larkin, eds., *Tudor Royal Proclamations*, 3 vols. (New Haven, 1964–1969), 3:34–35 (no. 709).

55. Carlson, *Martin Marprelate*, 112–15; on 114 he identifies the phrase "ancient orders" as "the bishops in the House of Lords." Carlson's account apparently is based upon Matthew Sutcliffe's slightly ambiguous account in *An answere vnto a certaine calumnious letter published by M. Iob Throckmorton* . . . (1595), especially f. 80 recto.

56. Martin Marprelate, *O read ouer D. John Bridges* [the Epistle] (1588), 6: books have been called in by the bishops "as things against their state." Their "state" may only mean their "eminence"; in any event, it has no argumentative force.

57. See Carlson, *Martin Marprelate*, 117 and n. 57. The STC (no. 1521) gives a date of 1590. Carlson's admittedly subjective criteria of attribution are much weakened by the differences in style that separate this tract from the rest of the Throckmorton/Martin oeuvre; see Carlson's own account, *Martin Marprelate*, 117–19.

58. [Henry Barrow?] *A petition* . . . ([Middelburg,] 1592), 17–18, 34–35. Cf. 7, 8, 27–29, and the implied parliamentary supremacy in legislation, 40–41.

59. Sutcliffe, *Answere to a certaine libel supplicatorie, or rather diffamatory* (1592), 48–49; see also 50, 65–68 (a reply to the historical argument), 140, 190 (an argument that presbyterianism would "overthrow infinite statutes, most of the common laws . . . finally the whole state," a position not unlike Cooper's), 194 (Scotland).

60. On Maitland and the politics of this period, see Maurice Lee, *John Maitland of Thirlestane* (Princeton, 1959).

61. Donaldson, "Attitude of Whitgift and Bancroft," 106–13; Calderwood, *History,* 5:77–78, 118–24.

62. Calderwood, *History,* 6:387.

63. Donaldson, "Polity," 225. My use of Donaldson in this section is extensive.

64. See p. 94.

65. APS, 4:282.

66. APS, 3:443.

67. Calderwood, *History,* 5:72–73 (emphasis added).

68. APS, 3:541–43.

69. This paragraph and the next is based upon my examination of APS.

70. For 1606, see Calderwood, *History,* 6:530–31; for 1630s see Chapter 5.

71. See p. 95.

72. Lee, "James VI and Revival," 52.

73. Ibid., 53; Calderwood, *History,* 5:437–39, 453–59.

74. Lee, "James VI and Revival," 56–61.

75. APS, 4:130.

76. Calderwood, *History,* 5:681. This reaction argues against Lee's contention that only much later was the act of 1597 understood as a continuous policy; Lee, "James VI and Revival," 51.

77. *Calendar of State Papers . . . Scotland, 1597–1603,* ed. John Duncan Mackie, 2 parts (Edinburgh, 1969), pt. 1, 146–48, 156–60.

78. Calderwood, *History,* 5:694.

79. Ibid., 694–95.

80. See *Trew law . . .* in James I, *The Political Works of James I,* ed. Charles Howard McIlwain (Cambridge, Mass., 1918), 62.

81. Ibid., 64.

82. Ibid., 22.

83. Ibid., 24. James's remarks were even stronger in 1598 than in the English edition of 1603 because the original text did not excuse the tumultuous Scottish reformation as being "extraordinarily wrought by God," as was inserted in 1603. See the edition: James I, *Basilikon doron,* ed. James Craigie (Edinburgh, 1944), 22–23.

84. James I, *Political Works,* 26.

85. James I, *Basilikon doron,* (Edinburgh, 1950), 4.

86. Ibid., 8–13; cf. John Hill Burton and David Masson, eds., *Register of the*

Privy Council of Scotland, 1545–1625, 14 vols. (Edinburgh, 1877–1898), 6:34–35 and n.

87. Calderwood, *History,* 5:74–75.

88. See James I, *Political Works,* 26, for the order; for Gledstanes see Annie Cameron, ed., *The Warrender Papers,* 2 vols. (Edinburgh, 1932), 2:381–83.

89. Calderwood, *History,* 5:757, 761.

90. Ibid., 5:681–82. This synod was preoccupied with the discussion of bishops' votes in Parliament.

Chapter 5

1. On union see David Harris Willson, *King James VI and I* (New York, 1967), 249–57; idem, "King James I and Anglo-Scottish Unity," in Aiken and Henning, *Conflict in Stuart England,* 41–55; Donaldson, "Foundations of Union," 282–314; Maurice Lee, *Government by Pen: Scotland under James VI and I* (Urbana, 1981), 31–38; Joel J. Epstein, "Francis Bacon and the Issue of Union, 1603–08," *Huntington Library Quarterly* 33 (1969–1970): 121–32.

2. *Constitutions & Canons Ecclesiastical 1604,* ed. H. A. Wilson (Oxford, 1923), canon 55.

3. If, as Mark Curtis has argued, Hampton Court was a less-than-total triumph of the bishops for the support of James, it was a very well-kept secret, not least by James himself, whose proclamations leave little doubt about the message he wished to transmit to the public. See Mark Curtis, "Hampton Court Conference and its Aftermath," *History* 46 (1961): 1–16; James F. Larkin and Paul L. Hughes, *Royal Proclamations of King James I, 1603–1625* (Oxford, 1973), 74–79, 87–90, and the pre–Hampton Court proclamation against seditious reform of the church, 60–63, to see that the result was all but inevitable, no matter how much James wished to appear evenhanded. William Barlow's report of the conference, of course, was officially sanctioned: *The summe and substance of the conference . . . at Hampton Court* (1604).

4. Joseph Foster, ed., *Alumni Oxonienis . . . 1500-1714,* 4 vols. (1891–1892; reprint ed., 4 vols. in 2, Nendeln, Lichtenstein, 1968), 4:1432. The account of Stoughton in P. W. Hasler, ed., *The History of Parliament: the House of Commons 1558–1603,* 3 vols. (1981), 3:454, casts some slight doubt on the identification of Stoughton the M.P. with the civil lawyer. But the author of *An assertion* was a civilian, and the account does accept that Stoughton the M.P. was its author. The assumption of two William Stoughtons so closely related in age, career, and values is farfetched.

5. Patrick Collinson, ed., *Letters of Thomas Wood, Puritan, 1566–1577,* in *Bulletin of the Institute of Historical Research Special Suppl.,* no. 5 (Nov. 1960), x, xxxvi.

6. William Stoughton, *An assertion for true and Christian church-policie* (1604; reprint eds., 1642), A4 recto. (This is the 1642 edition with a fleur-de-lis ornament with the wreathed motto, "In Domino Confido." See also n. 18, below.) However, this preface erroneously also attributes *A covnter-poyson, modestly written for the time* [1584] to Stoughton. The tract usually is ascribed to Dudley Fenner, as a later ms. note to a copy of this edition in the Union Theological Seminary Library points out. Stoughton certainly could not have described himself as a "poor minister," as is done in *A covnter-poyson*, 151.

7. *An abstract* . . . (n.p. [1584]) was notable for its use of civil and canon law to combat Stoughton's opponents in terms of a learning that he perhaps uniquely shared with them. However, *An abstract* did not directly raise the question of the episcopal or clerical claim to be an estate, another indication that the issue arose in England only in the late 1580s.

8. D'Ewes, *Journals of parliaments*, 340, 349, 373.

9. Roland G. Usher, *The Rise and Fall of the High Commission*, with a new intro. by Philip Tyler (Oxford, 1968), 187–88; Brian Levack, *The Civil Lawyers in England, 1603–1641: A Political Study* (Oxford, 1973), 50 n. 2, 164; Babbage, *Puritanism and Bancroft*, 139, 144.

10. STC, 2nd ed., rev. by W. A. Jackson, F. S. Ferguson, and Katharine Pantzer, vol. 2: I–Z (1976), 368 (no. 23318). In addition to the Oxford copies noted in the STC, the copy in the Union Theological Seminary Library was similarly defaced; the Huntington copy in the STC microfilms has no preface at all.

11. Collinson, *Elizabethan Puritan Movement*, 432.

12. Stoughton, *An assertion* (1604 edition), title page; cf. 10–11.

13. Ibid., 165–87, especially 165–69, 176.

14. Ibid., 349–51.

15. Ibid., 351–56, 362–63.

16. Ibid., 363–64.

17. William Covell, *A modest & reasonable examination* (1604), 5.

18. Charles Ripley Gillett, ed., *Catalogue of the McAlpin Collection*, 5 vols. (New York, 1927–1930), 2:169. See the date notes in the Huntington copy in the STC microfilms.

19. For the chronology and for Spelman's remembrance, see Linda Van Norden, "Sir Henry Spelman on the Chronology of the Elizabethan College of Antiquaries," *Huntington Library Quarterly* 13 (1948–1949): 131–60. Spelman originally wrote "some mislike" and changed it to "a little mislike"; 135 and n. 25.

20. Thomas Hearne, ed., *A collection of curious discourses*, re-ed. Joseph Ayloffe, 2 vols. (1771), 1:156. On the shift to sensitive topics, see Linda Van Norden, "The Elizabethan College of Antiquaries" (Ph.D. diss., UCLA, 1946), 342–43.

21. Van Norden, "Sir Henry Spelman," 145–46.

22. See pp. 58–59, 61–62.

23. Hearne, *Curious discourses* (1775 ed.), 1:293–95.

24. Ibid., 1:281–93. This is also the attribution in BL Harl. Ms. 305. The tenor of the discourse does not sit well with Dodderidge's other attitudes.

25. Robert Bowyer, *The Parliamentary Diary of Robert Bowyer, 1606–07*, ed. David Harris Willson (Minneapolis, 1931), 202n.: "A division of tenures was alleged by Mr. Tate which was triple that tenures were either from almoin, knights service or socage called in latin 1 *oratores*, 2 *billatores* [*sic*], 3 *laboratores.*" See also his interesting list of queries on the ancient Britons made to the Welsh antiquary William Jones; Hearne, *Curious discourses* (1771 ed.), 1:126–27.

26. Hearne, *Curious discourses* (1775 ed.), 1:299–303.

27. Ibid., 1:308–10.

28. Van Norden, "Sir Henry Spelman," 145–46.

29. Andrewes's specialty was extracting submissions from already marked men; Carlson, *Martin Marprelate*, 79, 81, 85.

30. This paragraph and the two following draw entirely on Lee, *Government by Pen*, 31–34, 40–42, 47–56, 60–68. Quotation from 50.

31. Ibid., 63.

32. APS, 4:281–82.

33. Lee, *Government by Pen*, 63–64. See also A. Ian Dunlop, "The Polity of the Scottish Church, 1600–1637," *Records of the Scottish Church Historical Society* 12 (1956): 161–84; Walter Roland Foster, "The Operation of Presbyteries in Scotland, 1600–1638," *Records of the Scottish Church Historical Society* 15 (1965): 21–33.

34. So described by Gordon Donaldson, *Scotland: James V to James VII* (Edinburgh, 1965), 204.

35. Melville, *Autobiography,* 664. Of course, one must take this description with a grain of salt.

36. Ibid., 653. Cf. John Spottiswoode's summary of this and the other sermons in his *History of the Church of Scotland*, ed. Michael Russell, 3 vols. (Edinburgh, 1847–1851), 3:177. William Barlow's sermon (STC 1452) was printed as *The first of the foure sermons . . . concerning the antiquity and superiority of bishops: Sept. 21. 1606* (1607).

37. William Barlow, *The sermon preached at Paules Crosse, the tenth day of November* [1605] (1606), D2 verso; cf. E3 verso, for an attempt to link the ideas of Knox and Buchanan to the Gunpowder Plot. This sermon, preached on the first Sunday after the plot, used many official documents.

38. John Buckeridge, *A sermon preached at Hampton Court before the king* (1606), A3 recto.

39. Launcelot Andrewes, *A sermon preached before the kings maiestie, at Hampton Court . . . the 28. of September, Anno. 1606* (1606), 8.

40. John King, *The fourth sermon preached at Hampton Court* . . . (Oxford, 1606).

41. John King, *A sermon preached at Whitehall the 5. day of November* (Oxford, 1608), 20, cf. 28, "Priests are foundations. They are *fulcra reip.*," which establishes beyond doubt what his three estates were. Conrad Russell first called my attention to this sermon.

42. Oliver Ormerod, *The picture of a puritan* (1605), E1 recto; Jon Dove, *A defence of church government* (1606), A4 verso, 10–11.

43. Peter Heylyn, *Cyprianus Anglicus* (1668), bk. 1, 48–49; King, *Fourth sermon*, 48–49.

44. Melville, *Autobiography*, 666–67.

45. Calderwood, *History*, 6:597–98.

46. *The Convocation Book of M DC VI. Commonly Called Bishop Overall's Convocation Book* . . . , Library of Anglo-Catholic Theology, no. 29 (Oxford, 1844). James would not allow the book to proceed because its startling consistency would have denied him the right to meddle in the affairs of the Netherlands (see 6–8). Barlow possessed a copy of the first part of the book; John Cosin later recalled that the book was "made" by Bancroft or "some other, at his appointment" (10–12).

47. *George Downame, Two sermons* (1608), 2nd sermon, 67, 87.

48. George Meriton, *A sermon of nobility* (1607), B2 verso, E2 recto, E3 recto.

49. Launcelot Andrewes, *The Works of Launcelot Andrewes, Sometime Bishop of Winchester*, 11 vols. (1841–1872; reprint ed., New York, 1967), 5:176–77 (preached 24 March 1606/1607). See also 4:209, 224, 306, 338, 354, and sermon cited in n. 39.

50. Thomas Bayly Howell, ed., *A Complete Collection of State Trials*, 33 vols. (1809–1826), 2:428, 470. In related proceedings in 1610, by contrast, Salisbury adhered to the king's view of estates, in which he was joined by such opposition figures as James Whitelocke and Nicholas Fuller, to judge from remarks as muddy as Hakewill's. See Howell, *State Trials*, 2:486–87; E. R. Foster, *Proceedings in Parliament*, 1:31, 48, and 2:109; Samuel Rawson Gardiner, ed., *Parliamentary Debates in 1610* (1862), 24, 37.

51. See p. 153.

52. Wilfrid R. Prest, "The Art of Law and the Law of God: Sir Henry Finch (1558–1625)," in *Puritans and Revolutionaries: Essays in Seventeenth-Century History Presented to Christopher Hill*, ed. Donald Pennington and Keith Thomas (Oxford, 1978), 94–117.

53. Sir Henry Finch, *Nomotechnia* (1613), f. 21 verso.

54. Sir Henry Finch, *Law, or, a discourse thereof* (1627), 86–87.

55. Knafla, *Tracts of Ellesmere*, 80–81, 254–55, 307; Carlson, *Martin Marprelate*, 75, 268. But see also a proclamation of Ellesmere's drafting, "concerning

the choice of Knights and Burgesses for the Parliament," in Larkin and Hughes, *Royal Proclamations,* 67: the knights and burgesses "do present the body of the third estate," and Parliament was a "lawful assembly of the three estates of the realm," a phrasing that must have meant to James, if not Ellesmere, the traditional estates.

56. Nicholas Tyacke, "Puritanism, Arminianism, and Counter-Revolution," in C. Russell, *Origins,* 137.

57. Ibid., 125–27; cf. Clarendon, *History,* 1:118–20.

58. H[enry] B[urton], *Israels fast* (1628), A3 recto. The whole sermon is virulently anti-Buckingham.

59. Peter Heylyn, *Augustus* (1632), especially 2, 124, 139, 142.

60. *The stumbling-block of disobedience* . . . , in Peter Heylyn, *The historical and miscellaneous tracts* (1681), 687–707; see also 708–27. Heylyn first wrote *The stumbling-block* in 1644.

61. Cited in Chrimes, *English Constitutional Ideas,* 126.

62. John Cowell, *The interpreter* (Cambridge, 1607), s.v. "Parliament"; John Minsheu, *Ductor in linguas* (1617), col. 8995b; Sir Walter Raleigh, *The prerogative of parliaments,* in *Works,* 8 vols. (Oxford, 1829), 8:170, 197, 213. *The prerogative of parliaments* was written in 1615 and first printed in 1628; see Pierre Lefranc, *Sir Walter Raleigh écrivain: l'oeuvre et les idées* (Paris, 1968), 53–54, 56 and n. 61.

63. William Camden, *Britain, or a chorographical description,* trans. Philemon Holland (1610), 177; cf., however, 163. Camden, following Fortescue, viewed English government as a mixture of regal and political authority; Frank Smith Fussner, "William Camden's 'Discourse Concerning the Prerogative of the Crown,'" *Proceedings of the American Philosophical Society* 101 (1957): 210, 211, 212.

64. Sir Henry Spelman, *Reliquiae Spelmannianae* (1723), 62–64. Spelman, however, viewed the Commons as a latecomer: see Pocock, *Ancient Constitution,* 91–127.

Chapter 6

1. Sir Thomas Hope, *A Diary of the Public Correspondence of Sir Thomas Hope . . . , 1633–1645,* ed. Thomas Thomson (Edinburgh, 1843), 106–07.

2. Donaldson, *Scotland,* 207. For the church in early Stuart Scotland see Walter Roland Foster, *The Church Before the Covenants* (Edinburgh, 1975); Dunlop, "Polity of the Scottish Church," and W. R. Foster, "Presbyteries in Scotland." Ussher patronized a less structured but similar system in Ireland.

3. The tension of the clerical and lay or nonprofessional elements in presbyterian theory and practice is stressed by Walter Makey, *The Church of the Covenant, 1637–1651* (Edinburgh, 1979), especially 123–30. See also David Stevenson, *The Scottish Revolution 1637–1644* (New York, 1973), 109.

4. This and the next four paragraphs are most heavily indebted to Stevenson, *Scottish Revolution*, 79–127. For proepiscopal interpretation of the 1581 confession see [Walter Balcanquhall,] *A large declaration* (1639), 140.

5. Stevenson, *Scottish Revolution*, 111–12.

6. Ibid., 109.

7. On the registers see ibid., 119–20; Makey, *Church of the Covenant*, 37–38. *The principall acts of the solemne generall assembly . . . at Glasgow the xxi of November 1638* (Edinburgh, 1639) makes heavy, sometimes moving use of the lost registers.

8. [Balcanquhall,] *Large declaration*, 251, 258, 262; Archibald Johnston, *Diary of Sir Archibald Johnston of Wariston, 1632–1639*, ed. George Morison Paul (Edinburgh, 1911), 401.

9. Charles I, *His majesties proclamation in Scotland, with an explanation of the meaning of the oath and covenant* (1639; reprint ed., Amsterdam, 1974), *Explanation*, 9, 11–17.

10. *The protestation of the Generall Assemblie . . .* [29 November 1638,] (1638; reprint ed., Amsterdam, 1971), B3 verso, STC 22044.

11. [Balcanquhall,] *Large declaration*, 392.

12. Archibald Johnston, reviser, *The declinator and protestation of the sometimes pretended bishops refuted* (Edinburgh, 1639), 20, and idem, *An answer to the profession and declaration made by James Marques of Hammilton* (Edinburgh, 1639), 24, 40, 42.

13. Johnston, *Declinator and protestation*, 77 (emphasis added); the same "may be" in the same context occurs as well on 20.

14. Johnston, *Answer to the profession*, especially 42–52.

15. [Balcanquhall,] *Large declaration*, 426.

16. APS, 5:256.

17. Stevenson, *Scottish Revolution*, 170–74.

18. Ibid., 176; APS, 5:286–87.

19. Charles I, *His maiesties declaration concerning his proceeding with his subiects of Scotland* (1640; reprint ed., Amsterdam, 1971), 22–23.

20. APS, 5:288–92, 298–99, 302–03.

21. Samuel Rawson Gardiner, ed., *The Hamilton Papers, 1638–1648* (1880), 266. Cf. Stevenson, *Scottish Revolution*, 361 n. 78, and Perez Zagorin, *The Court and the Country* (New York, 1970), 104.

22. Johnston, *Diary*, 351; Allyn Bailey Forbes, ed., *Winthrop Papers* 5 vols. (Boston, 1929–1947), 3:190–93.

23. *Calendar of State Papers, Domestic Series, 1639–40,* 524. Hereafter cited as CSPD.

24. Mary Frear Keeler, *The Long Parliament, 1640–41,* Memoirs of the American Philosophical Society, vol. 36 (Philadelphia, 1954), 94 (Bagshaw), 177 (Nathaniel Fiennes), 390 (John White, 1590–1645).

25. Edward Bagshaw, *A just vindication* (1660), 12; see also 6 for a tie to Montague of Boughton and 2 for an unflattering remembrance of a "great peer" who made merry "that he had often heard of a silenced preacher, but never of a silenced reader."

26. BL Stowe Ms. 424, ff. 4b–5a (church history), f. 18b (heresy), f. 23a–28b (High Commission).

27. Ibid., f. 15 b; cf. CSPD, 1639–1640, 521.

28. Bagshaw, *Just vindication,* 10, pinned all on a distinction between a bishop and a beneficed clerk. His reading, however, used canon law to find clerical exercise of civil jurisdiction both "dishonest and dishonorable"; the distinction also contradicts his vision of the primitive church: BL Stowe Ms. 424, ff. 9a, 15b.

29. BL Stowe Ms. 424, ff. 12b–13b, 15b (made with reference to beneficed clerks).

30. Ibid., f. 9a.

31. Bagshaw, *Just vindication,* 11–15.

32. [William Ker, earl of Lothian,] *A true representation of the proceedings of the kingdome of Scotland, since the late pacification* (n.p., 1640), STC 21929, implied part 2, half-titled "The proceedings of the Commissioners sent from the Parliament of Scotland to the King," 10–11.

33. Rothes to William Murray, August 1639, in S. R. Gardiner, *Hamilton Papers,* 99.

34. [Ker,] *True representation* (pt. 2), 32–33 (23 March).

35. Esther S. Cope, ed., in collaboration with Willson H. Coates, *Proceedings of the Short Parliament of 1640* (1977), 60, 98, 234, 245. For the precedents, ibid., 99, 108. D'Ewes, *Journals of parliaments,* 67–68.

36. Cope, *Proceedings,* 17 April, 107–08; 18 April, 98, 108; 20 April, 65, 99, 235–36.

37. Ibid., 65, 99, 236.

38. Ibid., 109.

39. See p. 58.

40. Perry Miller and Thomas H. Johnson, eds., *The Puritans,* 2 vols. (New York, 1963), 1:209–10.

41. Forbes, *Winthrop Papers,* 4:267. A possible indication of growing familiarity with the language of estates is Sir Thomas Peyton's comment that the failure of the Short Parliament reflected upon "the third estate" and not a few "private

men"; Dorothy Gardiner, ed., *The Oxinden Letters, 1607–1642* (1933), 173.

42. For Parker's life see Wilbur Kitchener Jordan, *Men of Substance* (Chicago, 1942), 9–37. Jordan missed the connection to Saye, for which see *Dictionary of National Biography . . . to 1900*, ed. Sir Leslie Stephen and Sir Sidney Lee, 21 vols. (1921–1922; reprint ed., 1949–1950) (hereafter cited as DNB), s.v. "Henry Parker" and "William Fiennes," and see Edwin F. Gay, "The Temples of Stowe and Their Debts: Peter and John Temple, 1603–1653," *Huntington Library Quarterly* 2 (1938–1939): 399–438.

For Parker's thought see Jordan, *Men of Substance,* and Margaret Atwood Judson, "Henry Parker and the Theory of Parliamentary Sovereignty," in *Essays in History and Political Theory in Honor of Charles Howard McIlwain,* ed. Carl Frederick Wittke (Cambridge, Mass., 1936), 138–67.

43. Thomason's copy [BL E. 204 (3)] of *A discourse concerning puritans* (1640) is noted on the title page as "by Henry Parker a Counsellor." Parker used "privado" in *The case of shipmony* (1640) [BL E. 204.4], 35, and in *Observations upon some of his majesties late answers and expresses* (1642), reproduced in William Haller, ed., *Tracts on Liberty in the Puritan Revolution, 1638–1647,* 3 vols. (New York, 1934), 2:30. (Parker's pagination is followed throughout.) Cf. Virgilio Malvezzi, *Il ritratto del privato politico christiano* (Bologna, 1635).

44. [Henry Parker,] *The vintners answer to some scandalous phamphlets* (1640). [Idem,] *The humble remonstrance of the Company of Stationers* (1643), reprinted in Edward Arber, ed., *Transcript of the Registers of the Company of Stationers of London, 1554–1640,* 5 vols. (1–4, 1875–1877; 5, Birmingham, 1894), 1:584–88. Henry Parker, *Of a free trade* (1648). [Idem,] *Mr. William Wheelers case* (1645). [Idem,] *The generall junto, or the councell of union* (n.p., 1642), BL 669, f. 18 (1); see Thomason's note.

45. [Parker,] *Case of shipmony,* 1–5, 7; cf. 23, 28 on "nature."

46. Ibid., 38–39.

47. Ibid., 32–35.

48. Ibid., 7, 9, 37.

49. Ibid., 22, 23, 26–27.

50. Ibid., 20, 28.

51. [Parker,] *Discourse concerning puritans,* 1–2.

52. Virgilio Malvezzi, *Romvlvs and Tarqvin,* trans. Henry Carey, earl of Monmouth (1637), 196–98. The paths of Malvezzi, his English publisher Richard Whitaker, Parker, and Saye cross at a number of junctures; the matter is complicated, however, and must await treatment elsewhere.

53. [Parker,] *Discourse concerning puritans,* 36; cf. Machiavelli, *Discourses,* bk. 3, chap. 1. [Parker,] *Case of shipmony,* 32.

54. Paolo Sarpi, *History of the inquisition,* trans. Robert Gentilis (1639). Parker usually made a few changes. Compare:

Discourse concerning puritans	*History of the inquisition*
1. p. 19 (line seven from bottom)–p. 20 (l. 22): with changes.	1. p. 77 (l. 23)–p. 78 (l. 11)
2. p. 20 (l. 27)–p. 21 (l. 19) with changes.	2. p. 54 (9 lines from bottom)–p. 55 (2 lines from bottom)
3. p. 21 (l. 26)–p. 22 (l. 24) with changes.	3. p. 70 (l. 13)–p. 71 (3 lines from bottom)
4. p. 17 (l. 12–l. 17) with changes.	4. p. 20 (last 6 lines but one)
5. p. 30 (ll. 11–18): with changes: and in answer to Calvin	5. p. 29 (ll. 17–20); p. 30 (l. 4)
6. p. 21 (ll. 20–25): with changes: n.b. the collation by cf. items 2 and 3	6. p. 67 (ll. 7–11)
7. p. 26 (bot.)–27 based on distinction given on →	7. p. 8 (ll. 1–3); p. 26 (ll. 14–18)
8. p. 31 (ll. 25–32)	8. [?] p. 25 (last 6 lines)–p. 26 (ll. 1–13)

55. Nelson P. Bard, "The Ship Money Case and William Fiennes, Viscount Saye and Sele," *Bulletin of the Institute for Historical Research* 50 (1977): 177–84.

56. [Parker,] *Discourse concerning puritans,* 9–10.

57. Ibid., 10, 52, 53. The addition of John Dod and Robert Cleaver was a breezy touch. As Saye and Brooke were associated together, so were Dod and Cleaver, who formed a puritan literary team. For an example of the association of the names Saye and Brooke, see Heylyn, *Cyprianus Anglicus,* 2:386.

58. [Parker,] *Discourse concerning puritans,* 8; there is also the most passing mention of Prynne and Bastwick, along with Burton, 5. H[enry] P[arker], *The altar dispute* (1641), A2.

59. [Parker,] *Discourse concerning puritans,* 58.

60. Robert Baillie, *Letters and Journals,* ed. David Laing, 3 vols. (Edinburgh, 1841–1842), 1:274–75, 280, 291, 309, 313–14.

61. Sir Simonds D'Ewes, *The Journal of Sir Simonds D'Ewes from the Beginning of the Long Parliament to the Opening of the Trial of the Earl of Strafford,* ed. Wallace Notestein (New Haven, 1923), 138–41; Sir John Northcote, *Note Book . . . ,* ed. A. H. A. Hamilton (1877), 50–53. Not all of Northcote is used by Notestein.

62. D'Ewes, *Journal,* ed. Notestein, 249, 280, 283.

63. Ibid., 334–38. Samuel Rawson Gardiner, *History of England . . . 1603– 1642,* 10 vols. (1883–1884), 9:281, is challenged by Anthony Fletcher, *The Outbreak of the English Civil War* (New York, 1981), 98; Gardiner's full judg-

ment—with an adequate discount made for use of the word "party"—is sufficient to answer Fletcher's objections.

64. CSPD, 1640–1641, 418, 484. BL Harl. Ms. 6424, ff. 6a–7a; *Journals of the House of Lords* (hereafter cited as LJ), 4:174.

65. D'Ewes, *Journal*, ed. Notestein, 340.

66. Edward Bagshaw, *Mr. Bagshaw's speech in parliament February the ninth, 1640* (1641), 3.

67. Weston and Greenberg, *Subjects and Sovereigns*, 74–75, 97–98, 305 n. 13; Bagshaw, *Just vindication*, 4, absurdly states that Bagshaw "told the house, that by the ancient laws of the land the crown of England was founded in the state of prelacy."

Chapter 7

1. *Reformation no enemie* (1641) is a new edition of Marprelate, *Hay any worke*. The usually unattributed *A dialogue, wherin is plainly layd open* (1640) is a new edition of the 1589 tract of the same name, but cf. Carlson, *Martin Marprelate*, 158–71, 340. This edition was published by "Dr. Martin Marprelate," a shrewd guess. For Stoughton see Chapter 5, n. 18.

2. D'Ewes, *Journal*, ed. Notestein, 343.

3. [Charles I] *Eikon Basilike*, ed. Philip Knachel (Ithaca, 1966), 125; cf. 107. See also the title of Ussher's scheme in Richard Baxter, *Reliquiae Baxterianae*, ed. Matthew Sylvester (1696).

Aspects of the story told here are found in James Spalding and Maynard Brass, "Reduction of Episcopacy as a Means to Unity in England, 1640–1662," *Church History* 30 (1961): 414–19; Winthrop S. Hudson, "The Scottish Effort to Presbyterianize the Church of England During the Early Months of the Long Parliament," *Church History* 8 (1939): 265–66; Charles Hamilton, "The Basis for Scottish Efforts to Create a Reformed Church in England, 1640–41," *Church History* 30 (1961): 171–78.

4. J. J. Scarisbrick, *Henry VIII* (Harmondsworth, Middlesex, 1971), 661–62. Mary Dewar, ed., *A Discourse of the Commonweal of this Realm of England. Attributed to Sir Thomas Smith* (Charlottesville, Va., 1969), 131–33.

5. Collinson, *Elizabethan Puritan Movement*, pt. 4, chap. 3, and idem, "Episcopacy and Reform."

6. Roland G. Usher, *Reconstruction of the English Church*, 2 vols. (New York, 1910), 2:351–52; see also 337, 351, 352, 358–60. Francis Bacon, *Works*, ed. James Spedding et al., 14 vols. (1857–1874; reprint ed., 1967), 10:129, 131. Conrad Russell has been helpful here.

7. DNB, 20:66; Ussher's visitation articles of 1615.

8. Ussher's biographer in the DNB, Alexander Gordon, believed that the

pamphlet was Ussher's though he offered no evidence for that view whatsoever. The attribution is made by Thomas Cooper in his article on Udall in the DNB. William Arthur Shaw, *A History of the English Church . . .* , 2 vols. (1900), 1:70, knew Udall's scheme to be "quite distinct" from Ussher's, but he did not know its origin. Notestein follows Gordon.

9. Baxter, *Reliquiae Baxterianae*, 244. Sir Simonds D'Ewes, *Autobiography and Correspondence of Sir Simonds D'Ewes, Bart*, ed. James Orchard Halliwell, 2 vols. (1845), 2:252–53. See also Baillie, *Letters and Journals*, 1:287 (28 December 1640).

10. Ussher's proposal was published in 1656 in two versions, both with similar titles beginning, *The reduction of episcopacie unto the form of synodical government received in the antient* [or *ancient*] *church*. The first version to appear is BL E. 894 (3) in the Thomason Collection. The second version was issued by Nicholas Bernard to correct what Bernard viewed as misleading changes and additions to the first, in the course of which Bernard added a misleading note of his own; BL E. 897 (1). There were other editions of the Bernard text.

The text to be found in Baxter, *Reliquiae Baxterianae*, 238–41, is titled "Episcopal and Presbyterial Government Conjoyned." It combines features of both editions.

11. For a recent review see Clayton Roberts, "The Earl of Bedford and the Coming of the English Revolution," *Journal of Modern History* 49 (1977): 600–16. But see the caveats of Derek Hirst, "Unanimity in the Commons, Aristocratic Intrigues, and the Origins of the English Civil War," ibid., 50 (1979): 67; Conrad Russell's "Parliament and the King's Finances," in C. Russell, *Origins*, 112–15, remains fundamental.

12. John Hacket, *Scrinia reserata* (1693), pt. 2, 143; idem, *Memoirs of the life of Archbishop Williams* (1715), 203–04.

13. LJ, 4:174, 177, 180.

14. Burgess had a leading place in Bedford's funeral procession; BL Harl. Ms. 477, f. 131 b.

15. Izaak Walton, *Lives . . .* , intro. George Saintsbury [1956], 370–71.

16. Hacket, *Scrinia reserata*, pt. 2, 143, and idem, *Memoirs of Williams*, 204; see also Thomas Fuller, *Church History of Britain*, 3 vols. (1837), 3:415.

17. Baillie, *Letters and Journals*, 1:303.

18. John Selden, *Table talk of John Selden*, ed. Sir Frederick Pollock (1927), 19.

19. Sir Ralph Verney, *Verney Papers, Notes of Proceedings in the Long Parliament . . .* , ed. John Bruce (1845), 10. Baillie, *Letters and Journals*, 1:300.

20. Calybute Downing, *Considerations toward a peaceable reformation in matters ecclesiastical* (1641), 5, 7–8. Thomason acquired this pamphlet in December 1641, to judge from its place order in the collection [BL E. 179 (7)], but it makes no sense to suppose it relates to that period. See also Calybute Downing, *A sermon preached to the renowned Company of the Artillery* (1642); the sermon, delivered in

September 1640, provoked Charles's wrath, and Downing disappeared into Warwick's substantial lands in Essex. (See DNB s.v. "Downing.")

21. For Dury, Pym, and Williams see H. R. Trevor-Roper, "Three Foreigners," in *Religion, the Reformation and Social Change* (1967), 237–91. For Morley, Hales, and the Tew circle see Wormald, *Clarendon*, 240–62, passim. For 1640 and 1641 see Trevor-Roper, "Fast Sermons of the Long Parliament," in *Religion, Reformation and Social Change*, 297, 299, 300.

22. John Dury, "A briefe declaration . . . of the severall formes of government received in those churches" in the proepiscopal anthology, *Certain briefe treatises* (Oxford, 1641), 123–27. *Eikon Basilike* may have echoed Dury on this point (102, 106).

23. [George Morley,] *A modest advertisement concerning the present controversie about church government* (1641), 7, 12.

24. [John Hales,] *The way towards the finding of a decision . . . concerning church government* (1641), 36–40.

25. On the timing of *An answer to a booke* see David Masson, *Life of John Milton*, 7 vols. (Cambridge, 1859–1894), 2:225.

26. *Certaine reasons tending to prove the vnlawfulnesse . . .* (1641), 10, 17.

27. Robert Baillie, *Vnlawfulnesse and danger of limited episcopacie* (1641), 19, 27. Alexander Henderson, *Vnlawfulnes and danger of limited prelacie* (1641), 8, 11–13.

28. BL Harl. Ms. 6424, f. 9b; this reference is taken from the Grays' transcript on deposit at the Yale Center for Parliamentary History, New Haven, Conn.

29. Hacket, *Scrinia reserata*, pt. 2, 163. The appropriate passages are set off in italics to identify them as Williams's notes. Hacket only says this episode happened when it became known that the king intended to go to Edinburgh. The Venetian ambassador knew of the king's plans as of a dispatch of 31 May (new style); *Calendar of State Papers . . . in the Archives of Venice*, ed. H. F. Brown and A. B. Hinds, (hereafter cited as CSPV), vol. 25, *1640–42* (1924), 153. Williams surely knew it earlier. Presumably the attempt took place before 17 May because Saye, Essex, Leicester, and Hertford received offices on that day.

30. CSPD, 1640-1641, 550, 551; cf. 539.

31. BL Harl. Ms. 6424, f. 88a (Grays' transcript); see BL Harl. Ms. 6424, ff. 9b (Grays' transcript); Baxter, *Reliquiae Baxterianae*, bk. 1, 62.

32. BL Harl. Ms. 6424, f. 54a describes a meeting attended by seventy or more divines. More were scheduled.

33. Verney, *Notes,* 75–77; BL Harl. Ms. 477, f. 59b.

34. Best text is in S. R. Gardiner, *Constitutional Documents,* 167–76. BL Harl. Ms. 6424, ff. 78–79, had notes on the bill that serve to identify it unquestionably as that of Williams. The bill (168) actually might be construed as abolishing the seats of bishops in the Lords; all depends on the meaning of the phrases "temporal court" and "standing temporal court." But, obviously, no such abolition was

intended. Lambe's job was to be removed by the abolition of the Court of Arches (179).

35. Nothing about Dering's participation is on record. The major happening was the younger Sir Henry Vane's proposal to put the church into commission. BL Harl. Ms. 163, f. 337a. For Notestein's doubts on the actual delivery of another of Dering's speeches see D'Ewes, *Journal,* ed. Notestein, 148, n. 18. There is a short paper in the Dering correspondence, BL Stowe Ms. 184, ff. 39a–40a, entitled "Humble considerations . . . ," which Dering endorsed " 18 June," followed by an erasure of a surname preceded by a legible "Mr." The sheet, very badly penned, discusses bishops pro and con, coming out pro with a brief description of episcopo-presbytery on f. 40a.

36. BL Harl. Ms. 478, f. 93a.

37. Sir Edward Dering, *A collection of speeches* (1641), BL E. 197 (1), 155–61. See 155: "An imperfect copy of these, without my knowledge or consent hath been three times printed before."

38. a) BL Burney 11. a. (25): *The order and forme for church, government by bishops and the clergie of this kingdome. Voted in the House of Commons on Friday, July 16, 1641. Whereunto is added Mr. Grimstons and Mr. Seldens arguments concerning episcopacie* (1641). Pp. 1–4 contain sixteen points, compressing into one point nos. 15 and 16 of b) and c).

b) BL Burney 11. a (20): Sir Harbottle Grimston, *Mr. Grimstons argument concerning bishops: with Mr. Seldens answer. Also severall orders concerning church government* (1641). Pp. 2–5 contain sixteen numbered and one unnumbered point.

c) BL E. 165 (9): very close but not identical in title and contents to b). Both versions print "Conge De Cleire."

The exchange between Grimston and Selden was a separate matter and was celebrated in its time. It occurred on 1 Feb. 1641. CSPD, 1640–1641, 450–51; D'Ewes, *Journal,* ed. Notestein, 309, n. 12; BL Harl. Ms. 6424, f. 108a. The last point in the versions given above incorporates an order of the Commons on cutting timber on certain ecclesiastical land of 16 July; BL Harl. Ms. 479, f. 70a. John More made a copy of the scheme in his diary; BL Harl. Ms. 479, ff. 173b–175a, but written back to front.

John Hampden objected to one of these versions and had it referred to Dering's committee on printing, from which no report ever emerged; BL Harl. Ms. 479, f. 86a; *Journals of the House of Commons* (hereafter cited as CJ), 2:221.

39. Note the elaborate obeisance toward the scheme made by Augustine Skinner, a strong puritan; BL Sloane Ms. 744, ff. 13a–14a.

40. An edition appeared in June 1642 under the title *Sixteene propositions in parliament*: BL E. 149 (35); 108. b. 41; with a slightly different imprint, 702. d. 8 (8). W. A. Shaw referred to the last of these as "more apocryphal than but possibly contemporary" with Williams's plan in his *History of the English Church*, 1:73,

n. 1. Shaw was shrewd to see his mid-1642 text was of mid-1641 provenance, but his failure to connect it with Dering was unfortunate. Yet another edition was purchased by Thomason on 31 January 1643, again with a title ignorant of the provenance of the scheme but not its attractions: *Acts for the utter abolishing of bishops . . . with . . . the order for church-government by a better way . . .* (1643) BL E. 87 (8), 5–6 (the "Better Way").

41. Clarendon, *History,* 1:311.

42. Ibid., 1:311.

43. See Appendix 1.

44. John Selden, *The privileges of the baronage in England, when they sit in parliament* (1642), 120–26. Although printed in 1642, the book was written before the fall of the bishops, perhaps before the Long Parliament. See the introductory statement (A3 verso), either by Selden or an editor.

45. D'Ewes, *Journal,* ed. Notestein, 337–38. Notestein identifies this Vaughan as Edward Vaughan. But no such individual sat in the Commons according to Keeler, *Long Parliament,* 371–72. Of the two Vaughans who did sit, Selden's friend John Vaughan is presumably intended.

46. Ibid., 467–68.

47. Ibid., 469; cf. Snow, *Parliament in Elizabethan England,* 109–10, for use of Hooker in the Short Parliament.

48. Selden, *Table talk,* 20.

49. Ibid., 18, 20, 64.

50. See p. 145.

51. BL Harl. Ms. 6424, f. 48a. The diary was identified as Warner's by Conrad Russell, "The Authorship of the Bishop's Diary of the House of Lords in 1641," *Bulletin of the Institute of Historical Research* 41 (1968): 229–36.

52. Verney, *Notes* 54; Weston and Greenberg, *Subjects and Sovereigns,* 98.

53. Heylyn, *Historical tracts,* 739 ff.; the preface, 738, states that the exclusion of the bishops was the motive of the exercise. John Warner also thought he was by right a peer.

54. John Selden, *Jani Anglorum facies altera* (1610), 126. Redman Wescot, the late seventeenth-century translator of *Jani Anglorum facies altera,* translated *ordo* as "estate," chiding Selden for his error; but perhaps Selden was deliberate in avoiding *gradus.* John Selden, *Tracts written by John Selden,* ed. and trans. Redman Wescot [pseud.] (1683), 94, 127–28.

55. John Selden, *Titles of honor* (1614), 282, 347 (2nd ed., 1631).

56. Ibid. (1631 ed.), see especially 695–701.

57. Ibid., 691–745. For Selden and Spelman see Pocock, *Ancient Constitution,* 91–123. It is worth noting that the 1614 *Titles of honor,* like *Jani Anglorum,* placed credence in the *Modus*; the 1631 edition rejected it.

58. Selden, *Table Talk,* 15: see quotation on p. 159 and add: "Indeed your latter earls and barons have it expressed in their patents that they shall be called to the

Parliament; ob[jection]: but one sit there by blood, the bishops not. Answer: 'tis true they sit not both there the same way; yet that takes not away the bishops' right. If I am a parson of a parish I have as much right to my glebe and my tithes, as you have to your land that your ancestors have had in that parish 800 years.

"2. The bishops were not barons because they had baronies annexed to their bishoprics; for few of them had so unless the old ones (Canterbury, Winchester, Durham). The new erected we are sure had none (as Glocester, Peterborough) besides few of the temporal lords had any baronies. But they are barons because they are called by writ to the Parliament; and bishops were in the Parliament ever since there is any mention or sign of a Parliament in England."

Ibid., 32–33: an "erroneous opinion" is "that the Lords sit only for themselves when the truth is they sit as well for the commonwealth, the knights and burgesses sit for themselves and others, some for more, some for fewer." Repunctuated.

59. Weston and Greenberg, *Subjects and Sovereigns*, 98.

60. *Privy Council Registers Preserved in the Public Record Office*, 12 vols. (1968), 12:36, 40–41.

61. Ibid., 47.

62. Peter Heylyn, *Ecclesia Restaurata*, ed. James Craigie Robertson, 2 vols. (Cambridge, 1849), 1:cxxvii–cxxix.

63. *The third speech of the lord George Digby . . . the 9th of Febr: 1640*. (1640), 15–16.

64. But see the Grand Remonstrance's curious remark that the May 1640 tumults helped prevent "harsher courses" against members of the recently dissolved Parliament: S. R. Gardiner, *Constitutional Documents*, 218.

65. *Privy Council Registers*, 12:125, 126.

66. D'Ewes, *Autobiography*, 2:268. BL Harl. Ms. 6424, f. 59b.

67. Cambridge University Additional (hereafter cited as Camb. Add.) Ms. 90, f. 95a (Yale Center for Parliamentary History Microfilm Y 641–4); CJ, 2:134.

68. BL Harl. Ms. 6424, ff. 59a, 60a. The importance of the Protestation is very properly emphasized by Fletcher, *Outbreak*.

69. BL Harl. Ms. 6424, f. 59a.

70. Camb. Add. Ms. 89, f. 51b, and Camb. Add. Ms. 90, f. 96a (both in Yale Center for Parliamentary History Microfilm Y 641–4); BL Harl. Ms. 6424, ff. 69–70a; *Parliamentary . . . History of England*, 24 vols. (1751–1762), 10:290–91; BL Harl. Ms. 163, f. 199a; BL Harl. Ms. 477, f. 80b.

71. BL Harl. Ms. 477, f. 109a; at this point Pym's strategy was to have the charges put into the bill.

72. Selden, *Table talk*, 15.

73. *The lives of all the lords chancellors*, 2nd ed., 2 vols. (1712), 2:386, 389–90.

74. Ibid., 2:386–87, 395–97.

75. Ibid., 2:398.

76. *Parliamentary History*, 9:287–88.

77. [Sir Thomas Aston,] *A collection of sundry petitions* (1642), 5; *A short treatise of archbishops and bishops* (1641), 1–2.

78. D'Ewes, *Autobiography*, 2:271–72.

79. Aston, *Remonstrance*, 2.

80. BL E. 198 (16); William Fiennes, Viscount Saye and Sele, *Two speeches of the right honourable William lord Viscount Say and Seale* (1641), 1, 2, 8.

81. BL E. 173 (16): *The substance of a conference* (1641), 3–5. See Sir Simonds D'Ewes, *The Journal of Sir Simonds D'Ewes from the First Recess of the Long Parliament to the Withdrawal of King Charles from London*, ed. Willson Havelock Coates (New Haven, 1942), 43 n. 2.

82. BL Harl. Ms. 6424, f. 78b.

83. John Evelyn, *Diary and Correspondence*, ed. William Bray, 4 vols. (1906), 4:84–85, 91, 110, 112, 128–29, 136–37, 139.

84. CSPD, 1641–1643, 44.

85. BL Harl. Ms. 479. f. 107b; LJ, 4:337, 339, 342, 345–46; BL Harl. Ms. 6424, f. 88b–89a.

86. Sir Charles Harding Firth, *The House of Lords during the Civil War* (1910), 95–96; BL Harl. Ms. 6424, f. 96b (Grays' transcript); Evelyn, *Diary*, 4:85, 110.

87. S. R. Gardiner, *Constitutional Documents*, 227, 228.

88. Clarendon, *History*, 1:436–37.

89. D'Ewes, *Journal*, ed. Coates, 228. For the phrase "good lords" see Mendle, "Politics and Political Thought," 239.

90. Fletcher, *Outbreak*, 176–77, is a good discussion of the counterproductivity of Williams's gambit.

91. D'Ewes, *Journal*, ed. Coates, 365 n. 6. BL Harl. Ms. 480, ff. 163a, 164a.

92. LJ, 4:490, 533, 543. Fletcher, *Outbreak*, 420–22, conveniently tabulates these protests.

93. Clarendon, *History*, 1:542–46. CSPV, 1640–1642, 289.

94. BL Harl. Ms. 480, ff. 36a–37b; cf. BL Harl. Ms. 477, f. 120b; BL Harl. Ms. 163, f. 256a.

95. D'Ewes, *Journal*, ed. Coates, 356, n. 4.

96. LJ, 4:506. Bulstrode Whitelocke, *Memorials of the English Affairs*, 4 vols. (Oxford, 1853), 1:156. Nehemiah Wallington, *Historical Notices . . . of the Reign of Charles I*, ed. Rosamond Anne Webb, 2 vols. (1869), 2:1. Cf. BL Harl. Ms. 162, f. 314b. Since this section was written, a printed edition of the diaries used here and in subsequent citations to the end of this chapter has appeared: Willson H. Coates, Anne Steele Young, Vernon F. Snow, eds., *The Private Journals of the Long Parliament, 3 January to 5 March 1642* (New Haven, 1982).

97. LJ, 4:523; BL E. 134 (13), 3–5.

98. LJ, 4:534–37. For Tavistock and Totnes see Historical Manuscripts Commission, *5th Report* (1876), app., 4–5.

99. LJ, 4:537–43. Henry Oxinden thought enough of Pym's stentorian ordeal to turn it into a figure in a love letter: D. Gardiner, ed., *Oxinden Letters*, 289.

100. LJ, 4:543.

101. Ibid., 544, 549. The seamen were thanked on the second occasion for "their modest way of coming, not in multitudes."

102. Clarendon, *History*, 1:549–50 (includes a text); Camb. Add. Ms. 89, f. 27b (Yale Center for Parliamentary History Microfilm Y-641). See *Persecutio undecima* (1647), 64–67, for the time and the phrase "daily assaults."

103. BL 669. f. 4 (54): *To the honvrable the Hovse of Commons . . . the humble petition of many thousand poore people, in and about the citie of London* [1642].

104. BL Harl. Ms. 480, f. 81b; BL Harl. Ms. 162, f. 360b.

105. BL Additional (hereafter cited as Add.) Ms. 14827, f. 23b.

106. BL Harl. Ms. 162, f. 362b; LJ, 4:559; Historical Manuscripts Commission, *Manuscripts of the House of Lords, Addenda, 1514–1714*, ed. Maurice Bond, n.s., vol. 11 (1962), 306–07.

107. BL Add. Ms. 14827, ff. 25, 29.

108. LJ, 5:563–64, 570, 572–73.

109. BL Add. Ms. 14827, f. 31a; Fletcher, *Outbreak*, 201.

110. Out of a notional membership of 150 lords spiritual and temporal with which it began in November 1640, average attendance in February 1642 had dropped to under 40. Between 60 and 70 peers attended sessions in January; the bishops, of course, had dropped away by late December and early January: a two-month decline (including the bishops) of about 50 percent. Firth, *House of Lords*, 74, 112–13; Fletcher, *Outbreak*, 243. Fletcher thinks that Pym's speech of 25 January had much to do with the collapse, but he excludes it from the category of intimidation; I cannot agree.

111. Henry Carey, earl of Monmouth, *A speech made in the House of Peeres, . . . on Thursday the 13. of Ianuary. 1641* (1641), A3 recto.

112. BL Add. Ms. 14827, ff. 24b–25a. Strode was joined by Holles, who was careful, however, to preserve space for the good lords.

113. Dering, *Collection*, 164.

114. John Philipps Kenyon, *The Stuart Constitution . . .* (Cambridge, 1966), 241.

115. Wallington, *Historical Notices*, 2:2.

116. Robert Bell, ed., *Memorials of the Civil War: Comprising the Correspondence of the Fairfax Family*, 2 vols. (1849), 2:295.

117. [Aston,] *Collection*, A2 recto.

Chapter 8

1. The most notable examples for the early seventeenth century include Tyacke, "Puritansim, Arminianism, and Counter-Revolution," and Conrad Russell, "Introduction" and "Parliament and the King's Finances" in C. Russell, *Origins*; Conrad Russell, "Parliamentary History in Perspective," *History* 61

(1976): 1–27; idem, *Parliaments and English Politics, 1621–1629* (Oxford, 1979); idem, "The Parliamentary Career of John Pym, 1621–29," in *The English Commonwealth, 1547–1640*, ed. Peter Clark, Alan G. R. Smith, and Nicholas Tyacke (New York, 1979): all are brilliant studies. Also relevant and valuable is Kevin Sharpe's "Introduction: Parliamentary History, 1603–1629: in or out of Perspective?" in *Faction and Parliament . . .* , ed. Kevin Sharpe (Oxford, 1978); also see essays by R. C. Munden, "James I and 'the Growth of Mutual Distrust': King, Commons, and Reform, 1603–04," and J. N. Ball, "Sir John Eliot and Parliament, 1624–1629," both in Sharpe, *Faction and Parliament*. These studies demonstrate the folly of reading the civil war back into the first decades of the century.

The attempt to relate the political culture of 1640–1642 to the earlier period is, perhaps, less well advanced. Fletcher, *Outbreak*, does justice to "Confrontation" and "Accommodation" (these are chapter headings); the distinction, however, is somewhat artificial. Fletcher's book is nonetheless quite the soundest history of the period, including S. R. Gardiner's work. Less successful is Paul Christianson, "The Peers, the People, and Parliamentary Management in the First Six Months of the Long Parliament," *Journal of Modern History* 49 (1977): 575–99. See also Mark Kishlansky, "The Emergence of Adversary Politics in the Long Parliament," ibid., 617–40, and Roberts, "Earl of Bedford." In addition to the critique of these articles by Hirst, "Unanimity in the Commons," see J. H. Hexter, "Power Struggle, Parliament, and Liberty in Early Stuart England," *Journal of Modern History* 50 (1978): 1–50.

2. Kishlansky, "Emergence of Adversary Politics," 618–25.

3. Hall, *Admonition*, 83.

4. Margaret Cavendish, duchess of Newcastle, *The Life of William Cavendish, Duke of Newcastle*, ed. C. H. Firth (New York, 1906), 134.

5. Clarendon, *History*, 3:322. Roberts, "Earl of Bedford," 614, tends to concur that Bedford and Pym could not deliver the Commons on the financial issue. Cf. C. Russell, *Origins*, 115.

6. Fletcher, *Outbreak*, 180.

7. *The Autobiography of Sir John Bramston, K. B.* (1845), p. 74. Thomas Hobbes also reflected upon the theme in *Leviathan*, ed. C. B. Macpherson (Harmondsworth, Middlesex, 1968), 360 (pt. 2, chap. 28), 390–91 (pt. 2, chap. 30).

8. See p. 84.

9. Cecily Veronica Wedgwood, *Thomas Wentworth, First Earl of Strafford, 1593–1641: A Revaluation* (1964), 73.

10. S. R. Gardiner, *Constitutional Documents*, 231.

11. For example, [Henry Parker,] *Observations*, 28, with reference to the confrontation at Hull; cf. Parker's *Some few observations upon his majesties late answer* (1642), 8–9.

12. *Liber Famelicus of Sir James Whitelocke,* ed. John Bruce ([Westminster], 1858), 114.

13. S. R. Gardiner, *Constitutional Documents,* 83, 84, 85, 91, 97.

14. Cf. Sharpe, *Faction and Parliament,* 29.

15. On the general question of localism see John Stephen Morrill, *The Revolt of the Provinces* (New York, 1976).

16. Clarendon, *History,* 1:345.

17. C. Russell, *Origins,* 29.

18. *Privy Council Registers,* 12:64 (6 December 1640).

19. *A speech spoken by Sr. Thomas Wroth knight . . . February, 25. 1642* (1642). A2 recto. BL Harl. Ms. 480, f. 172b: Wroth made a speech at the bar comparing "this house to the day of judgment."

20. Fletcher, *Outbreak,* 303.

21. BL Harl. Ms. 164, f. 70a.

22. BL Harl. Ms. 162, f. 375b. D'Ewes continued, in cipher: "I was very much moved with this dangerous and ignorant speech." On Martin, see C. M. Williams, "The Anatomy of a Radical Gentleman: Henry Marten," in Pennington and Thomas, *Puritans and Revolutionaries,* 118–38.

23. Clarendon, *History,* 1:579.

24. Verney, *Notes,* 184. This passage is from line 16 of the cipher (not including the unciphered line) to line 20, all but the four last numbers. Verney used only a simple substitution cipher with no known doublets; the difficulties arise only from his own errors in enciphering. The solution is as follows; it will be seen that the vowels are numbers 14–18 inclusive:

```
a  b c  d  e  f g(orj) h i  j(org) k l  m  n  o  p  q r s t  u,v w  x  y   z
14 6 10 13 15 2 11      7 16 11     4 20 27 28 17 12 - 3 8 5 18  18 22 25? -
                                                                    or
                                                                     9
```

The bracketed "t" in the transcription was an "r," presumably in error.

25. BL Harl. Ms. 163, ff. 32b–33a. For the common view of the militia ordinance see Lois G. Schwoerer, *"No Standing Armies!"* (Baltimore, 1974), 33–50.

26. BL Harl. Ms. 163, f. 33a.

27. Ibid., f. 58b; first four words in cipher.

28. Ibid., f. 79b.

29. BL 669, f. 6 (7). It probably appeared in the second week of April 1642.

30. [Richard Overton; sometimes misattributed to John Lilburne,] *Englands birth-right justified* (1645) began with *A question answered*; it was cited in most of Lilburne's 1640s' pamphlets. Lilburne always referred to it by its page number— 150—in Husbands, *Exact collection.*

A question answered was known in Aberdeen, where John Spalding noted that some people thought it was "made" by the "English Parliament"; John Spalding, *The History of the Troubles and Memorable Transactions* . . . , 2 vols. (Edinburgh, 1828), 2:41.

31. Charles I, *His maiesties message to the House of Peers* (1642), BL 669, f. 5 (6), dated 22 April. See also Appendix 2.

32. *A plea for moderation* (1642), BL E. 143 (7).

33. Ibid., A3 recto, A4 recto.

34. Ibid., B1 recto–B2 recto.

35. Ibid., B2 verso.

36. This very important letter is quoted and discussed by Fletcher, *Outbreak*, 304–05.

37. See p. 6.

38. The house took up the *Answer* as early as 23 June; BL Harl. Ms. 163, f. 207b. But on 23 July the house was still considering the reply to the king's answer to the declaration of 26 May. See note 39, below. In November the reply was published with the excuse that the press of affairs prevented the Lords from voting on it; Husbands, *Exact collection,* 686.

39. BL Harl. Ms. 163, ff. 288b, 22 July; 291b, 292b, 23 July.

40. [Parker,] *Observations,* 23–24.

41. Ibid., 23, 31, 35, 37.

42. Sir John Spelman, *The case of our affaires* (1643; reprint ed., Exeter, 1975), 10.

Appendix 1

1. Wormald, *Clarendon,* 10–12, 240–41, 276.

2. See p. 144.

3. Wormald, *Clarendon,* 281. I. M. Green, *The Re-Establishment of the Church of England 1660–1663* (Oxford, 1978).

4. Wormald, *Clarendon,* 18, 240–41, 276, 280.

5. Ibid., 241.

6. Ibid., 277–80; this section effectively contradicts Wormald's own argument. Note Hyde's contempt of Laudian notions of episcopal peerage.

7. Wormald, *Clarendon,* 282–325.

8. See p. 20.

9. Kurt Weber, *Lucius Cary, Second Viscount Falkland* (New York, 1940), 143–56, based primarily on the Clarendon State Papers.

10. Henry Octavius Coxe and Sir Charles Firth, general eds., *Calendar of the Clarendon State Papers Preserved in the Bodleian Library,* 5 vols. (Oxford, 1869–1970), vol. 1 (1869) ed. Octavius Ogle and William Henry Bliss, no. 1503; cf. nos. 1447, 1460, 1470, 1476, 1481, 1506, 1513, 1530.

11. William Laud, *The Works of the Most Reverend Father in God, William Laud, D. D. Sometime Lord Archbishop Of Canterbury*, ed. William Scott and James Bliss, 7 vols. (1847–1860; reprint ed. New York, 1975), 3:244. See also R. W. Harris, *Clarendon and the English Revolution* (Stanford, Calif., 1983), 29, 42, 47.

Appendix 2

1. Heylyn, *Cyprianus Anglicus*, pt. 2, 321–23. The attribution probably arose out of the very mixed feelings of Heylyn toward Selden—he was brilliant, on the one hand, and had proved treacherous to the cause after having defended it so remarkably, on the other. See also Spalding, *History of the Troubles*, 2:41.

2. John Milton, *Complete Prose Works of John Milton*, Don M. Wolfe, general editor, 7 vols. to date (New Haven, 1953–). See vol. 2, ed. Ernest Sirluck, 18, 38. Sirluck did not know of Heylyn's attribution: "no author has been suggested."

3. John Marsh, *An argument or, debate in law of the great question concerning the militia* (1642), A2 recto.

4. Marsh (ibid.) relies heavily upon Henry Bracton, Dyer, and deductions from statutes. His sense of equity initially, 8–9, is of construction, not, as with *A question answered*, virtually a separate kind of rationale. At the end of the tract, 41–43, Marsh employs a more expansive notion; still he sandwiches the general position around a great many legal particulars.

5. [Parker,] *Observations*, 21, 25, 36–37. *Questions resolved . . .* (24 September 1642), BL E. 118 (38), 1, 3; Peter Bland, *Resolved vpon the question. Or a question resolved* (29 September 1642), BL E. 119 (4), 5; *The vindication of the parliament and their proceedings* (15 October 1642), BL E. 122 (19), 2.

6. *Touching the fundamentall lawes* (24 February 1643), BL E. 90 (21).

7. Milton, *Prose*, 2:19 and n. 29, 38 and n. 3.

8. William Haller, *Liberty and Reformation in the Puritan Revolution* (New York, 1955), 73; Schwoerer, *"No Standing Armies!"* 41–42. Husbands, *Exact collection*, 470.

Bibliography

Manuscripts

British Library:
  Additional:
    14827
  Cotton:
    Nero C. x.
    Appendix 47
  Harley:
    162–164
    477–480
    6424
  Sloane:
    744
  Stowe:
    184
    424
Cambridge University Library:
  Additional 89, 90 (Microfilm Y-641 at Yale Center for Parliamentary History, New Haven, Conn.)
Pierpont Morgan Library, New York:
  MA 276

Printed Works

Acts and Proceedings of the General Assemblies of the Kirk of Scotland from the Year M.D.L.X. Edited by Thomas Thomson. 3 vols. Edinburgh: Bannatyne and Maitland Clubs, 1839, 1840, 1845.

Acts for the utter abolishing of bishops . . . with . . . the order for church-government by a better way. . . . London, 1643.

Acts of the Parliaments of Scotland. Edited by Thomas Thomson and Cosmo Innes. 11 vols. Edinburgh, 1814–1844.

A dialogue. Wherin is plainly laide open. [1589?] Reprint. 1640.

Aelfric. *Aelfric's Lives of Saints,* part 3. Edited by Walter W. Skeat. London: Early

English Text Society, no. 94 (original series), 1890.

Allen, J. W. *A History of Political Thought in the Sixteenth Century.* London: Methuen, 1961.

Andrewes, Launcelot. *A sermon preached before the kings maiestie, at Hampton Court . . . the 28. of September, Anno. 1606.* London, 1606.

——. *The Works of Launcelot Andrewes, Sometime Bishop of Winchester.* 11 vols. Oxford: John Henry Parker, 1841–1872. Reprint. New York: AMS Press, 1967.

Aristotle. *The Politics.* Edited by and translated by Sir Ernest Barker. New York: Oxford University Press, 1962.

[Aston, Sir Thomas.] *A collection of sundry petitions.* London, 1642.

——. *A remonstrance against presbitery.* London, 1641.

Aylmer, John. *An harborowe for faithfull and trewe subiectes.* Strasbourg [*sic*: London], 1559.

Babbage, Stuart Barton. *Puritanism and Richard Bancroft.* London: S.P.C.K., 1962.

Bacon, Francis. *Works.* Edited by James Spedding, Robert Leslie Ellis, and Douglas Denon Heath. 14 vols. London: Longmans & Co., 1857–1874. Reprint. New York: Garrett Press, 1967.

Bagshaw, Edward. *A just vindication.* London, 1660.

——. *Mr. Bagshaw's speech in parliament February the ninth, 1640.* London, 1641.

Baillie, Robert. *Letters and Journals.* Edited by David Laing. 3 vols. Edinburgh: Bannatyne Club Publications, no. 73, 1841–1842.

——. *Vnlawfulnesse and danger of limited episcopacie.* London, 1641.

[Balcanquhall, Walter.] *A large declaration.* London, 1639.

Ball, J. N. "Sir John Eliot and Parliament, 1624–1629." In *Faction and Parliament: Essays on Early Stuart History,* edited by Kevin Sharpe. Oxford: Clarendon Press, 1978.

Bancroft, Richard. *Daungerous positions and proceedings, published and practised within this iland of Brytaine. . . .* London, 1593.

——. *A sermon preached at Paules Crosse the 9 Februarie, . . . 1588.* London, 1588.

[——.] *A survey of the pretended holy discipline.* London, 1593.

[——, supposed author.] *Tracts Ascribed to Richard Bancroft.* Edited by Albert Peel. Cambridge: Cambridge University Press, 1952.

Bard, Nelson P. "The Ship Money Case and William Fiennes, Viscount Saye and Sele," *Bulletin of the Institute for Historical Research* 50 (1977):177–84.

Barlow, William. *The first of the foure sermons . . . concerning the antiquity and superiority of bishops: Sept. 21. 1601.* London, 1607.

——. *The sermon preached at Paules Crosse, the tenth day of November* [1605]. London, 1606.

——. *The summe and substance of the conference . . . at Hampton Court.* London, 1604.

[Barrow, Henry?] *A petition directed to her most excellent maiestie.* [Middelburg?] 1592.

Batany, Jean. "Des 'trois fonctions' aux 'trois états?'" *Annales* 18 (1963):933–38.

Baumer, Franklin LeVan. *The Early Tudor Theory of Kingship.* New Haven: Yale University Press, 1940. Reprint. New York: Russell & Russell, 1966.

Baxter, Richard. *Reliquiae Baxterianae.* Edited by Matthew Sylvester. London, 1696.

Bell, Robert, ed. *Memorials of the Civil War: Comprising the Correspondence of the Fairfax Family.* 2 vols. London: Richard Bentley, 1849.

Bilson, Thomas. *The true difference between christian svbiection and vnchristian rebellion.* London, 1586.

Biondi, Giovanni Francesco. *An history of the civill warres of England.* Translated by Henry Carey, earl of Monmouth. Vol. 1. London, 1641.

Bland, Peter. *Resolved vpon the question. Or a question resolved.* London, 1642.

Boethius. *King Alfred's Anglo-Saxon Version of Boethius De Consolatione Philosophiae.* Edited and translated by J. S. Cardale. London: W. Pickering, 1829.

Bowyer, Robert. *The Parliamentary Diary of Robert Bowyer, 1606–07.* Edited by David Harris Willson. Minneapolis: University of Minnesota Press, 1931.

Bramston, Sir John. *The Autobiography of Sir John Bramston, K. B.* Preface by Richard Neville-Griffin, Baron Braybrooke. London: Camden Society Publications, no. 32 (1st series), 1845.

Bruce, John, ed. *Letters of Queen Elizabeth and King James VI of Scotland.* London: Camden Society Publications, no. 46 (1st series), 1849.

Buckeridge, John. *A sermon preached at Hampton Court before the king.* London, 1606.

B[urton], H[enry]. *Israels fast.* London, 1628.

Burton, John Hill, and Masson, David, eds. *Register of the Privy Council of Scotland, 1545–1625.* 14 vols. Edinburgh: H. M. General Register House, 1877–1898.

Caesar, Julius. *The Gallic War.* With a translation by H. J. Edwards. Cambridge Mass.: Harvard University Press, 1958.

Calderwood, David. *The History of the Kirk of Scotland.* Edited by Thomas Thomson. 8 vols. Edinburgh: Wodrow Society, 1842–1849.

Calendar of State Papers, Domestic Series, . . . 1625 [–1649]. Edited by John Bruce, et al. 23 vols. London: various publishers, 1858–1897.

Calendar of State Papers . . . in the Archives of Venice. Edited by H. F. Brown and A. B. Hinds. Vols. 1–38, 1603–1675; vol. 25, 1640–1642. London: H. M. S. O., 1864–1940, 1924.

Calendar of State Papers . . . Scotland, 1597–1603. Edited by John Duncan Mackie. 2 parts. Edinburgh: H. M S. O., 1969.

Cam, Helen. "The Theory and Practice of Representation in Medieval England." *History* 38 (1953). Reprinted with revision in *Historical Studies of the English Parliament*, edited by E. S. Fryde and Edward Miller. 2 vols. Cambridge: Cambridge University Press, 1970.

Camden, William. *Britain, or a chorographical description*. Translated by Philemon Holland. London, 1610.

Cameron, Annie, ed. *The Warrender Papers*. With introduction by Robert Rait. 2 vols. Edinburgh: Scottish Historical Society Publications, no. 19, 3rd series, 1932.

Carey, Henry, earl of Monmouth. *A speech made in the House of Peeres, . . . on Thursday the 13 of Ianuary. 1641*. London, 1641.

Carlson, Leland. *Martin Marprelate, Gentleman: Master Job Throckmorton Laid Open in His Colors*. San Marino, Calif.: Huntington Library, 1981.

———. "Martin Marprelate: His Identity and His Satire." In Leland Carlson and Ronald Paulson, *English Satire*. Los Angeles: William Andrews Clark Memorial Library, University of California, 1972.

Carozzi, Claude. "Les fondements de la tripartition sociale chez Adalbéron de Laon." *Annales* 33 (1978):633–702.

Cavendish, Margaret, duchess of Newcastle. *The Life of William Cavendish, Duke of Newcastle*. Edited by C. H. Firth. New York: E. P. Dutton, 1906.

Cawdrey, Robert. *Table alphabetical . . . of hard vsvall English wordes*. London, 1604.

Certain briefe treatises. Oxford, 1641.

Certaine reasons tending to prove the vnlawfulnesse. . . . London, 1641.

[Charles I, supposed author.] *Eikon Basilike*. Edited by Philip Knachel. Ithaca: Cornell University Press for the Folger Shakespeare Library, 1966.

Charles I. *His majesties answer to the xix propositions of both houses of parliament*. London, 1642 [British Library Shelfmark E. 151 (25)].

———. *His maiesties declaration concerning his proceeding with his subiects of Scotland*. London, 1640. Reprint. Amsterdam: Theatrum Orbis Terrarum, 1971.

———. *His maiesties message to the House of Peers* [22 April 1642]. London, 1642.

———. *His majesties proclamation in Scotland, with an explanation of the meaning of the oath and covenant*. London, 1639. Reprint. Amsterdam: Theatrum Orbis Terrarum, 1974.

Chrimes, Stanley Bertram. *English Constitutional Ideas of the Fifteenth Century*. Cambridge: Cambridge University Press, 1936.

———. "Sir John Fortescue and His Theory of Dominion." *Transactions of the Royal Historical Society*, 4th series, 17 (1934):117–47.

Chrimes, Stanley Bertram, and Brown, Alfred L., eds. *Select Documents of English Constitutional History, 1307–1485*. New York: Barnes & Noble, 1961.

Christianson, Paul. "The Peers, the People, and Parliamentary Management in the First Six Months of the Long Parliament." *Journal of Modern History* 49 (1977):575–99.

Clarke, Maud V. *Medieval Representation and Consent, A Study of Early Parliaments in England and Ireland, with Special Reference to the* Modus Tenendi Parliamentum. London: Longmans, Green & Co., 1936. Reprint. New York: Russell & Russell, 1964.

Collinson, Patrick. *The Elizabethan Puritan Movement.* London: Jonathan Cape, 1967.

———. "Episcopacy and Reform in England in the Later Sixteenth Century." In *Studies in Church History,* vol. 3, edited by G. J. Cuming. Leiden: E. J. Brill, 1966.

———, ed. *Letters of Thomas Wood, Puritan, 1566–1577.* In *Bulletin of the Institute of Historical Research Special Supplement* no. 5. London, November 1960.

Constitutions & Canons Ecclesiastical 1604. Edited by H. A. Wilson. Oxford: Clarendon Press, 1923.

The Convocation Book of M DC VI. Commonly Called Bishop Overall's Convocation Book. . . . Library of Anglo-Catholic Theology, no. 29. Oxford: John Henry Parker, 1844.

Cooper, Thomas. *An admonition to the people of England.* London, 1589.

Cope, Esther S., with Willson H. Coates, eds. *Proceedings of the Short Parliament of 1640.* London: Camden Society Publications, no. 29 (4th series), 1977.

Covell, William. *A modest & reasonable examination.* London, 1604.

Cowell, John. *The interpreter.* Cambridge, 1607.

Coxe, Henry Octavius, and Firth, Sir Charles, general editors. *Calendar of the Clarendon State Papers Preserved in the Bodleian Library.* 5 vols. Oxford: Clarendon Press, 1869–1970. Vol. 1 (1869), edited by Octavius Ogle and William Henry Bliss.

Crawford, S. J., ed. *The Old English Version of the Heptateuch, Aelfric's Treatise on the Old and New Testament and his Preface to Genesis.* London: Early English Text Society Publications, no. 160 (original series), 1922.

Cross, Claire. *The Royal Supremacy in the Elizabethan Church.* New York: Barnes & Noble, 1969.

Curtis, Mark. "Hampton Court Conference and its Aftermath." *History* 46 (1961):1–16.

Danielsson, Bror. *Sir Thomas Smith, 1513–1577. Literary and Linguistic Works (1542, 1549, 1568).* Stockholm: Almqvist & Wiskell, Stockholm Studies in English no. 12, 1963.

Dering, Sir Edward. *A collection of speeches.* London, 1641.

Dewar, Mary. *Sir Thomas Smith: A Tudor Intellectual in Office.* London: University of London, Athlone Press, 1964.

————, ed. *A Discourse of the Commonweal of this Realm of England, Attributed to Sir Thomas Smith.* Charlottesville, Va." University Press of Virginia for the Folger Shakespeare Library, 1969.

D'Ewes, Sir Simonds. *Autobiography and Correspondence of Sir Simonds D'Ewes, Bart.* Edited by James Orchard Halliwell. 2 vols. London: R. Bentley, 1845.

————. *Journal of Sir Simonds D'Ewes from the Beginning of the Long Parliament to the Opening of the Trial of the Earl of Strafford.* Edited by Wallace Notestein. New Haven: Yale University Press, 1923.

————. *Journal of Sir Simonds D'Ewes from the First Recess of the Long Parliament to the Withdrawal of King Charles from London.* Edited by Willson Havelock Coates. New Haven: Yale University Press, 1942.

————. *Journals of all the parliaments . . . of Queen Elizabeth.* Revised by Paul Bowes. London, 1682.

Dictionary of National Biography . . . to 1900. Edited by Sir Leslie Stephen and Sir Sidney Lee. 21 vols. 1921–1922. Reprint. London: Oxford University Press, 1949–1950.

Digby, George, earl of Bristol. *The third speech of the lord George Digby . . . the 9th of Febr: 1640.* [London,] 1640.

Donaldson, Gordon. "The Attitude of Whitgift and Bancroft to the Scottish Church." *Transactions of the Royal Historical Society,* 4th series, 24 (1942): 95–115.

————. "Foundations of Anglo-Scottish Union." In *Elizabethan Government and Society,* edited by Stanley Thomas Bindoff, Joel Hurstfield, and C. H. Williams. London: University of London, Athlone Press, 1961.

————. "Lord Chancellor Glamis and Theodore Beza." *Scottish Historical Society Miscellany* 9 (1951):89–113.

————. "The Polity of the Scottish Church, 1560–1600." *Records of the Scottish Church Historical Society* 11 (1953):212–226.

————. *Scotland: James V to James VII.* Edinburgh: Oliver & Boyd, 1965.

————. "Scottish Presbyterian Exiles in England, 1584–88." *Records of the Scottish Church Historical Society* 14 (1963):67–80.

————. *The Scottish Reformation.* Cambridge: Cambridge University Press, 1960.

Dove, John. *A defence of church government.* London, 1606.

Downame, George. *Two sermons.* London, 1608.

Downing, Calybute. *Considerations toward a peaceable reformation in matters ecclesiastical.* London, 1641.

————. *A sermon preached to the renowned Company of the Artillery.* London, 1642.

Dubuisson, Daniel. "L'Irlande et la théorie mediévale des 'trois ordres.'" *Revue de l'Histoire des Religions* 188 (1975):35–63.

Duby, Georges. *The Three Orders: Feudal Society Imagined.* Translated by Arthur Goldhammer. Chicago: University of Chicago Press, 1980.

Dumézil, Georges. *Archaic Roman Religion.* Translated by Philip Krapp. 2 vols. Chicago: University of Chicago Press, 1970.

Dunkel, Wilbur. *William Lambarde, Elizabethan Jurist, 1536–1601.* New Brunswick: Rutgers University Press, 1965.

Dunlop, A. Ian. "The Polity of the Scottish Church, 1600–1637." *Records of the Scottish Church Historical Society* 12 (1956):161–84.

Dury, John. "A briefe declaration . . . of the severall formes of government received in those churches." In *Certaine briefe treatises.* Oxford, 1641.

Dyer, James. *Cy ensuont ascuns nouel cases collectes per le iades tresreuerend iudge, mounsieur Jasques Dyer.* London, 1585.

Ellis, Henry, ed. *Original Letters Illustrative of English History.* 2nd series. 4 vols. London: Harding & Lepard, 1827.

Elton, Geoffrey. *"The Body of the Whole Realm": Parliament and Representation in Medieval and Tudor England.* Charlottesville: University Press of Virginia, 1969.

———, ed. *The Tudor Constitution: Documents and Commentary.* Cambridge: Cambridge University Press, 1968.

Elyot, Thomas. *The boke named the governour.* London: 1531. Facsimile reprint. Menston, Yorks.: Scolar Press, 1970.

Epstein, Joel J. "Francis Bacon and the Issue of Union, 1603–08." *Huntington Library Quarterly* 33 (1969–1970):121–32.

Evelyn, John. *Diary and Correspondence.* Edited by William Bray. 4 vols. London: G. Routledge & Sons, 1906.

[Fenner, Dudley?] *A covnter-poyson, modestly written for the time.* London [1584].

Fiennes, William, Viscount Saye and Sele. *Two speeches of the right honourable William lord Viscount Say and Seale.* London, 1641.

Finch, Sir Henry. *Law, or, a discourse thereof.* London, 1627.

———. *Nomotechnia.* London, 1613.

Firth, Sir Charles Harding. *The House of Lords during the Civil War.* London: Longmans, Green & Co., 1910.

Fletcher, Anthony. *The Outbreak of the English Civil War.* New York: New York University Press, 1981.

Forbes, Allyn Baily, ed. *Winthrop Papers.* 5 vols. Boston: Massachusetts Historical Society, 1929–1947.

Fortescue, Sir John. *De Laudibus Legum Angliae.* Edited by Stanley Bertram Chrimes. Cambridge: Cambridge University Press, 1942.

Foster, Elizabeth Read, ed. *Proceedings in Parliament, 1610.* 2 vols. New Haven: Yale University Press, 1966.

Foster, Joseph, ed. *Alumni Oxoniensis . . . 1500–1714.* 4 vols. 1891–1892. Reprint (4 vols. in 2). Nendeln, Lichtenstein: Kraus, 1968.

Foster, Walter Roland. *The Church Before the Covenants.* Edinburgh: Scottish Academic Press, 1975.

——. "The Operation of Presbyteries in Scotland, 1600–1638." *Records of the Scottish Church Historical Society* 15 (1965):21–33.

Foxe, John. *Actes and monuments.* London, 1563.

Franklin, Julian H. *John Locke and the Theory of Sovereignty: Mixed Monarchy and the Right of Resistance in the Political Thought of the English Revolution.* New York: Cambridge University Press, 1978.

——, ed. and trans. *Constitutionalism and Resistance in the Sixteenth Century: Three Treatises by Hotman, Beza, and Mornay.* New York: Pegasus, 1969.

Fuller, Thomas. *Church History of Britain.* 3 vols. London: T. Tegg, 1837.

Fussner, Frank Smith. "William Camden's 'Discourse Concerning the Prerogative of the Crown.'" *Proceedings of the American Philosophical Society* 101 (1957):204–15.

Gardiner, Dorothy, ed. *The Oxinden Letters, 1607–1642.* London: Constable & Co., 1933.

Gardiner, Samuel Rawson, ed. *Constitutional Documents of the Puritan Revolution, 1625–1660.* 3rd. ed. Oxford: Oxford University Press, 1906.

——, ed. *The Hamilton Papers, 1638–1648.* London: Camden Society Publications, no. 27 (2nd series), 1880.

——. *History of England . . . 1603–1642.* 10 vols. London: Longmans, Green & Co., 1883–1884.

——. *Parliamentary Debates in 1610.* Westminster: Camden Society Publications, no. 81 (1st series), 1862.

Gardiner, Stephen. *The Letters of Stephen Gardiner.* Edited by James Arthur Muller. Cambridge: University Press, 1933.

——. *A Machiavellian Treatise.* Edited and translated by Peter Samuel Donaldson. Cambridge: Cambridge University Press, 1974.

——. *De vera obedientia.* Roane [Geneva?], 1553. Reprint. Leeds: Scolar Press, 1966.

Gay, Edwin F. "The Temples of Stowe and Their Debts: Peter and John Temple, 1603–1653." *Huntington Library Quarterly* 2 (1938–1939):399–438.

Gilbert, Felix. "Fortescue's 'Dominium Regale et Politicum.'" *Medievalia et Humanistica,* fasc. 2 (1944):88–97.

Gillett, Charles Ripley, ed. *Catalogue of the McAlpin Collection.* 5 vols. New York, 1927–1930.

Green, I. M. *The Re-Establishment of the Church of England, 1660–1663.* Oxford: Oxford University Press, 1978.

Grimston, Sir Harbottle. *Mr. Grimstons argument concerning bishops: with Mr. Seldens answer. Also severall orders concerning church government.* [London,] 1641.

Hacket, John. *Memoirs of the life of Archbishop Williams.* London, 1715.

———. *Scrinia reserata.* London, 1693.

[Hales, John.] *The way towards the finding of a decision . . . concerning church government.* London, 1641.

Hall, Arthur. *An Account of a Quarrel between A. H., Esq., and Melchisedech Mallorie, Gent.* Reprinted in *Miscellanea antiqua Anglicana,* edited by Robert Triphook. London: R. Triphook, 1816. Includes *An Admonition by the Father of F. A.*

Haller, William. *Liberty and Reformation in the Puritan Revolution.* New York: Columbia University Press, 1955.

———. *Tracts on Liberty in the Puritan Revolution, 1638–1647.* 3 vols. New York: Columbia University Press, 1934.

Hamilton, Charles. "The Basis for Scottish Efforts to Create a Reformed Church in England, 1640–41." *Church History* 30 (1961):171–78.

Hanson, Donald W. *From Kingdom to Commonwealth: The Development of Civic Consciousness in English Political Thought.* Cambridge, Mass.: Harvard University Press, 1970.

Harrington, James. *The Political Works.* Edited and with an introduction by J. G. A. Pocock. Cambridge: Cambridge University Press, 1975.

Harris, R. W. *Clarendon and the English Revolution.* Stanford, Calif.: Stanford University Press, 1983.

Harrison, William. *The Description of England.* Edited by Georges Edelen. Ithaca: Cornell University Press for the Folger Shakespeare Library, 1968.

Hartley, T. E., ed. *Proceedings in the Parliaments of Elizabeth I, 1558–1581.* 2 vols. Wilmington, Del.: Michael Glazier, 1981.

Hasler, P. W., ed. *The History of Parliament: The House of Commons 1558–1603.* 3 vols. London: H. M. S. O. for the History of Parliament Trust, 1981.

Heal, Felicity. *Of Prelates and Princes: A Study of the Economic and Social Position of the Tudor Episcopate.* Cambridge: Cambridge University Press, 1980.

Hearne, Thomas, ed. *A collection of curious discourses.* Reedited by Joseph Ayloffe. 2 vols. London, 1771. Another cited edition, London, 1775.

Heinze, Rudolph W. *The Proclamations of the Tudor Kings.* Cambridge: Cambridge University Press, 1976.

Henderson, Alexander. *Vnlawfulnes and danger of limited prelacie.* London, 1641.

Hexter, J. H. "Power Struggle, Parliament, and Liberty in Early Stuart England." *Journal of Modern History* 50 (1978):1–50.

Heylyn, Peter. *Augustus.* London, 1632.

———. *Cyprianus Anglicus.* London, 1668.

———. *Ecclesia Restaurata.* Edited by James Craigie Robertson. 2 vols. Cambridge: For the Ecclesiastical History Society, 1849.

———. *The historical and miscellaneous tracts.* London, 1681.

Hinton, R. W. K. "The Decline of Parliamentary Government under Elizabeth I and the Early Stuarts." *Cambridge Historical Journal* 13 (1957): 116–32.

——. "English Constitutional Theories from Sir John Fortescue to Sir John Eliot." *English Historical Review* 75 (1960):410–25.

Hirst, Derek. "Unanimity in the Commons, Aristocratic Intrigues, and the Origins of the English Civil War." *Journal of Modern History* 50 (1978):51–71.

Historical Manuscripts Commission. *5th Report.* London: H. M. S. O., 1876.

——. *Manuscripts of the House of Lords, Addenda, 1514–1714.* Edited by Maurice Bond. Vol. 11 (new series). London: H. M. S. O., 1962.

Hobbes, Thomas. *Leviathan.* Edited by C. B. Macpherson. Harmondsworth, Middlesex: Penguin Books, 1968.

Hooker, Richard. *Of the Laws of Ecclesiastical Polity.* Edited by Ronald Bayne. 2 vols. London: J. M. Dent, 1907.

Hope, Sir Thomas. *A Diary of the Public Correspondence of Sir Thomas Hope . . . , 1633–1645.* Edited by Thomas Thomson. Edinburgh: Bannatyne Club Publications, no. 76, 1843.

Hotman, François. *Francogallia.* Latin text by Ralph E. Giesey. Translated by J. H. M. Salmon. Edited by Giesey and Salmon. Cambridge: Cambridge University Press, 1972.

Howell, Thomas Bayly, ed. *A Complete Collection of State Trials.* 33 vols. London: Longman, Hurst, Rees, Orme, & Browne, 1809–1826.

Hudson, Winthrop S. *John Ponet (1516?–1556), Advocate of Limited Monarchy.* Chicago: University of Chicago Press, 1942. Includes John Ponet's *A shorte treatise of politike power,* 1556.

——. "The Scottish Effort to Presbyterianize the Church of England During the Early Months of the Long Parliament." *Church History* 8 (1939):255–82.

Hughes, Paul L., and Larkin, James F., eds. *Tudor Royal Proclamations.* 3 vols. New Haven: Yale University Press, 1964–1969.

Hulme, Harold. "Charles I and the Constitution." In *Conflict in Stuart England: Essays in Honour of Wallace Notestein,* edited by William Appleton Aiken and Basil Duke Henning. London: Jonathan Cape, 1960.

Hume, David. *History of England.* 8 vols. London: Baynes & Son, 1822.

Hurstfield, Joel. *Freedom, Corruption and Government in Elizabethan England.* Cambridge, Mass.: Harvard University Press, 1973.

Husbands, Edward, ed. *An exact collection.* London, 1643.

Hyde, Edward, earl of Clarendon. *The History of the Rebellion. . . .* Edited by W. Dunn Macray. 6 vols. Oxford: Clarendon Press, 1888.

——. *The History of the Rebellion . . . , Also, His Life.* 2 vols. Oxford: University Press, 1843.

James I. *Basilikon doron.* Edited by James Craigie. Edinburgh: Scottish Text Society Publications, nos. 16, 18 (3rd series), 1944, 1950.

——. *The Political Works of James I.* Edited by Charles Howard McIlwain. Cambridge, Mass.: Harvard University Press, 1918.

John, of Worcester. *The Chronicle of John of Worcester 1118–1140.* Edited by J. R. H. Weaver. Oxford: Clarendon Press, 1908.

Johnston, Archibald, reviser. *An answer to the profession and declaration made by James Marques of Hamilton.* Edinburgh, 1639.

————, reviser. *The declinator and protestation of the sometimes pretended bishops refuted.* Edinburgh, 1639.

————. *Diary of Sir Archibald Johnston of Wariston, 1632–1639.* Edited by George Morison Paul. Edinburgh: Scottish Historical Society Publications, no. 61 (1st series), 1911.

Jordan, Wilbur Kitchener. *Men of Substance.* Chicago: University of Chicago Press, 1942.

Journals of the House of Commons, 1547– . [London.] Printed by order of the House of Commons, 1803– .

Journals of the House of Lords, 1509– . n.p., n.d.

Judson, Margaret Atwood. "Henry Parker and the Theory of Parliamentary Sovereignty." In *Essays in History and Political Theory in Honor of Charles Howard McIlwain,* edited by Carl Frederick Wittke. Cambridge, Mass.: Harvard University Press, 1936.

Keeler, Mary Frear. *The Long Parliament, 1640–41.* Memoirs of the American Philosophical Society, vol. 36. Philadelphia: American Philosophical Society, 1954.

Kenyon, John Philipps. *The Stuart Constitution: Documents and Commentary.* Cambridge: Cambridge University Press, 1966.

[Ker, William, earl of Lothian.] *A true representation of the proceedings of the kingdome of Scotland, since the late pacification.* n. p., 1640.

King, John. *A sermon preached at Whitehall the 5. day of November.* Oxford, 1608.

————. *The fourth sermon preached at Hampton Court . . . .* Oxford, 1606.

Kirk, James. "'The Polities of the Best Reformed Kirks': Scottish Achievements and English Aspirations in Church Government after the Reformation." *Scottish Historical Review* 59 (1980):22–53.

Kishlansky, Mark. "The Emergence of Adversary Politics in the Long Parliament." *Journal of Modern History* 49 (1977):617–40.

Knafla, Louis A. *Law and Politics in Jacobean England: the Tracts of Lord Chancellor Ellesmere.* Cambridge: Cambridge University Press, 1977.

Lambarde, William. *Archeion, or A Discourse upon the High Courts of Justice in England.* Edited by Charles Howard McIlwain and Paul L. Ward. Cambridge, Mass.: Harvard University Press, 1957.

Lambert, Malcolm. *Medieval Heresy: Popular Movements from Bogomil to Hus.* New York: Holmes & Meir, 1977.

Larkin, James F., and Hughes, Paul L. *Royal Proclamations of King James I, 1603–1625.* Oxford: Clarendon Press, 1973. Vol. 1 of *Stuart Royal Proclamations,* incomplete.

Laud, William. *The Works of the Most Reverend Father in God, William Laud, D. D. Sometime Lord Archbishop of Canterbury.* 7 vols. Edited by William Scott and James Bliss. 1847–1860. Reprint. New York: AMS Press, 1975.

Lee, Maurice. *Government by Pen: Scotland under James VI and I.* Urbana: University of Illinois Press, 1981.

——. "James VI and the Revival of Episcopacy in Scotland: 1596–1600." *Church History* 43 (1974):50–64.

——. *John Maitland of Thirlestane.* Princeton: Princeton University Press, 1959.

Lefranc, Pierre. *Sir Walter Raleigh écrivain: l'oeuvre et les idées.* Paris: Armand Colin, 1968.

Le Goff, Jacques. *La civilisation de l'Occident médiéval.* Paris: Arthaud, 1972.

——. "Les trois fonctions indo-européennes, l'historien et l'Europe féodale." *Annales* 34 (1979):1187–215.

——. *Time, Work, and Culture in the Middle Ages.* Translated by Arthur Goldhammer. Chicago: University of Chicago Press, 1980.

Levack, Brian. *The Civil Lawyers in England, 1603–1641: A Political Study.* Oxford: Clarendon Press, 1973.

Littleton, C. Scott. *The New Comparative Mythology.* Berkeley: University of California Press, 1966.

The lives of all the lords chancellors. 2 vols. 2nd ed. n.p., 1712.

Machiavelli, Niccolò. *Machiavels discourses upon the first decade of T. Livius.* Translated by Edward Dacres. London, 1636.

——. *Opere.* Edited by Mario Bonfantini. Milan: Ricciardi, 1963.

McIlwain, Charles Howard. *Constitutionalism Ancient and Modern.* Ithaca: Cornell University Press, 1958.

Maitland, Frederic William, Introduction to *Memoranda de Parliamento.* London: Rolls Series, 1893. Reprinted in Maitland, *Selected Essays,* edited by Harold Dexter Hazeltine, Gaillard Lapsley, and Percy Henry Winfield; Cambridge: Cambridge University Press, 1936; and in Maitland, *Selected Historical Essays,* edited by Helen Cam; Cambridge: Published in association with the Selden Society of the University Press, 1957.

Makey, Walter. *The Church of the Covenant, 1637–1651.* Edinburgh: John Donald Publishers, 1979.

Malvezzi, Virgilio. *Il ritratto del privato politico christiano.* Bologna, 1635.

——. *Romvlvs and Tarqvin.* Translated by Henry Carey, earl of Monmouth. London, 1637.

Marprelate, Martin [pseud.]. *The Marprelate Tracts [1588–1589].* Menston, Yorks.: Scolar Press, 1970.

——. *Reformation no enemie.* London, 1641.

Marsh, John. *An argument or, debate in law of the great question concerning the militia.* London, 1642.

Masson, David. *Life of John Milton.* 7 vols. Cambridge: Macmillan & Co., 1859–1894.

Melville, James. *Autobiography and Diary of Mr. James Melvill with a Continuation of the Diary.* Edited by Robert Pitcairn. Edinburgh: Wodrow Society, 1842.

Mendle, Michael J. "Politics and Political Thought, 1640–42." In *The Origins of the English Civil War,* edited by Conrad Russell. London: Macmillan & Co., 1973.

Mercer, Eric. *Furniture, 700–1700.* New York: Meredith Press, 1969.

Meriton, George. *A sermon of nobility.* London, 1607.

Migne, Jacques Paul, ed. *Patrologia cursus completus . . . series latina.* 221 vols. Paris, 1844–1864.

Milton, John. *Complete Prose Works of John Milton.* Don M. Wolfe, general editor. 7 vols. to date. New Haven: Yale University Press, 1953–   .Vol. 2 (1959), edited by Ernest Sirluck.

Miller, Perry, and Johnson, Thomas H., eds. *The Puritans.* 2 vols. New York: Harper & Row, 1963.

Minsheu, John. *Ductor in linguas.* London, 1617.

Mohl, Ruth. *The Three Estates in Medieval and Renaissance Literature.* New York: Columbia University Press, 1933. Reprint. New York: F. Unger, 1962.

[Morley, George.] *A modest advertisement concerning the present controversie about church government.* London, 1641.

Morrill, John Stephen. *The Revolt of the Provinces.* New York: Barnes & Noble, 1976.

Munden, R. C. "James I and 'the Growth of Mutual Distrust': King, Commons, and Reform, 1603–04." In *Faction and Parliament: Essays on Early Stuart History,* edited by Kevin Sharpe. Oxford: Clarendon Press, 1978.

Neale, J. E. *Elizabeth I and her Parliaments.* 2 vols. London: Jonathan Cape, 1969.

Niccoli, Ottavia. *I sacerdoti, i guerrieri, i contadini. Storia di un'immagine della società.* Turin: G. Einaudi, 1979.

Northcote, Sir John. *Note Book of Sir John Northcote.* Edited by A. H. A. Hamilton. London: J. Murray, 1877.

The order and forme for church, government by bishops and the clergie of this kingdome. Voted in the House of Commons on Friday, Iuly 16. 1641. Whereunto is added Mr. Grimstons and Mr. Seldens arguments concerning episcopacie. [London,] 1641.

Ormerod, Oliver. *The picture of a puritan.* London, 1605.

[Overton, Richard.] *Englands birth-right justified.* [London,] 1645.

Owst, Gerald Robert. *Literature and Pulpit in Medieval England.* Cambridge: Cambridge University Press, 1933.

P[arker], H[enry]. *The altar dispute.* London, 1641.

[Parker, Henry.] *The case of shipmony.* [London,] 1640.

[————.] *A discourse concerning puritans.* London: 1640.

[————.] *The generall junto, or the councell of union.* n.p., 1642.

[————.] *The humble remonstrance of the Company of Stationers.* London, 1643. Reprinted in *Transcript of the Registers of the Company of Stationers of London, 1554–1640,* edited by Edward Arber. 5 vols. London: privately printed, 1875–1877, vols. 1–4; Birmingham: privately printed, 1894, vol. 5.

[————,] *Mr. William Wheelers case.* London, 1645.

[————.] *Observations upon some of his majesties late answers and expresses.* [London,] 1642.

————. *Of a free trade.* London, 1648.

[————?] *A question answered: how laws are to be understood, and obedience yeelded?* . . . [London, 1642.]

[————.] *Some few observations upon his majesties late answer.* [London,] 1642.

[————.] *The vintners answer to some scandalous phamphlets.* London, 1640.

Parliamentary . . . History of England. 24 vols. London, 1751–1762.

Pecock, Reginald. *The Repressor of Over Much Blaming of the Clergy.* Edited by Churchill Babington. 2 vols. London: Longman, Green, Longman & Roberts, 1860.

Penry, John. *Th' appelation of John Penri.* [La Rochelle,] 1589.

Persecutio undecima. London, 1647.

A plea for moderation. London, 1642.

Pocock, J. G. A. *The Ancient Constitution and the Feudal Law.* New York: W. W. Norton & Co., 1967.

————. *The Machiavellian Moment: Florentine Political Thought and the Atlantic Republican Tradition.* Princeton: Princeton University Press, 1975.

Pollard, Albert Frederick. *The Evolution of Parliament* 2nd ed. London: Longmans, Green & Co., 1934.

————. Review of *English Constitutional Ideas,* by Stanley Bertram Chrimes. *History* 22 (1937):164–65.

Pollard, Alfred William, ed. *Fifteenth-Century Prose and Verse.* London: A. Constable, 1903. Reprint. New York: Cooper Square Publishers, 1964.

Pollard, A. W., and Redgrave, G. R. *A Short-Title Catalogue . . . , 1475–1640.* London: Bibliographical Society, 1946. 2nd ed., rev. by W. A. Jackson, F. S. Ferguson, and Katharine Pantzer, vol. 2: I–Z. London: Bibliographical Society, 1976.

Ponet, John. *A shorte treatise of politike power.* [Strasburg?] 1556.

Prest, Wilfrid R. "The Art of Law and the Law of God: Sir Henry Finch (1558–1625)." In *Puritans and Revolutionaries: Essays in Seventeenth-Century History Presented to Christopher Hill,* edited by Donald Pennington and Keith Thomas. Oxford: Clarendon Press, 1978.

The principall acts of the solemne generall assembly . . . at Glasgow the xxi of November 1638. Edinburgh, 1639.

Privy Council Registers Preserved in the Public Record Office. Vol. 12. London: H. M. S. O., 1968.

The protestation of the Generall Assemblie. . . . [29 November 1638] Glasgow, 1638. Reprint. Amsterdam: Theatrum Orbis Terrarum, 1971.

Prynne, William. *The fourth part of a brief register . . . of parliamentary writs.* London, 1664.

Questions resolved. . . . [London, 1642.]

Raleigh, Sir Walter. *Works.* 8 vols. Oxford: Oxford University Press, 1829.

Roberts, Clayton. "The Earl of Bedford and the Coming of the English Revolution." *Journal of Modern History* 49 (1977):600–616.

Roskell, John. "The Social Composition of the Commons in a Fifteenth-Century Parliament." *Bulletin of the Institute of Historical Research* 24 (1951):152–72.

Russell, Conrad. "The Authorship of the Bishop's Diary of the House of Lords in 1641." *Bulletin of the Institute of Historical Research* 41 (1968):229–36.

———. "Introduction," and "Parliament and the King's Finances." In *The Origins of the English Civil War,* edited by Conrad Russell. London: Macmillan & Co., 1973.

———. "The Parliamentary Career of John Pym, 1621–29." In *The English Commonwealth, 1547–1640,* edited by Peter Clark, Alan G. R. Smith, and Nicholas Tyacke. New York: Barnes & Noble, 1979.

———. "Parliamentary History in Perspective." *History* 61 (1976):1–27.

———. *Parliaments and English Politics, 1621–1629.* Oxford: Clarendon Press, 1979.

Sarpi, Paolo. *History of the inquisition.* Translated by Robert Gentilis. London, 1639.

Sayles, George Osborne. *The King's Parliament of England.* New York: W. W. Norton, 1974.

Scarisbrick, J. J. *Henry VIII.* Harmondsworth, Middlesex: Penguin Books, 1971.

Schwoerer, Lois, G. *"No Standing Armies!"* Baltimore: Johns Hopkins University Press, 1974.

Selden, John. *Jani Anglorum facies altera.* London, 1610.

———. *The privileges of the baronage in England, when they sit in parliament.* London, 1642.

———. *Table talk of John Selden.* Edited by Sir Frederick Pollock. London: Quaritch, 1927.

———. *Titles of honor.* London, 1614. 2nd ed. London, 1631.

———. *Tracts written by John Selden.* Edited and translated by Redman Wescot [pseud.]. London, 1683.

Sergent, Bernard. "Les trois fonctions des Indo-Européens dans la Grèce ancienne: bilan critique." *Annales* 34 (1979):1155–87.

Seyssel, Claude de. *La monarchie de France.* . . . Edited by Jacques Poujol. Paris: Librairie d'Argences, 1961.

Sharpe, Kevin. "Introduction: Parliamentary History, 1603–1629: in or out of Perspective?" In *Faction and Parliament: Essays on Early Stuart History,* edited by Kevin Sharpe. Oxford: Clarendon Press, 1978.

Shaw, William Arthur. *A History of the English Church during the Civil Wars and under the Commonwealth, 1640–1660.* 2 vols. London: Longmans, Green & Co., 1900.

A short treatise of archbishops and bishops. London, 1641.

Sixteene propositions in parliament. London, 1642.

Skeel, Caroline. "The Influence of the Writings of Sir John Fortescue." *Transactions of the Royal Historical Society,* 3rd series, 10 (1916):77–114.

Smith, Sir Thomas. *De republica Anglorum.* Edited by L. Alston. Cambridge: University Press, 1906.

Snow, Vernon F. *Parliament in Elizabethan England: John Hooker's Order and Usage.* New Haven, Conn.: Yale University Press, 1977.

Spalding, James, and Brass, Maynard. "Reduction of Episcopacy as a Means to Unity in England, 1640–1662." *Church History* 30 (1961):414–32.

Spalding, John. *The History of the Troubles and Memorable Transactions* . . . . 2 vols. Edinburgh: Bannatyne Club, 1828.

Spelman, Sir Henry. *Reliquiae Spelmannianae.* London, 1723.

Spelman, Sir John. *The case of our affaires.* [Oxford,] 1643. Reprint. Exeter: Rota, 1975.

Spottiswoode, John. *History of the Church of Scotland.* Edited by Michael Russell. 3 vols. Edinburgh: Spottiswoode Society, 1847–1851.

Starkey, Thomas. *England in the Reign of King Henry the Eighth. A Dialogue between Cardinal Pole and Thomas Lupset.* Edited by J. M. Cowper. London: Early English Text Society no. 12 (extra series), 1872.

Stevenson, David. *The Scottish Revolution 1637–1644.* New York: St. Martin's Press, 1973.

Stone, Lawrence, ed. *Social Change and Revolution in England, 1540–1640.* London: Longmans, 1966.

[Stoughton, William?]. *An abstract of certaine acts of parlement.* n.p. [1584.]

Stoughton, William. *An assertion for true and christian church-policie.* [Middelburg, 1604]. Two other editions, 1642.

Strype, John. *Works.* 21 vols. in 25. Oxford: Clarendon Press, 1812–1840.

Stubbs, William. *The Constitutional History of England in Its Origin and Development.* 3 vols. 3rd ed. Oxford: Clarendon Press, 1884.

The substance of a conference. . . . London, 1641.

Sutcliffe, Matthew. *An answere to a certaine libel supplicatorie, or rather diffamatorie.* London, 1592.

————. *An answere vnto a certaine caluminious letter published by M. Iob Throckmorton.* London, 1595.

Taviani, Huguette. "Le mariage dans l'hérésie de l'An Mil." *Annales 32* (1977):1074–89.

Thompson, W. D. J. Cargill. "Sir Francis Knollys' Campaign against the *Jure Divino* Theory of Episcopacy." In *The Dissenting Tradition: Essays for Leland H. Carlson,* edited by C. Robert Cole, and Michael E. Moody. Athens, Ohio: Ohio University Press, 1975.

To the honovrable the Hovse of Commons . . . the humble petition of many thousand poore people, in and about the citie of London. [London, 1642].

Touching the fundamentall lawes. London, 1643.

Travers, Walter. *A full and plaine declaration of ecclesiasticall discipline.* London, 1574.

Trevor-Roper, H. R. *Religion, the Reformation and Social Change.* London: Macmillan & Co., 1967.

Twysden, Sir Roger. *Certaine Considerations Upon the Government of England.* Edited by J. M. Kemble. London: Camden Society Publications, no. 45 (1st series), 1849.

Tyacke, Nicholas. "Puritanism, Arminianism, and Counter-Revolution." In *The Origins of the English Civil War,* edited by Conrad Russell. London: Macmillan & Co., 1973.

Usher, Roland G. *Reconstruction of the English Church.* 2 vols. New York: D. Appleton & Co., 1910.

————. *The Rise and Fall of the High Commission.* New introduction by Philip Tyler. Oxford: Clarendon Press, 1968.

Ussher, James. *The reduction of episcopacie unto the form of synodical government received in the antient* [or *ancient*] *church.* 2 editions. London, 1656.

Van Norden, Linda. "The Elizabethan College of Antiquaries." Ph.D. dissertation, University of California at Los Angeles, 1946.

————. "Sir Henry Spelman on the Chronology of the Elizabethan College of Antiquaries." *Huntington Library Quarterly* 13 (1948–1949):131–60.

Verney, Sir Ralph. *Verney Papers, Notes of Proceedings in the Long Parliament, temp. Charles I.* Edited by John Bruce. London: J. B. Nichols & Son for Camden Society Publications, no. 31 (1st series), 1845.

The vindication of the parliament and their proceedings. London, 1642.

Wallington, Nehemiah. *Historical Notices . . . of the Reign of Charles I.* Edited by Rosamond Anne Webb. 2 vols. London: R. Bentley, 1869.

Walton, Izaak. *The Lives of John Donne, Henry Wotton, Richard Hooker, George Herbert, and Robert Sanderson.* Introduction by George Saintsbury. London: Oxford University Press [1956].

Warnicke, Retha. *William Lambarde, Elizabethan Antiquary, 1536–1601.* [London:] Phillimore [1973].

Weber, Kurt. *Lucius Cary, Second Viscount Falkland.* New York: Columbia University Press, 1940.

Wedgwood, Cecily Veronica. *Thomas Wentworth, First Earl of Strafford, 1593–1641: A Revaluation.* London: Jonathan Cape, 1964.

Weston, Corinne Comstock. "Beginnings of the Classical Theory of the English Constitution." *Proceedings of the American Philosophical Society* 100 (1966): 133–44.

———. "Concepts of Estates in Stuart Political Thought." In *Representative Institutions in Theory and Practice, Studies Presented to the International Commission for the History of Representative and Parliamentary Institutions, no. 39.* Brussels: Éditions de la Librairie Encyclopédique, 1970.

———. *English Constitutional Theory and the House of Lords, 1556–1832.* London: Routledge & Kegan Paul, 1965.

———. "The Theory of Mixed Monarchy Under Charles I and After." *English Historical Review* 75 (1960):426–43.

Weston, Corinne Comstock, and Greenberg, Janelle Renfrow. *Subjects and Sovereigns; The Grand Controversy over Legal Sovereignty in Stuart England.* Cambridge: Cambridge University Press, 1981.

Whitelock, Dorothy, ed. *English Historical Documents, 500–1042.* 2nd ed. New York: Oxford University Press, 1979.

Whitelocke, Bulstrode. *Memorials of the English Affairs.* 4 vols. Oxford: University Press, 1853.

Whitelocke, Sir James. *Liber Famelicus of Sir James Whitelocke.* Edited by John Bruce. [Westminster:] Camden Society Publications, no. 70 (1st series), 1858.

Whitgift, John. *The Works of John Whitgift.* Edited by John Ayre. 3 vols. Cambridge: Parker Society Publications, nos. 46–48, 1851–1853.

Wilkinson, Bertie. *Constitutional History of England in the Fifteenth Century (1399–1485).* London: Longmans, Green & Co., 1964.

———, ed. *The Creation of Medieval Parliaments.* New York: John Wiley & Sons, 1972.

———. "The Deposition of Richard II and the Accession of Henry IV." *English Historical Review* 54 (1939):215–39. Reprinted in *Historical Studies of the English Parliament*, edited by E. S. Fryde and Edward Miller. 2 vols. Cambridge: Cambridge University Press, 1970.

Williams, C. M. "The Anatomy of a Radical Gentleman: Henry Marten." In *Puritans and Revolutionaries: Essays in Seventeenth-Century History Presented to Christopher Hill*, edited by Donald Pennington and Keith Thomas. Oxford: Clarendon Press, 1978.

Williamson, Arthur. *Scottish National Consciousness in the Age of James VI.* Edinburgh: John Donald Publishers, 1979.

Willson, David Harris. "King James I and Anglo-Scottish Unity." In *Conflict in*

Stuart England: Essays in Honour of Wallace Notestein, edited by William Appleton Aiken and Basil Duke Henning. London: Jonathan Cape, 1960.

———. *King James VI and I.* New York: Oxford University Press, 1967.

Wormald, B. H. G. *Clarendon: Politics, History, and Religion.* Cambridge: Cambridge University Press, 1952.

Wright, Herbert Gladstone. *Life and Works of Arthur Hall of Grantham.* Manchester: University Press, 1919.

Wright, Thomas, ed. and trans. *The Political Songs of England, from the Reign of John to that of Edward II.* London: Camden Society Publications, no. 6 (1st series), 1839.

Wroth, Sir Thomas. *A speech spoken by Sr. Thomas Wroth knight, . . . February, 25. 1642.* London, 1642.

Wulfstan II, archbishop of York. *Die "Institutes of Polity, Civil and Ecclesiastical."* Edited by Karl Jost. Berne: Francke, 1959.

———. *A Wulfstan Manuscript.* Edited by Henry Royston Loyn. Early English Mss. in facs. no. 17. Copenhagen: Rosenkilde & Bagger, 1971.

Zagorin, Perez. *The Court and the Country.* New York: Atheneum, 1970.

Index

Abbot, George, archbishop of Canterbury, 112

Aberdeen, 106, 224 (n. 30)

Adalbero, bishop of Laon, 27–28, 37

Adam, 110

Adamson, Patrick, archbishop of Saint Andrews, 73, 76, 78, 79

Aelfric, abbot of Eversham, 25, 37, 182, 192 (n. 12)

Alfred, king of Wessex, 23–26, 37, 182

Allen, J. W., 52

Alston, L., 52

Andrewes, Launcelot, bishop of Winchester, 20, 105–06, 108–10, 208 (n. 29)

Anne of Denmark, queen of England, 108

Answer to the xix propositions, 2, 4, 21, 22, 26, 30, 32, 35, 37–41, 59–60, 63, 111, 134, 139, 147–48, 151, 161, 171, 180–82, 190 (n. 13); circumstances and analysis of, 5–20; "government," two senses of in *Answer*, 16–19, 190 (n. 27)

Antiquaries, College of, 103–04, 106, 108, 207 (n. 19)

Appelants, 43

Aquinas, Saint Thomas, 42

Aristotle, 49, 67

Army Plot, 158, 164, 176

Arras, 29

Array, commissions of, 13

Artillery, Honourable Company of the, London, 144

Aston, Sir Thomas, 18, 161, 170, 176

Athens, 65

Aylmer, John, bishop of London, 48–51, 60, 61, 74, 84–86, 173, 196 (n. 38), 204 (n. 50)

Bagshaw, Edward, 123–26, 137–38, 141, 150, 160, 212 (nn. 25, 28), 215 (n. 67)

Baillie, Robert, 135–36, 143–45

Balcanquhall, Walter, 118, 120, 122, 140; and *A large declaration*, 122

Banbury, 123

Bancroft, Richard, archbishop of Canterbury, 20, 37, 60, 65, 77–81, 86–90, 98, 100, 102, 106, 108–10, 112, 185, 202 (n. 34), 209 (n. 46); sermon at Paul's Cross, 65, 78–80, 86, 88; *Dangerous positions*, 79, 109; *Pretended holy discipline*, 79

Barlow, William, bishop of Lincoln, 108–10, 209 (n. 46)

Barrow, Henry, 87

Bastwick, Dr. John, 156, 214 (n. 58)

Batany, Jean, 23

Baxter, Richard, 142

Beaufort, Henry, bishop of Lincoln and Winchester, 34

Bernard, Nicholas, 216 (n. 10)

Berwick, Treaty of, 120

Beza, Theodore, 68–71, 79, 80, 202 (n. 14)

Bilsen, Thomas, bishop of Winchester, 81, 204 (n. 42)

Biondi, Giovanni Francesco, 19, 191 (n. 36)

Bishops (I), and bishops' exclusion bill (i.e., bill to remove clergy from civil employment), 8, 20, 140, 148, 155–58, 160–62, 164, 177 [*See also* Bishops (II)]; whether *jure divine*, 20, 65; Bilson on, 81, 204 (n. 42); Andrewes on, 105, 110; Sir Henry Spelman on, 113; Bagshaw on, 124; Parker on, 130–31, 133; root-and-branch movement against, 135–36, 139, 142–43, 156, 158, 161–62; convergence of the bishops and the Few, 141, 159–61, 169–70, 180; Aston on, 161; attempted praemunire against, 163; attacked in Grand Remonstrance, 164; attacks upon, December 1641–January 1642, 165–68; petitions against, 166–70. *See also* Episcopo-presbytery

Bishops (II), right to be in parliament: whether by right of barony, 54–55, 58, 104, 124, 140, 147, 150, 153, 159; by right of peerage otherwise conceived, 140–41, 151–55, 159–60; whether bishops' presence or assent essential to House of Lords, 124, 126, 139–40, 147–49; Bancroft on, 79, 108–10; according to Selden, 153–55, 159. *See also* Bishops (III), Estates (I, II, III)

Bishops (III), asserted to be an estate: by Hyde, 7–9, 19–20, 148; by Bancroft, 79, 108; by Richard Hooker, 80; by Cooper, 81–82, 99–100; by proclamation suppressing Marprelate press, 86, the denial of which was seditious, 38, 63, 86; by Covell, 102; by Andrewes, 110; by Hall, Laud, or both, 126–27; by Strangwaies, 136; by Selden, 149–50, and Pym's response, 150, 152–53; by Williams, Warner and Bridgeman, 150–51, 159. *See also* Bishops (II), Estates (I, II, III, IV)

Bishops (IV), denied to be an estate: by Martin Marprelate, 83–85, 99; by Stoughton, 99; by a grand committee of the House of Lords, 127; by Falkland, 148; by Strode, 149; implicitly by Saye and St. John, 161–62. *See also* Bishops (II), Estates (I, IV, V)

Bishops' Wars, 115, 120

Black, David, 91

Bockelson, John (John of Leyden), 29

Bodin, Jean, 67, 80

Boethius, 25

Bostock, Robert, 132

Bowes, Robert, 89

Bracton, Henry, 59, 226 (n. 4)

Bramston, Sir John, 173

Bridgeman, Sir Orlando, 151

Bridges, Dr. John, dean of Salisbury and later bishop of Rochester, 84, 86

Buchanan, George, 208 (n. 37)

Buckeridge, John, bishop of Rochester and Ely, 108–10

Buckinghamshire, petitioners from, 166

Burgess, Cornelius, 143–45, 216 (n. 14)

Burton, Henry, 112, 134, 156, 214 (n. 58)

Cade, John (Jack), 18

Caesar, Gaius Julius, 23

Calamy, Edmund, 143–44

Calderwood, David, 89, 96

Calvin, Jean, 80

Cam, Helen, 32

Camden, William, 103, 113, 210 (n. 63)

Campbell, Archibald, eighth earl of Argyll, 120

Canons of 1604, 98

Canterbury, archdiocese of, 103; court of Arches, 98–99; convocations of, 126–27, 150–52

Canute, king of the English, Danes, and Norwegians, 61

Carey, Henry, earl of Monmouth, 132, 169

Carlson, Leland, 77, 87, 204 (nn. 55, 57)

Carozzi, Claude, 27–28

Cartwright, Thomas, 64–68, 77, 102, 128

Cary, Lucius, Viscount Falkland, 6, 7, 9, 10, 19, 20, 136, 144, 148, 155, 180, 184–85; his circle at Great Tew, 184–85

Cavendish, Margaret, duchess of Newcastle, 172

Cecil, Robert, first earl of Salisbury, 93, 209 (n. 58)

Cecil, William, Baron Burghley, 33, 59, 60, 62, 88

Certaine reasons tending to prove the unlawfulnesse and inexpediencie of all diocesan episcopacie (even the most moderate), 144–45

Charles I, king of England, 3, 5–11, 14, 17, 19, 20, 38, 40, 41, 115, 117, 120–22, 124–25, 135, 137, 141, 143, 145–47, 162–66, 169, 173, 175–76, 178–79, 183–84, 217 (n. 20)

Chaucer, William, 87

Chrimes, S. B., 33–35, 52

Cleaver, Robert, 134, 214 (n. 57)

Clotworthy, Sir John, 122

Cluny, monastery of, 28

Cobb, Richard, 186

Coke, Sir Edward, 113, 159

Constantine, emperor of Rome, 91

Cooper, Thomas, biographer, 216 (n. 8)

Cooper, Thomas, bishop of Winchester, 77, 80–86, 90, 99–101

Copinger, Edmund, 29

Coriolanus, Caius Martius, 131

Cosin, John, bishop of Durham, 209 (n. 46)

Cotton, John, 128

Cotton, Sir Robert, 103

Council, 3, 10, 12, 17, 43, 55, 80, 95, 156

Council, privy. *See* Council

Council of the North, 173

Covell, William, 102

Cowell, Dr. John, 108, 113

Culpeper, Sir John, Baron Culpeper, 6, 7, 9, 10, 19, 20, 148, 155, 180, 185

Custos regni, revival of in 1641, 44

Danvers, Sir John, 129

Denmark, 130

Dering, Sir Edward, 146–47, 169, 180, 218 (n. 35), 219 (n. 40)

Devereux, Robert, third earl of Essex, 157, 217 (n. 29)

Devon, petition from, 167

D'Ewes, Sir Simonds, 136, 142, 157, 161, 168, 178, 179, 182, 224 (n. 22)

Digby, George, second earl of Bristol, 136, 151, 156, 158, 162

Digby, John, first earl of Bristol, 158, 162, 180

Digges, Dudley, 173

Dod, John, 134, 214 (n. 57)

Dodderidge, Sir John, 104, 208 (n. 24)

Dominic, Saint, 132

Donaldson, Gordon, 72

Dove, John, 109

Downame, George, 110

Downing, Calybute, 143–44, 185, 216–17 (n. 20)

Duby, Georges, 22–24, 27–29, 192 (n. 1), 193 (n. 28)

Dumézil, Georges, 23–25, 37, 112, 193 (n. 34)

Dury, John, 144

Dyer, James, 36, 226 (n. 4)

Dykes, John, 95

Eadmer, of Canterbury, monk, 29

Edinburgh, 114, 122, 176, 217 (n. 29); riot in, December 1596, 91

Edward I, king of England, 31

Edward VI, king of England, 18, 47, 141

Egerton, Sir Thomas, Baron Ellesmere and Viscount Brackley, 41, 111–12, 139, 180, 209–10 (n. 55)

Elizabeth I, queen of England, 3, 5, 38, 48, 51, 72, 88–89, 93, 99, 103, 147

Elphinstone, James, first Baron Balmerino, 91

Elton, Geoffrey, 36, 49, 50, 63

Elyot, Sir Thomas, 42, 43, 53

Elyott, Sir William, 161

Episcopo-presbytery, 124, 140–47, 184. *See also* Scotland (II)

Essex, petitions from, 166

Estates (I), concepts of and development of Parliament, 30–37

Estates (II), the three, defined as clergy (or bishops), nobility (or Lords Temporal), and commons: 1, 21–22, 68, 73, 74; connection with medieval triad of *oratores, bellatores, laboratores*, 2–3, 21–30, 74, 192 (n. 1); postulated connection with archaic Indo-European thought structures, 23–24. *See also* Estates (III), Scotland (III)

Estates (III), the three, defined as clergy (or bishops), nobility (or Lords Temporal), and commons, assertions of: by Hyde, 7–9, 19–20, 148; by Twysden, 19; by Smith, 55; by Harrison, 55; by Hall, 62; by Beza, 70, 202 (n. 14); by Cooper, 81–84, 99–101; by proclamation suppressing Marprelate press, 86; by Robert Cecil, 93; by Sutcliffe, 87–88, 102; by court divines in 1606 and after, 108–10; by Heylyn, 112; by Coke, 113; by Cowell, 113; by Minsheu, 113; by Raleigh, 113; by Camden, 113; by Strangwaies, 136, 141; by Selden, 149–50; by Tate with respect to tenures, 208 (n. 25); by a royal proclamation, 209–10 (n. 55). *See also* Bishops (III), Estates (II), Scotland (II, III)

Estates (IV), the three, defined as king, Lords, and Commons (or near equivalents), assertions and usages of: 1, 2, 21, 113; in *Answer*, 5–8, 11–18, 40–41; Hume's view of, 30; in fifteenth century, 32–33; *TLS* controversy concerning, 33; by Gardiner, 46–47; by Aylmer, 49, 84; by Lambarde, 55, 102, 104; by John

Hooker, 58, 121, 153; by Burghley, 59, 88; by Hall, 61, 84–85, 101–02, 139; by Hotman, 70–71, 202 (n. 15); by Martin Marprelate, 77, 83–85, 87, 89, 99–100; by *A petition delivered to her most excellent maiestie* (1592), 87, 102; by Stoughton, 98–102; and attacked by Covell, 102; in meetings of the college of Antiquaries, 103–06; nearly disappear from 1606 to 1640, 111; possibly by Hakewill in 1610, 111; possibly by the young John Selden, 111, 153; by Sir Henry Finch, 111; by Ellesmere, 111; by Burton, 112; by Heylyn, 112; revival of, in 1640, 133; by a grand committee of the House of Lords in April 1640, 127; by Saye, 128; by Parker, 130, 132, but not compatible with Parker's developed views, 179, 182; by Bagshaw, 137, 141; by Wroth, 177; by Harley, 177, turned against Harley by royalists, 181; by *A plea for moderation* (1642), 180; by Sir John Spelman, 183; by Prynne, 200 (n. 78). *See also* Estates (V); Mixed government; Monarchy, aristocracy, democracy; Presbyterianism

Estates (V), the three, defined as king, Lords, and Commons, functions of: a code language (along with mixed government) for presbyterianism or radicalism, 3, 11, 19, 41–42, 64, 175; a royalist ploy, before the *Answer*, 15, 41, 61–62, 101–02, 111–12, 138–39, 180–81. *See also* Bishops (IV), Estates (IV); Mixed government; Monarchy, aristocracy, democracy; Presbyterianism

Estates (VI), two, three or four, otherwise and variously defined, 32–33, 57–58, 85, 104, 126–27, 153. *See also* Scotland (III)

Exchequer, chancellorship of, 173

Exeter, 56; petition from, 167

Familists, 29

Field, John, 79

Fiennes, Nathaniel, 122, 123, 136, 138, 163, 178, 179, 182

Fiennes, William, Viscount Saye and Sele, 122–34 passim, 138, 145, 151, 157, 160–62, 179, 213 (nn. 52, 57), 217 (n. 29)

Finch, Sir Henry, 111, 113

Finch, John, Baron Finch of Fordwich, 124, 126

Five Members, 165, 169

Fletcher, Anthony, 214–15 (n. 63), 222 (n. 110)

Fortescue, Sir John, 19, 36, 42, 52, 56, 59, 61, 113, 180, 194 (n. 53), 210 (n. 63); his phrase, *dominium politicum et regale*, 19, 42, 52, 55, 60, 112, 181

Fox, Charles, 33

France, 71, 130

Francis, Saint, 132

Fulham Palace, 45

Fuller, Nicholas, 209 (n. 50)

Gardiner, Samuel Rawson, 136, 214–15 (n. 63)

Gardiner, Stephen, bishop of Winchester, 46–47, 50–51, 60–61, 74, 198 (n. 52)

Gauden, John, bishop of Worcester, 141, 184

Geneva, 20, 68, 80

Gerald, bishop of Cambrai, 27, 37

Gilby, Anthony, 98

Glasgow, University of, 69

Gledstanes, George, 94, 96

Goodwin, Arthur, 158

Gordon, Alexander, 215–16 (n. 8)

Grand Remonstrance, 164, 174, 220 (n. 64)

Great Britain, James's scheme of union of England and Scotland into, 97–98, 104

Greenberg, Janelle Renfrow, 19, 39, 201 (n. 90)

Greenwood, George, 33

Greville, Robert, second Baron Brooke, 126, 133–34, 214 (n. 57)

Grey, Lady Jane, 61

Grimston, Sir Harbottle, 218 (n. 38)

Grindal, Edmund, archbishop of Canterbury, 141

Groby, Leicestershire, 99

Grocers' Hall, London, 166

Gunpowder Plot, sermons on, 108, 109, 208 (n. 37)

Hacket, John, fanatic, 29

Hacket, John, Williams's chaplain and later bishop of Coventry and Lichfield, 143, 145–46, 217 (n. 29)

Hakewill, William, 111

Hales, John, 144, 184

Hall, Arthur, 41, 59, 61–62, 68, 74, 84, 101, 103–04, 111, 139, 172, 181, 200–01 (n. 84)

Hall, Joseph, bishop of Exeter, 126–27, 143

Haller, William, 188

Hamilton, James, third marquis and first duke of Hamilton, 116–19

Hampden, John, 133, 166, 218 (n. 37)

Hampden's Case, 133

Hampton Court: conference at, in 1604, 64, 79, 98, 206 (n. 3); meetings at, in 1606, 108–10

Harley, Sir Robert, 177, 181

Harrington, James, 16

Harrison, William, 53–55

Hartwell, Abraham, 105

Haselrigg, Sir Arthur, 169

Hastings, Henry, third earl of Huntingdon, 98

Henderson, Alexander, 142, 145

Henry I, king of England, 30

Henry III, king of England, 62

Henry VI, king of England, 34

Henry VIII, king of England, 37, 50, 84, 86, 126, 141

Herefordshire, 181

Hertfordshire, petition from, 166

Heylyn, Peter, 109, 112, 152, 156, 187, 226 (nn. 1, 2)

High Commission, 123

Hinton, R. W. K., 39, 52, 53

Hobbes, Thomas, 223 (n. 7)

Holinshed, Raphael, 57, 78

Holles, Denzil, first Baron Holles of Ifield, 166, 168, 222 (n. 112)

Holles, John, second earl of Clare, 168

Home, Sir George, second earl of Dunbar, 106–07

Homilies, Book of (1547), 46

Hooker, John, 51, 56–61, 74, 103, 113, 127, 150, 153, 200 (nn. 81, 90), 219 (n. 47)

Hooker, Richard, 80, 144, 185

Hooker, Thomas, 128

Hope, Sir Thomas, 114–16, 119, 120

Hotman, François, 70–71

Huguenots, 70–71

Hume, David, 30

Hyde, Edward, first earl of Clarendon, 2, 5–10, 19, 20, 144, 148–49, 151, 152, 155, 164, 167, 173, 176, 181; religious position of, 184–86

Inns of Court, 99. *See also* Lincoln's Inn, Middle Temple

Institute of Historical Research, 33

Ireland, 114, 125, 141

James VI, king of Scotland, and I, king of England, 3, 5, 15, 29, 37, 41, 42, 63, 64, 71–79 passim, 88–100 passim, 103–16 passim, 119–21, 141, 203 (n. 25), 205 (n. 83), 209 (n. 46), 210 (n. 55); *Basilikon doron*, 94–95, 98, 109, 120; *Trew law*, 94; "no bishop, no king," 3, 28, 64, 79, 98, 139, 180; same implied in letter of Elizabeth to James, 72; implied in *Basilikon doron*, 95

John, king of England, 153

Johnston, Archibald, Lord Wariston, 116–22

Jones, William, 208 (n. 25)

Justinian, emperor of the Romans, 110

Kent, 146, 147; petition from, 168

King, John, bishop of London, 109

Kirton, Edward, 136

Knox, John, 48, 208 (n. 37)

Lambarde, William, 55, 58–61, 102–04, 111, 159, 198–99 (n. 67), 200 (n. 84)

Lambe, Sir John, dean of the Arches, 145, 146, 218 (n. 34)

Lambeth Palace, 45, 152

Langland, William, 87

Larnar, William, 167

Laud, William, archbishop of Canterbury, 108, 112, 115, 122, 124–27, 135, 139, 143, 151, 152, 159, 165, 184–86

Lee, Maurice, 203 (n. 25), 205 (n. 76)

Le Goff, Jacques, 22, 23, 27, 29, 192 (n. 1), 193 (n. 28)

Leicestershire, 98, 99

Leigh, Francis, Baron Dunsmore, later first earl of Chichester, 167

Leslie, John, sixth earl of Rothes, 120, 125

Leutard, heretic, 29

Levack, Brian, 99

Levellers, 179

Lewkenor, Edward, 99

Liège, 29

Lilburne, John, 157, 167, 185, 224 (n. 30)

Lincoln's Inn, 129, 187

Lollards, 30

London, 6, 45, 165–67, 169; diocese of, 109; petition from, 135, 136; riots in, 156–57

Lunsford, Thomas, 165

Lupset, Thomas, 43

Lyon, John, seventh Baron Glamis, 69–71

Machiavelli, Niccolò, 46, 47, 60, 132, 195 (n. 8)

Magna Charta, 180

Maitland, Frederic William, 32, 33, 193 (n. 31)

Maitland, Sir John, first Baron Maitland of Thirlestane, 88, 91

Malvezzi, Virgilio, marquis of Castel Guelfo, 129, 131–33, 213 (n. 52)

Marprelate, Martin, pseud., 50, 77, 80–87, 99, 100, 106, 112, 138, 173, 204 (nn. 56, 57). See also Throckmorton, Job

Marsh, John, 187–88, 226 (n. 4)

Marshall, Stephen, 143, 144

Martin, Henry, 158, 177–79

Mary, queen of Scots, 76

Mary I, queen of England, 47

Melville, Andrew, 68, 69, 76, 91, 108–10, 118, 202 (n. 10)

Melville, James, 71, 72, 76, 95, 108

Menenius, 131

Merchant Adventurers, 129

Meriton, George, 110

Merton, barons' declaration at, 19

Middelburg, 87

Middle Temple, 123, 125, 160

Minsheu, John, 113

Mixed government: absence of in early seventeenth century, 1, 2, 111; reversal of positions on (and on the estates) in 1641–42, 3, 4, 134–35, 138, 147–70 passim, 176–77, 181; in Answer, 15–19; Weston's views on, 38–41, 45; not used by Fortescue, 42; not used by Elyot, 43; used loosely by Starkey, 44–45; implied by Gardiner, 47; used by Ponet, 47–48; used by Aylmer, 50, 84–85; used by Smith, 52–55; used by Hall, 61, 84; before embrace by presbyterians, 62–63; after embrace by presbyterians, 64, 76–77, 82–83, 88; used by Cartwright and Travers, 64–68; not entailed by Scottish estates-revision, 73–74, 127; used by

Throckmorton/Marprelate, 76–77, 82–87; almost connected to presbyterianism by Bancroft and Cooper, 80–82, 84; used by Stoughton, 98–102; by Ellesmere, 111; revival of in 1640, 123, 138; used by Saye, 128; used by Parker, 130–32. For royalist use of, see Estates (V). See also Estates (III, IV); Monarchy, aristocracy, democracy; Presbyterianism

Modus tenendi parliamentum, 32, 57–59, 104, 113, 200 (n. 78)

Monarchy, aristocracy, democracy (One, Few, Many), 1, 3; in Answer, 5, 13, 15; glossed as estates in Answer, 40–41, and by Aylmer, 49; need to define perceived by Elyot, 43, by Ponet, 48, by Smith, 53, in sixteenth century, 58, by Stoughton, 101–02; understood by Gardiner, 47; implied by Ponet, 47–48, 60; used by Smith, 53, but not reflected in his social categories, 54; in presbyterian church polity, 66; use by Machiavelli and his translator Dacre, 195 (n. 8). See also Estates (IV, V), Mixed Government, Presbyterianism

Montague, Edward, Baron Montague of Kimbolton, known as Viscount Mandeville, later second earl of Manchester, 157, 169

Montague, Edward, first Baron Montague of Broughton, 212 (n. 25)

Montague, Sir Henry, first earl of Manchester, 123

Montague, Richard, dean of the King's Chapel, later bishop of Norwich, 109

More, Sir Thomas, 52

More Fields, London, 167

Morley, George, bishop of Winchester, 144, 184

Moses, 108

Netherlands, 99, 130, 209 (n. 46)

Newcomen, Matthew, 143

Niccoli, Ottavia, 24

Nicholas, Sir Edward, 6, 162, 163

Nineteen Propositions, 6, 10–12, 14, 16, 17, 19, 44

Noah, 47

Norman Conquest, 160

Norton, Thomas, 62, 68

Notestein, Wallace, 216 (n. 8)

Octavian (Augustus), princeps and emperor of Rome, 112
Oldcastle, Sir John, styled Lord Cobham, 30
One, Few, Many. *See* Monarchy, aristocracy, democracy
Ordainers, 43
Orléans, 29
Ormerod, Oliver, 109
Overall, John, dean of Saint Paul's, later bishop of Norwich, 20, 110; the Convocation Book associated with his name, 110
Oxford University, 61, 161; Christ Church, 98; Saint Edmund Hall, 129
Oxinden, Henry, 222 (n. 99)

Parker, Henry, 9, 128–34, 138, 179, 182, 187–88, 213 (n. 52); *Case of shipmony*, 129–34, 138, 182; *Discourse concerning puritans*, 129–34; *Observations*, 130, 181, 182, 188; attribution of *A question answered* to, 179, 187–88
Parker, Sir Nicholas, 128
Parker, Sir Philip, 136
Parliament, bicameral sovereignty of and the theory of the ordinance, 177–79
Parliaments: *1295 (Model)*: 31; *1586–87*: Cope's Bell and Book in, 76; *1640 (Short)*: 38, 122, 123, 125, 127, 134, 137–38, 147, 150–51, 165; *1640–53 (Long)*: 38, 44, 123–24, 129, 135, 139, 155–56, 175–76; House of Lords, Committee on Religious Innovations, 142; House of Commons, Committee on the Ministers' Remonstrance, 143; militia bill, 12; ACTS AND STATUTES OF: *1351*: Statute of Provisors, 123; *1539*: Act of Proclamations, 84, 86; *1559*: Act of Supremacy, 83; *1641*: Triennial Act, 17, 44, 142; act to prevent the present Parliament from being dissolved without its own consent, 17; *1642*: Bishops' Exclusion Act (Clerical Disabilities Act), *see* Bishops (I)
Peace of God, 27
Pecock, Reginald, bishop of Chichester, 30
Pennington, Isaac, 136
Penry, John, 83, 85, 87

Peyton, Sir Thomas, 212 (n. 41)
Philip IV, king of Spain, 132
Physicians, College of, 143
Pierrepont, Henry, Baron Pierrepont of Holme Pierrepont, known as Viscount Newark, later first marquis of Dorchester, 160
A plea for moderation, 180–81
Pocock, J. G. A., 39
Pole, Reginald, cardinal and archbishop of Canterbury, 43, 45
Pollard, A. F., 31–34, 36
Pollard, Alfred William, 87
Pollock, Sir Frederick, 33
Polybius, 57
Ponet, John, bishop of Rochester and Winchester, 47–48, 50–51, 60–61, 74, 196-97 (n. 28)
Presbyterianism, 71, 76, 124, 141, 146; and mixed government, 3, 15, 41–42, 51–52, 63–68, 76–77, 82–83, 86–88, 98–102; compared to Cluniac movement, 29; and Richard Bancroft, 77–80, 86. *See also* Episcopo-presbytery, Estates (IV), Mixed government, Scotland (VI)
Prideaux, Dr. John, bishop of Worcester, 143
Primitive episcopacy. *See* Episcopo-presbytery
Protestation, 158, 163
Prynne, William, 57, 156
Pym, John, 10, 127, 134–36, 144, 145, 149, 150, 152, 153, 157, 158, 162, 163, 165–68, 173, 176, 178, 220 (n. 71), 222 (nn. 99, 110)

A question answered. See Parker, Henry

Raleigh, Sir Walter, 113
Ratton, Sussex, 128
Redgrave, G. R., 87
Rich, Sir Robert, second earl of Warwick, 143, 167, 217 (n. 20)
Richard II, king of England, 34, 35, 153, 160
Richard III, king of England, 35
Richardson, H. G., 31
Rome: church of, 47; republic, 54, 57, 65, 112
Rous, Francis, 157, 182
Russell, Conrad, 176, 209 (n. 41)

Russell, Francis, fourth earl of Bedford, 135, 142, 167, 173, 176
Russell, John, bishop of London, 33–35
Ruthven lords, 72, 73, 88

Saint James's Palace, London, 158
St. John, Oliver, 162, 167
Saint Paul's Cathedral, London, 156; churchyard, 132
Sanderson, Robert, bishop of Lincoln, 143
Sarpi, Paolo, 132, 133, 213–14 (n. 54)
Sayles, G. O., 31
Schilders, Richard, 87, 99
Schwoerer, Lois, 188
Scotland (I): 52, 62–64, 83, 88, 97–98, 104, 113, 122, 174; importance of religious ideas in, to formation of *Answer*, 1; National Covenant and Covenanters, 3, 115–22, 125–27, 133, 142; Articles of Perth, 114; King's Covenant, 116–17; confession of faith (1581), 116, 118; Committee of the Estates, *see* Scotland (V); and Edward Bagshaw's reading, 123–25
Scotland (II), bishops: 3, 58–59, 69, 90–91, 96; denial of rank as an estate declared to be treason, 38, 41, 63, 73–75; denial of rank as an estate by presbyterians, 69, 75, noted by Bancroft, 78–79; condemned as an estate by General Assembly (1581), 69; defended as an estate by Glamis and Lennox, 69–73; importance of Parliament to, 75; under attack (1586–96), 88–91; said to be indirectly abolished as an estate by Act of Annexation, 89, 94, 107; revival of claim to be an estate (1596–97), 92; act of 1597 restoring bishops to Parliament, 92–93, 96; and Synods of Fife (1598, 1599), 95, 96; further revival in early seventeenth century, 106, 114; renewed attack upon (1630s), 115; kept from and abjured by General Assembly (1638), 117; bishops' "declinator and protestation" to exclusion, 118; claim to be an estate (1638–39), 118–20; claim denied by Covenanters, 119–21; asserted by Charles to be an estate in first Bishops' War, 121–22; assertion denied by Covenanters' commissioners at Whitehall (March 1640), 125–26;

episcopo-presbytery in Scotland, 141–42, 145. *See also* Scotland (III)
Scotland (III), estates: ideas on, 3, 22, 74, 99, 114, 127; three (clergy or bishops, nobility, commons), 68–69, 72–74, 88–91, 93–96, 98, 114, 116–19, 121–22, 202 (n. 10); scheme to use commissioners as clerical estate (1596), 92; three without bishops (nobles, lairds, shire commissioners), 90–91, 119, 120; four, 90. *See also* Scotland (II)
Scotland (IV), General Assembly: 68, 72–73, 75, 93, 107, 118, 126; commissioners of, 92; postponed meeting of, scheduled for July 1605, in Aberdeen, 106; the Tables, 119; General Assembly at Glasgow (1581) adopts *Second book of discipline*, 69; General Asssembly at Edinburgh (October 1581), 71–72; General Assembly at Dundee (March 1598), 93–94; General Assembly at Glasgow (1638), 115–19, 121
Scotland (V), Parliament: 68–69, 72–75, 81, 91, 117, 122; Lords of the Articles, 90, 121; *Parliament of 1584*: Black Acts, 73–75, 78, 118–19, 121, 126; *Parliament of 1587*: Act of Annexation, 78, 89, 94, 107, 119, 126; Act "anent the Parliament," 89; *Parliament of 1592*: Act "for abolishing of acts contrary the true religion," 90; change in style of enactment clauses, 90; change in style of listing of the Lords of the Articles, 90–91; *Parliament of 1597*: Act to restore bishops to Parliament (declares prelacy to be one of the three estates), 92, 118, 122, 126; *Parliament of 1606*: Act "anent the king's majesty's prerogative," 107; Act "anent the restitution of the estate of bishops," 107, 119, 122, 126; *Parliament of 1639*: 114, 120; intended Act recissory, 121, 125; intended Act "anent the constitution of parliaments," 121, 125; intended Act revising the Lords of the Articles, 121; *Committee of Estates* (1640): fulfills legislative program of Parliament of 1639, 122, 125; Act "anent the Large Declaration," 122
Scotland (VI), presbyterianism in: 3, 64, 68–69, 71–73, 75, 88–89, 91, 104, 114–15, 141; Bancroft's views on, 78–79;

presbyterian ministers summoned to
Hampton Court (1606), 108–09; in later
1630s, 115; non-clerical representation in
presbyteries and assemblies, 115, 117
Selden, John, 33, 140, 143, 149–55,
159–61, 180, 187, 226 (n. 1); *Jani
Anglorum facies altera*, 153, 219 (n. 54);
Privileges of the baronage, 149, 154, 219 (n.
44); *Table Talk*, 33, 111, 143, 150, 154,
218 (n. 35), 219 (n. 58); *Titles of honor*,
153, 154
Seton, Sir Alexander, first earl of
Dunfermline, 106–07
Seymour, Edward, duke of Somerset, the
Protector, 46, 47
Seymour, William, first marquis of Hertford,
217 (n. 29)
Seyssel, Claude de, archbishop of Turin, 71,
194 (n. 37)
Shaw, W. A., 216 (n. 8), 218–19, (n. 40)
A short treatise of archbishops and bishops,
161
Sidney, Robert, second earl of Leicester, 217
(n. 29)
Sirluck, Ernest, 187, 188
Skinner, Augustine, 218 (n. 39)
Smectymnuus, 143, 144
Smith, Sir Thomas, 18, 51–61, 74, 198
(nn. 49, 52); *De republica Anglorum*, 18,
52–56, 198 (n. 67), 199 (n. 69)
Somerset, petition from, 177
Southwark, 123
Spalding, John, 224 (n. 30)
Sparta, 49, 50, 57, 65, 84
Spelman, Sir Henry, 103, 113, 153, 159, 182,
207 (n. 19), 210 (n. 64)
Spelman, Sir John, 182, 183
Spottiswoode, John, archbishop of Saint
Andrews, 106, 107
Spurstow, William, 143
Stafford, John, bishop of Bath and Wells, 33,
35, 194 (n. 37)
Stapleton, Sir Philip, 163
Star Chamber, 157
Starkey, Thomas, 43–45
Stationers, Company of, London, 129
Stewart, James, earl of Arran, 75, 88
Srewart, John, first earl of Traquair, 120, 121
Stoughton, William, 98–103, 106, 138, 206
(n. 4), 207 (nn. 6, 7); allusion to, 84
Stowe, Buckinghamshire, 128

Strangwaies, Sir John, 136, 141
Strode, William, 136, 149, 150, 169, 222
(n. 112)
Stuart, Esmé, sixth sieur d'Aubigny and first
duke of Lennox, 71–73
Stuart, James, fourth duke of Lennox and
first duke of Richmond, 167
Stubbs, William, 31, 33
Suffolk, petitions from, 136, 168
Surrey, petition from, 168
Sussex, petition from, 99
Sutcliffe, Matthew, 87, 88, 102, 204 (n. 55),
205 (n. 59)

Tate, Francis, 104, 208 (n. 25)
Tavistock, Devon, petition from, 167
Temple, John, 128
Temple, Sir Peter, 133
Ten Propositions, 10, 162
Thirning, William, chief justice of the
Common Pleas, 33
Thomas, William, 47
Thomason, George, 129, 132, 188, 216
(n. 20), 219 (n. 40)
Throckmorton, Job, 76, 77, 82, 85–87, 100,
173, 204 (n. 57). *See also* Marprelate,
Martin
Totnes, Devon, petition from, 167
Tower of London, 77, 145, 152, 158, 165,
186
Travers, Walter, 64–68, 77, 102
Triplet, Thomas, 185
Troyes, Treaty of (1421), 33, 34
Twysden, Sir Roger, 19
Tyler, Walter (Wat), 18, 182

Udall, Ephraim, 142, 216 (n. 8)
Udall, John, 142
Ussher, James, archbishop of Armagh,
141–43, 145, 210 (n. 2), 215–16 (n. 8),
216 (n. 10)
Uxbridge, negotiations at, 184

Vane, Sir Henry, the younger, 218 (n. 35)
Van Norden, Linda, 106
Vaughan, John (?), 149, 219 (n. 45)
Venice, 80, 94; dukes of, 14, 94
Venn, John, 167
Verney, Sir Ralph, 178, 224 (n. 24)
Vindiciae contra tyrannos, 71

Vintners, Company of, 129
Visitation Articles (1547), 46

Wallington, Nehemiah, 169
Warner, John, bishop of Rochester, 151, 219
    (nn. 51, 53)
Warwickshire, grand jury at, 87
Wentworth, Sir Thomas, first earl of
    Strafford, 151, 152, 155–57, 162, 164,
    173, 180
Westminster, 156; Palace Yard, 157
Westminster School, 98
Weston, Corinne Comstock, 2, 19, 38–40,
    43, 45, 48, 51–53, 60, 63, 201 (n. 90)
Wheeler, William, 129
Whitaker, Richard, 213 (n. 52)
White, John, 185
Whitehall, 125, 145
Whitelocke, Bulstrode, 33
Whitelocke, Sir James, 174–75, 209 (n. 50)

Whitgift, John, archbishop of Canterbury, 67,
    68, 77, 78, 102, 201 (n. 8)
Wilkinson, Bertie, 35
Williams, John, bishop of Lincoln,
    archbishop of York, 142–46, 150, 151,
    156, 159, 160, 165, 180, 217 (nn. 29, 34),
    218 (n. 40)
Winthrop, John, 128
Winthrop, John, Jr., 122
Wood, Thomas, 98
Wormald, Brian, 184–86
Wren, Matthew, bishop of Ely, 161
Wriothesley, Thomas, fourth earl of
    Southampton, 167
Wroth, Sir Thomas, 177, 224 (n. 19)
Wulfstan II, archbishop of York, 25–26, 182
Wyclif, John 30, 87

York, 6, 7, 181; archbishop of, 45
Young, Thomas, 143

ABOUT THE AUTHOR

Michael Mendle teaches history at The University of Alabama. He received his bachelor of arts degree from Wesleyan University and his doctorate from Washington University.